ASIAN STUDIES ASSOCIATION OF AUSTRALIA
Southeast Asia Publications Series

NO. 15

TRADE, TRADERS AND TRADING IN RURAL JAVA

ASIAN STUDIES ASSOCIATION OF AUSTRALIA
Southeast Asia Publications Series

EDITORIAL COMMITTEE

TRADE, TRADERS AND TRADING IN RURAL JAVA

JENNIFER ALEXANDER

A publication of the
Asian Studies Association of Australia

SINGAPORE
OXFORD UNIVERSITY PRESS
OXFORD   NEW YORK
1987

Oxford University Press
Oxford New York Toronto
Petaling Jaya Singapore Hong Kong Tokyo
Delhi Bombay Calcutta Madras Karachi
Nairobi Dar es Salaam Cape Town
Melbourne Auckland

and associates in
Beirut Berlin Ibadan Nicosia

ISBN 0 19 588865 0

Sole distributors in Australia and New Zealand for the
Asian Studies Association of Australia
George Allen & Unwin Australia

National Library of Australia
C.I.P. Entry

Alexander, Jennifer.
Trade and trading in rural Java.

Bibliography.
Includes index.
ISBN 0 19 588865 0.
ISBN 0 04 150085 7 (Allen & Unwin).

1. Markets – Indonesia – Java. 2. Markets – Social
aspects – Indonesia – Java. 3. Marketing – Indonesia –
Java. 4. Market towns – Indonesia – Java. I. Asian
Studies Association of Australia. II. Title. (Series:
Southeast Asia publications series; 15).

381′.1′095982

Typeset in the Philippines by Vera-Reyes, Inc.
Printed in Malaysia by Peter Chong Printers Sdn. Bhd.
Published by Oxford University Press, Pte. Ltd.,
Unit 221, Ubi Avenue 4, Singapore 1440

For Lanei who shared the fieldwork, and for Paul, who although he cannot type, helped in numerous other ways.

Acknowledgements

My research in Java was sponsored by the Indonesian Institute of Sciences (Lembaga Ilmu Pengetahuan Indonesia), and by the Population Studies Centre (Pusat Penelitian Kependudukan) and the Centre of Village and Regional Studies (Pusat Penelitian Studi Pedesaan dan Kawasan) both at Gadjah Mada University, Yogyakarta. Special thanks are due to Dr Masri Singarimbun and Dr Soetatwo Hadiwigeno, the Directors of these institutes, who were always willing to help me with my work. Indonesian officials, at both *kabupaten* and *kecamatan* level, were unfailingly helpful, but two who deserve particular attention are the Mantri Pasar Prembun, Pak Marjuni, and the Market Bank official, Pak Anis Helmy.

It would be impossible to repay my obligations to my hosts in the village of Babadsari, Pak and Bu Lurah Siswowijoyo, who extended unfailing hospitality and kindness to me and my family throughout the fieldwork. Bu Boesono and her family, Mbak Maryani and Mbak Ningsih took a particularly active interest in my research, and most of the villagers in Babadsari helped me in some way or other. My friends and informants among the *bakul* are too numerous to list, but I must single out Bu Menik, Bu Samilah, Mbak Sri, Bu Sugi, Bu Nyai and Bu Badriyah. They faced my never-ending questions with patience, kindness and unfailing courtesy.

In its original form this work benefited considerably from the advice and encouragement of my three thesis supervisors. Drs Rudy de Iongh, my initial supervisor, and his colleagues Pak Sumaryono and Dr George Quinn in the Indonesian and Malayan Studies Department, stimulated my interest in the Javanese rural economy and helped me acquire a knowledge of Javanese language and culture. When I transferred to Anthropology, Dr Doug Miles and Professor Peter Lawrence clarified my analysis and accepted the wearying task of bringing some order to my chaotic manuscript. I gratefully acknowledge their help and also thank Michael Allen, Glen.Chandler, Darryl Feil and Peter Hinton for comments on particular chapters. The task of rewriting the thesis was made much easier by advice and encouragement by my PhD examiners, Dr Ben White, Professor Hildred Geertz and Professor Jim Fox, and from Dr Chris Gregory.

I am grateful to Dr Anthony Reid, Chairman of the Editorial Committee of the ASAA Southeast Asia Publications Series, for supporting this publication, and to Dr Jennifer Brewster for her editorial advice.

Sydney   JENNIFER ALEXANDER
1986

Contents

Plates

Figures

Tables

Maps

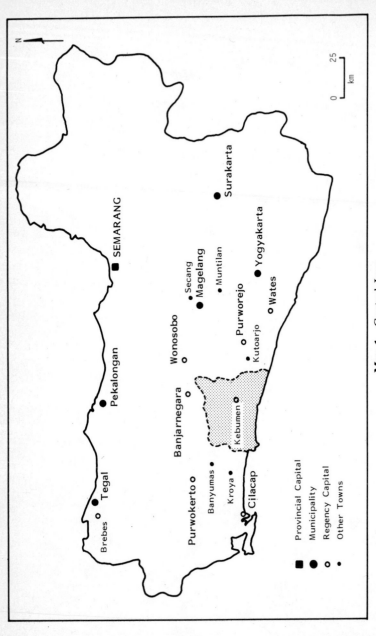

Map 1 Central Java

Introduction

MARKET days transform Javanese towns. Twice a week, two thousand traders and their customers crowd into the *pasar* and spill over along the margins of the narrow roads, to engage in a frantic four hours of buying and selling. Seemingly a world apart from the stylized ceremonies of the court and the bureaucracy, or the painstaking drudgery of the rice fields, the *pasar* is bustling and exciting, its activities unrestrained, at times even vulgar. The large noisy crowds, the disordered heaps of commodities, and the thousands of individual transactions, can make the *pasar* appear an impossible subject for ethnographic analysis,

One common response to the complexity of the *pasar* is a broad survey of geographical topics such as the distribution of market places, the home villages of traders and the material flow of commodities. Another, diametrically opposite, is to concentrate on detailed life histories of individual traders. The first produces the quantitative information which is too often equated with practical research; the second seems a complement, drawing readers into an understanding of the ways the rural poor organize their lives. But even in combination, such studies provide little insight into the systemic aspects of the market. Neither social relationships nor cultural norms, neither kinship, neighbourhood and patron–client ties nor credit arrangements and bargaining conventions appear in their reports.

Perhaps for this reason, we have been slow to appreciate that a market, like kinship or religion, is always a cultural construct. Javanese traders plan, execute and justify economic actions in the concepts of Javanese culture, and the meanings of these concepts must always be treated as problematic. There are Javanese terms which might be glossed as 'capital', 'profit' and 'price' and, no doubt, some Javanese sometimes use them in precisely the same sense as an economist. But this is merely the first step towards analysis, for glosses are only a clue to the range of meanings and the way in which they are combined. *Rega* can be translated as 'price', but understanding activities in the market place requires the knowledge that no commodity has a single price, that there is no 'just price', that fixed prices can be lowered by bargaining, and that selling prices are not calculated by adding a mark-up to the cost.

I have approached the markets of Central Java from three perspectives: trade, traders and trading. Trade, treats the market as a system of material exchanges, examining the geographical distribution of market places, and the production and circulation of commodities. Traders, sees the market as a social system, describing the types of traders, their careers, and the social institutions which link them into complex webs of social relationships. Trading, a perspective which is too often ignored,[1] conceptualizes the market as a structured flow of information, showing how traders make their living by acquiring information and concealing it from others. Although the boundaries are necessarily fuzzy, each of the three parts of this study takes one perspective as its theme.

Chapter 1 provides an ethnographic context, describing those aspects of Javanese social structure and the political economy of Kebumen which are particularly germane to a study of markets in the region. Because most market place participants are women, the contribution of women to household incomes and the distribution of wealth, which is the major constraint on trading success, are treated in depth. The marketing system, conceptualized as the flow of commodities through time and space, is the major topic of Chapters 2 and 4. Apart from the point of production, commodities in rural Java are sold at four locations: *pasar*, *depot*, *warung* and *toko*. *Warung* are 'stalls' selling household commodities and prepared food, common in the town and ubiquitous in villages. *Toko* (shops) sell factory manufactured goods, retailing to the wealthier townspeople and wholesaling to village *warung* owners. *Depot* (warehouses) bulk agricultural produce. Chapter 2 describes the hierarchy of *pasar* in Kebumen, examining the relationship of market places to market towns, the periodicity of markets, and the reasons why traders work in one market rather than another. Chapter 4 describes petty commodity production, emphasizing the extent to which production decisions are orientated towards maximizing household employment, and the critical role of a stable clientele in maintaining a viable enterprise.

Javanese distinguish two main categories of traders: *juragan* and *bakul*. *Juragan* are 'wholesalers', often men, mainly located in *depot*; *bakul* are predominantly women, dealing with varying success with a wide range of agricultural and manufactured commodities, whose trading activities are centred on the *pasar*. Twice a week, more than two thousand traders and their customers throng the streets and market places of Prembun market town, tripling its usual population. Chapter 3 broadly characterizes *bakul* by the commodities in which they deal, to demonstrate how commodity characteristics affect such aspects of marketing strategies as the unit of sale, the use of credit, and relationships with other traders.

Chapters 5 and 6 examine in greater depth the two largest sectors of the market: cloth trading and the bulking of agricultural produce. Successful cloth traders are especially adept at manipulating credit facilities, and the ways in which they accomplish this is the main theme of the chapter. An analysis of institutionalized forms of credit, most notably the distinction between *langganan tetep* and *ngalap-nyaur*, demonstrates that credit does not provide finance for those who lack it, but stabilizes relationships between wholesalers and relatively wealthy traders. The difference between successful and poor cloth traders owes little to marketing skills, shrewdness or tenacity: it is a product of their access to credit, which in turn reflects their class position.

The concentration of Javanese traders at the lowest levels of the marketing system is usually attributed to aspects of their social structure, and to *pasar* trading practices, such as a lack of stable trading relationships and the prevalence of bargaining as a means of price setting, which disadvantage them in competition with Indonesian-Chinese wholesalers. Chapter 6 describes a *depot*, specializing in the bulking and distribution of chillies, which challenges the conventional view. One of eight similar enterprises in Prembun, the *depot* is run by three women who have slowly built up their turnover to above twelve tonnes a day during the main harvests. Selling mainly on credit to a group of semi-permanent clients, the *depot* buys agricultural produce at several sites in Central Java and sells it as far away as Jakarta.

Much of the discussion of the *depot* is concerned with social relationships between the *depot* operators and their suppliers and distributors, but the last section examines the *depot*'s articulation of the supply and distribution networks centred on it by setting prices. The *depot*'s price-setting function is a function of its nodal position in an information network which enables the *depot*'s operators to reconstruct prices throughout the system. It is discontinuities in information which make possible discontinuities in profits, and the *depot*'s high returns are achieved by taking advantage of temporary disjunctions in price information.

The last two chapters further investigate the links between price-setting and information flow, through an analysis of bargaining. Transcriptions of protracted bargaining sessions for expensive commodities illustrate bargaining techniques, such as 'sales patter', altering currency units, interchanging items and interrupting negotiations. The two parties to a transaction have different goals and use strongly contrasting strategies. Buyers, aware that their price information may be wrong, are essentially defensive, utilizing few bids and small increments in the hope of buying at the bottom of the current range. Sellers attack, scattering their offers among numerous items to test the buyer's knowledge, in the hope of selling for as high a price as possible.

The final chapter develops an explanation of bargaining, emphasizing disparities in information and consequent differences in bargaining strategies. Bargaining is seen as a three-stage process: an 'initial' stage where the trader establishes the broad parameters of her customer's knowledge; the 'plateau' stage where the trader attempts to obtain a premium for quality; and the 'settlement' stage where a price is agreed.

FIELDWORK IN KEBUMEN

As with many women students in the seventies, my research interests were strongly influenced by the growth of women's studies. The relatively copious literature on Javanese women[2] provided ample evidence of considerable female autonomy, and as I had studied Indonesian, Javanese and Dutch, the relative importance of cultural and economic factors in maintaining high female status seemed an interesting question to research. My initial research plan was thus little more than an intention to investigate those aspects of rural Javanese social structure which might account for the high status of Javanese women. Although I wanted to live in a village to facilitate close interaction with a limited number of people, it was clear that trading in the market was the major occupation for many women, and I accordingly sought a village in close proximity to several markets.

By the end of my first period of fieldwork, however, I was completely absorbed in the complexity of the marketing system, and the fact that the majority of traders and customers were women became almost irrelevant. During a year in Sri Lanka I had purchased most household requirements at a weekly rural market and found bargaining in a language I spoke poorly a puzzling, almost frightening, experience. Despite my much better command of the language, bargaining in Java seemed no easier, while the markets were several times larger and much more frequent.

At the same time it was becoming apparent that a detailed investigation of women's status in rural Java would, at best, replicate previous research of considerable quality. Although there are some regional differences and the new marriage law is having noticeable effects, kinship and family structure in Kebumen seem broadly congruent with Hildred Geertz's (1961) comprehensive account. And the social and economic consequences of the major contribution which women and children make to household budgets have been amply demonstrated by scholars such as Hart (1977), T. Hull (1975; 1977), V. Hull (1975; 1976; 1979), Singarimbun and Manning (1976), Stoler (1977), and White (1975; 1976a).

In contrast, the literature on Javanese markets left more questions open to investigation.[3] The two major studies by Dewey (1962a) and Geertz (1963b), which have strongly influenced anthropological conceptions of peasant markets, were based on fieldwork in East Java between 1952 and 1958 and there have been major social and economic changes in the ensuing three decades. Better transport has made it possible for even small traders to cover considerable distances, and legislation has reversed the previously favoured position of Indonesian-Chinese in wholesale trade. Dewey's research concentrated on the bulking and distribution of agricultural produce, and on the reasons—mainly a more adaptive social structure in her view—for the Chinese domination of wholesaling: precisely the two aspects most affected by ensuing changes. Geertz's account was principally concerned with the possibilities of 'modernization', and while exhibiting characteristic flashes of insight, suffered from the unilineal model of economic development current at that time.[4]

My research was located in the *kabupaten* (regency) of Kebumen, a region with a population of one million on the coastal rice plain of south Central Java. Before arriving in Indonesia, I had selected the *kecamatan* (district) of Kutowinangun because this was the site of an extensive economic survey in the 1930s (Ochse and Terra 1934) which would provide some historical depth to my investigations.[5] But while I lived in Kutowinangun, the focus of my research gradually shifted to Prembun, the main market town in the adjoining *kecamatan*.

After visiting several villages, I decided to live in Babadsari. This had been the initial recommendation of the Kutowinangun district head (*camat*), who described it as a pleasant place, accessible to several regional markets. His recommendation probably was also influenced by the *lurah* (village headman) of Babadsari. Pak Lurah is a man of great intellectual curiosity and unparalleled political skills, whose experience as village headman under the Dutch, during the Japanese occupation and the fight for Independence made him well equipped to deal with errant foreigners. A small section at the front of Pak Lurah's house, room enough for a bed and a table, was partitioned off, and I lived with him, his wife and their grandson. A married son, his wife and their child occupied another section of the house, and there were usually other members of Pak Lurah's family in residence. Staying with the village headman, while probably inevitable for at least the initial field trip to Java, poses some problems: it identifies the researcher with the authorities in a highly stratified society, and no market trader was bold enough to visit me at home. But I had ample opportunity to talk to people elsewhere, at the market or at their own homes, and it provided privacy which is often scarce for fieldworkers.

Babadsari, well known throughout the region for its cloth traders, proved an ideal site for my research. Although it is roughly equidistant, about five kilometres, from the two market towns of Kutowinangun and Prembun, I concentrated on Prembun. The main Kutowinangun market place was being rebuilt during my first two trips, with a consequent dislocation of activities, and Prembun had one of the four livestock markets in the *kabupaten*, as well as important coconut and bicycle markets.

Living in Babadsari for the fifteen months of my three field trips[6] also made it possible to observe the many activities which provided the essential context for a study of the market place (*pasar*) itself: agriculture, petty commodity production, itinerant traders and village shops. Every morning, before six, I accompanied traders from Babadsari and the adjoining villages to market: walking, taking a pony cart or using a minibus. Once at the market, I wandered about talking to friends, watching transactions and occasionally minding a stall. At the end of the market day, around one o'clock, I was often invited to traders' home villages or to help them dispose of commodities such as coconuts at the processing plants. Sometimes I visited Prembun on non-market days, but more commonly I went to other market places in the *kabupaten*. My regular visits were to the small mountain village of Krakal, another village market in Ungaran, two *kecamatan* markets in the side-road towns of Ambal and Demangsari, and the main *kabupaten* market in Kebumen.

Although I had studied Javanese for three years, it was not until my second trip that I was confident enough to abandon Indonesian. By this time many villagers in Babadsari regarded me as something of an 'expert' on markets and regularly consulted me on prices. But I was often made aware of my lack of comprehensive knowledge. Once, during my second field trip, I attempted to strike up an acquaintance with an elderly and very shy trader by purchasing a small pottery bowl from her. As is customary, we bargained without specifying currency units. I replied to her offer of 'four' with 'one', and in a few minutes we settled on 'two'. Then, much to the amusement of bystanders and the complete amazement of the pottery seller, I handed over two Rp 100 notes. As I later learned, the seller was bargaining in Rp 10 units, although the traders who told me graciously pretended I was taking pity (*kasihan*) on a poor old woman, rather than simply being foolish. After fifteen months' experience, I still find it very difficult to accept the very low prices of locally made handicrafts, or to understand how the poorest third of village households survive on their incomes.[7]

My findings are based on participant observation and informal interviews, both in the village and in the market places. Aware of, if not accepting, the common criticism that anthropological studies are irrelevant for policy formation because they are not based on quantitative data, I attempted a formal questionnaire-based survey early in my second field trip. After twenty-odd interviews it was obvious that, despite the ubiquity of survey methods in market studies, the precision implied by the statistical analysis of such data is spurious, because the information is unreliable. This is not because the traders were unwilling to answer questions or because they told lies: most vendors were remarkably tolerant of my enquiries and while they sometimes avoided answering, they seldom lied.[8] The reason is because only after detailed research does the fieldworker know what questions to ask; and some of the most important information is not accessible to direct questioning. Traders who normally buy from wholesalers, for example, need not be aware of such apparently simple points as the production site of their stock, and for reasons discussed later, few traders can provide useful quantitative information on topics such as profit margins.

In view of these difficulties, I limited my use of survey techniques to two topics. Several times I conducted market censuses, concentrating on very basic information such as the traders' ages, sex, places of residence and the commodities they sold. Apart from the first, each census took three market days, dealing with a different sector of the town each day, and providing the opportunity to speak with up to 600 traders each day. During my last field trip, I interviewed a stratified sample of fifty Babadsari households in some depth with the intention of testing hypotheses about the ways in which traders' careers and sources of finance were governed by their class position.

The most important source of information, however, was the hours I spent watching the business activities of thirty women traders. Most days were spent with one or other of these women, not only talking and watching in the market place, but also accompanying them while they bought new stock, paid their debts and chased their debtors. I did not pay them and while I gave them numerous small gifts, these were more than reciprocated. Some became close friends, and all seemed to believe that exchanging details of their world for details of mine was a reasonable bargain.

While the fieldwork was focused on these women, however, this is not a synthesis of thirty case studies of individuals. Rather I treated each woman as the entry point to a system, using introductions from her to interview her suppliers and distributors, and repeating the process until I reached both production and retail sites of the commodity. Using such a 'network' approach makes it possible to gradually build up an understanding of the marketing system as a whole, checking information obtained at one level against material gathered at the next. This is particularly important with price information, which requires a comprehensive knowledge of the context of transactions before it can be interpreted.

Inasmuch as the study is based on case studies, it is case studies of the marketing of particular commodities rather than case studies of individuals. Thus, although I use the contrasting fortunes of Bu Menik and Bu Samilah to describe some of the features of cloth trading (see Chapter 5), I had five other major informants among the cloth traders. Sometimes, of course, the network approach was inapplicable. A close friend traded in dried fish and often pressed me to accompany her on the 200 kilometre journey to Semarang to buy new supplies, but as most of the fish is produced outside Java, the next stages in the network would be difficult to follow up. Similarly, while I had two good informants among the copper sellers and was friendly with the others, I was unable to obtain quantitative data on the link between production and retailing despite several invited visits to their village.[9]

1. In this, as with so many other topics with which I am concerned, Geertz (1979) is the major exception.

2. Among the most important works on Javanese women are Geertz (1961), Hart (1977; 1978), Hering (1976), V. Hull (1975; 1976; 1979), Sajogyo (1983), Soewondo (1968), Stoler (1977), Vreede de Steurs (1960), and the series of articles in Volume 13 of *Archipel* (1977).

3. In addition to the major studies by Geertz and Dewey, other accounts of Javanese markets include Adam (1916), Anderson (1978; 1980), Chandler (1979; 1981; 1982; 1984), Jellinek (1976; 1977; 1978a; 1978b), and Peluso (1981; 1982).

4. For a major statement of the theory, see Rostow (1960). See also Geertz (1963a; 1965). For some critical views see Alexander and Alexander (1979; 1982) and White (1976a).

5. My initial plan was to include a historical account of the development of peasant marketing in Kebumen, drawing heavily on the Declining Welfare reports (*Onderzoek naar de Mindere Welvaart*) hereafter *Mindere Welvaart*, and archival sources. However, it quickly became apparent that the rise of regional markets was closely related to other economic changes during the colonial and post-colonial periods and that it would be misleading to isolate markets from the political economy as a whole.

6. My first field trip lasted from September 1979 to May 1980, the second from November 1980 to March 1981, and the third from November 1982 to February 1983. During my first two trips I was accompanied by my husband and daughter.

7. At the time of fieldwork, the exchange rate was about Rp 600 to the U.S. dollar, although, as White (1976a; 1979) notes, such comparisons are not very useful. At the same time a kilogram of rice cost Rp 250. In 1976, 30% of rural Javanese lived beneath the International (World Bank) poverty line of U.S.$50 per annum. But according to the National Poverty Line, 80% of rural inhabitants lived beneath the poverty line (White 1979:94).

8. The problems are exacerbated, however, when the fieldworker employs a team of assistants to administer the questionnaires, and I wonder if the results justify the considerable expense. Epstein (1982), for example, employed a team of eight assistants in her study of Papua New Guinea markets and Beals (1975) used at least seven assistants in the Oaxacan study.

9. A possible reason is that this is probably the most important 'trade secret' in the market place. See pp. 165–75.

1

The Village and the Region

KEBUMEN

IN the 1930s Kebumen was regarded as one of the most heavily populated and poorest regions in Central Java.[1] Today its population density of 800 per square kilometre is still high for a rural area, but my impression is that it is no longer among the poorest districts. The town of Kebumen is the administrative centre of Kabupaten Kebumen (see Map 2). Located 110 kilometres west of Yogyakarta, the town has a population of nearly 34 000. Kabupaten Kebumen consists of twenty-two districts (*kecamatan*)[2] and 460 villages (*desa*), with a total area of 1279 square kilometres and had 1 048 880 inhabitants in 1981.

The southern Javanese highway runs roughly parallel to the railway line built in the 1880s,[3] and divides the fertile southern plain from the stony hilly region. South of the main highway, the minor roads are gravelled and are negotiable throughout the year, except perhaps during the rainy season when flooding often disrupts transport. In the more remote hilly northern villages, roads are often elementary and well nigh impassable by motor transport.

The southern section of the *kabupaten*, part of the extensive southern Javanese plain, was planted in sugar during the colonial period and the cane was processed at a mill situated in Prembun.[4] As a result, the fields (*sawah*)[5] in this area are well irrigated and drained, although breakdowns in the irrigation system are not infrequent. The hillier northern sections have been deforested, run-off is rapid and erosion is severe in some areas. Nevertheless, the soil can be cultivated and is heavily planted in sweet potato, peanuts and cassava.

11

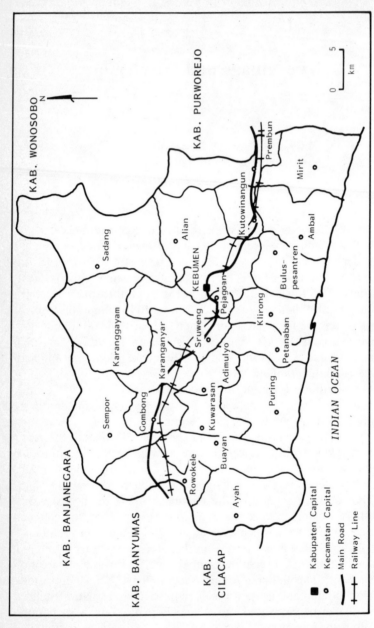

Map 2 Kabupaten Kebumen

Rice is grown throughout the region, but the bulk of the produce is consumed within the household or sold to neighbours. Imported rice, from both other regions within Indonesia and overseas, is handled by the government agency BULOG which was established in 1963. This rice is mainly sold in small stores at fixed prices. A little locally produced rice is sold in market stalls and is also price controlled. Thus rice, which is the preferred staple food of the Javanese, is marketed through strictly controlled outlets which prevent local traders making more than small profits.[6]

Many rural families cannot afford to eat rice more than once a day and for these households, sweet potatoes, maize and cassava are the staple foods of most meals.[7] My impression is that most of these foods are also produced by the consuming households or purchased direct from neighbours who have a temporary surplus. Both sweet potato and cassava are bulky and perishable commodities, which also limit their suitability for the usual marketing channels, but chips and sweets manufactured from them are sold in vast quantities.

Because rice is less profitable than other crops, land which is not being used to produce staples for home consumption is planted with specialized cash crops. Highly perishable foodstuffs in regular demand are planted in tiny plots and sold in small quantities to traders in the village. Such crops include spinaches, eggplant, long beans, some varieties of chillies, and bananas. Tree crops such as mango and *rambutan* might also be included in this category in that few households have more than a single tree, although they are usually sold unpicked. Very little of these commodities is sold outside the *kabupaten*. Less perishable foodstuffs are grown on a larger scale and villages tend to concentrate on particular crops. Citrus is widely grown on the former rice fields of Babadsari, for example, while other villages specialize in yam beans or chillies. Peanuts, soybeans and coconuts are more widely grown. The region has an extensive export trade in these foodstuffs and it is not uncommon for them to find a final buyer as far away as Singapore.

Local manufacturing is also mainly limited to goods which will be retailed within the region. Bricks and tiles, some cheaper types of clothing, regional styles of waxed cloth (*batik*), household items made from recycled materials, and prepared foods made from soybean, arrowroot and cassava are all important in this context. *Su'un* noodles and coconut oil are the only manufactured items sold in any quantity outside the region.

A limited range of food is imported into Kabupaten Kebumen. Apart from rice, the most important items are onions and dried fish from north Central Java, and cabbages, beans and carrots from the interior highlands. In addition, a wide range of prepared foods ranging from prawn crackers to tinned fish is imported in small quantities.

The major imports, however, are manufactured goods. All textiles are imported, some as raw materials for *batik*, as are most children's clothing and underclothes. Cigarettes, beverages, medicines (both Western and traditional herbal medicine or *jamu*) and kerosene are staples which are not produced locally, and a wide range of manufactured goods ranging from plastic ware and aluminium household ware to iron bedsteads and motorbikes is also freely available.

These features of the regional economy have important effects on the structure of the markets, and some points should be emphasized, even at this early stage. Firstly, the staple foodstuffs are not distributed through the major marketing channels and very few local traders are involved in their marketing. Secondly, the scattered and small-scale production of cash crops and local manufactures provides numerous opportunities for bulking functions and numerous entry points for small traders, and places a high economic value on local knowledge. Thirdly, the relatively large amount of imported commodities makes it possible for wholesalers to take advantage of economies of scale: obtaining profits by buying in bulk and breaking down into smaller packages for resale. This is particularly true of goods produced in large factories such as the better quality cigarettes, kerosene, and some types of clothing. Finally, good transport makes it possible for medium-scale traders to buy direct from the manufacturer and producer in other regions and thus bypass the wholesaler.

THE JAVANESE

The Javanese, the major ethnic group in the Kebumen region, inhabit the central, eastern and north-western parts of the island of Java. An unusual aspect of Javanese settlement patterns is that while the population density is very high, there are few large urban centres. Most of the million people of Kebumen live in the 460 rural villages with about three thousand inhabitants situated on the higher areas of land which cannot be used for wet rice fields. Settlements are often continuous and the divisions between villages are administrative rather than geographical boundaries. The towns (*kota*), so designated because of their position in the administrative structure, are little larger than the villages. Prembun, for example, has 4500 people and the population of the administrative capital of Kebumen is only 34 000.

Scholars agree that Javanese society is highly stratified, although they differ considerably in their descriptions of its structure (Geertz 1960; Koentjaraningrat 1960; 1967). Koentjaraningrat (1960:89), for example, described two major groups: the *wong cilik* who are the peasantry and the lower strata of the urban population, and the *priyayi* who are the administrative and intellectual elite. A small nobility, the *ndara*, was confined to four court centres, and has had little significance since the war. In a later paper, Koentjaraningrat (1967:245) expanded this feudalistic model to incorporate a largely urban small trader and merchant group, the *wong saudagar*. Koentjaraningrat also divided Javanese society into two vertical divisions based on the strength of their ties to Islam. The *wong santri* adhere to the five basic tenets of Islam: praying five times daily, fasting during the month of Ramadan, abstaining from pork and alcohol, attending the mosque on Fridays and desiring to make the pilgrimage to Mecca. The *wong abangan* are less strict Muslims, who are more irregular in Islamic practices and incorporate aspects of Hinduism, Buddhism and Javanese folk religion in their beliefs. These two major religious divisions or *aliran* are found among all four social divisions.[8]

Clifford Geertz, whose major study *The Religion of Java* (Geertz 1960) has become the standard work on these questions, divides the population in a slightly different manner. He describes three *aliran* which are approximately coterminous with the *santri*, the *abangan* and the *priyayi*. His horizontal division is also a trichotomy: the village people, most of whom are *abangan*; the *santri*, who include small traders and some villagers; and the *priyayi*, who are the administrative elite. Geertz (ibid.) stresses that these are ideal types constructed as a framework for his analysis of Javanese culture. It is also important to remember that they derive from fieldwork in a relatively remote area of East Java, soon after the Indonesian Revolution and before the modern Indonesian education system was established. While, no doubt, the divisions have been blurred in the ensuing thirty years, the basic validity of

Geertz's distinctions was made clear to me when I spent three months in a Central Javanese village whose inhabitants used the *santri/abangan* terminology.

The framework is of less value in Kebumen, however, where people use neither the *santri/abangan* distinction nor the *santri/abangan/priyayi* trichotomy. Other Central Javanese regard Kebumen and its neighbours as more strongly Muslim than their own areas, and from this viewpoint the entire population might be described as *santri*. The people describe themselves, however, as Muslims with a relatively strong commitment to Indonesian nationalism. Most villages have at least one mosque, often two or three, and *pesantren* (religious training centres) are scattered throughout the rural areas. The call to prayers echoes through the village each morning, many people appear to pray five times a day, most adults fast during Ramadan, and the mosque is full of men each Friday at noon. *Kebatinan* organizations of meditators, which are usually associated with *abangan* culture and which are common in Solo and Yogyakarta, are almost unknown in the region. *Wayang kulit* (leather puppet play) is seldom performed and the traditional Javanese dress is rarely seen, even on ceremonial occasions. Villagers are apt to point out, however, that many of the symbols Geertz associated with *santri*—the wearing of the *peci* (fez-shaped cap), for example—now symbolize a commitment to Indonesia rather than a religious orientation. They accept that there are considerable individual differences in adherence to orthodox Islam, but explain these in terms of personal commitment rather than subcultural norms. There are some areas of the *kabupaten*—mainly villages along the south coast—with few mosques or religious teachers, but this is ascribed to the poverty of the inhabitants. That people in such areas are also regarded as 'bad' characters and thieves, is seen as a consequence of the lack of mosques rather than the cause.

Despite their own views, there seem sufficient grounds to regard the people of Kebumen as *santri*, but other factors also have to be considered. The few performances of *wayang kulit* or *wayang golek* (wooden puppets) are mainly due to their considerable expense; certainly those that are held draw thousands of people from adjoining villages. *Slametan*, ritual gifts of food, which Geertz (1960) described as the central institution of *abangan* culture, are a constantly recurring feature of village life, marking all important occasions, from stages in an individual's life cycle to the opening of a new school. Moreover, the area has never been a stronghold of Islamic political parties: Kebumen as a whole has voted for the PNI (Sukarno's party) and the government-sponsored GOLKAR.

The major social division in Kebumen, apparent to both the villager and the anthropologist, is between the *pegawai negeri* and the masses. The former term strictly refers to civil servants, but it is extended to include all those who have a regular income from the government: civil servants, teachers, military men and pensioners. The members of this group are better educated, fluent in Indonesian, organized in unions and associations, and control political power in both the villages and towns. The regular meetings which reoccur so frequently in all areas of Kebumen life—the bi-weekly meeting of farmers, the weekly meeting of the savings association (*arisan*) for richer villagers, the monthly meeting of women with young babies, the monthly meeting of schoolteachers and their wives, to mention only a few—are all dominated by the *pegawai negeri*. To a large extent this political elite is also the economic elite, at least within the village. Not only do its members have regular incomes, but they are in a much better position to obtain the loans and permits needed to establish businesses, and to acquire land for cash cropping.

The bulk of society consists of farmers, small traders and labourers. Cut off from political power, these people provide the audience at political meetings which are conducted in languages—High Javanese or Indonesian—which they understand only imperfectly. Most of the farmers have only small areas of land and the small traders make low profits. Their children leave school early, because their parents cannot afford the fees and their households need their labour. As far as I am aware, this group believes as strongly in the tenets of Islam as the *pegawai negeri*, but they fall well short of orthodox practice. It is difficult to pray five times a day while trading in the market, and even small contributions to the mosque are outside their reach.

An important point in this context is the frequent equation in the literature of *santri* and trading (Castles 1967; Geertz 1960; 1963b; 1965; Koentjaraningrat 1960; 1967). Geertz pointed out that many *santri* lived in the confined area close to the mosque and that these quarters were often the centres of local manufacturing. It is also historically true that the Javanese traders who established *batik* and cigarette manufacturing on a scale large enough to compete with the Chinese were often adherents of reformist

Islamic organizations such as Muhammadiyah. With this ethnographic basis it is tempting to draw on Weber and argue that reformist Islam has had a similar function to Protestant Christianity in the rise of capitalism: to legitimate the accumulation of wealth and to promote active attempts to seek it.

Whatever the value of the hypothesis when applied to Modjokuto in the 1950s, it has little validity in the Kebumen region of the 1980s. There is a strong Muhammadiyah movement in Kebumen, and many traders belong to it. As with many other Indonesian organizations it sponsors a savings association (*arisan*) and thus provides a means to accumulate finance. But there is no evidence that the more successful traders are likely to be members of Muhammadiyah, indeed no evidence that traders are more heavily involved in it than other sections of the population. As with other groups of more than local affiliations, Muhammadiyah is dominated by *pegawai negeri*.

The cultural stratification of Javanese society remains important in the use of language, though here again some distinctions are blurred as Indonesian, which lacks the status markers of Javanese, is increasingly used. Javanese is the language used in the home and the market place, but children past the third year of primary school are educated solely in Indonesian, which is the language of the bureaucracy. The version of Javanese used in the research region is more informal and less refined than the standard Javanese of the court towns of Yogyakarta and Surakarta (Solo). Subtle differences occur in some vowel sounds and there are a number of regional variations in vocabulary. Although the Javanese in the Kebumen area are aware of the complexity of language styles (and are ever ready to engage in a discussion of them with a foreigner), most villagers have a very restricted knowledge of the more refined, *Krama*, forms. While they recognize these forms, they are not skilled at manipulating language levels and they themselves frequently comment on the fact that their language knowledge is deficient.

Two minor ethnic groups, which are however economically important, are the Chinese[9] and Arabs. Both live mainly in the large towns; indeed, Chinese are not permitted to live in villages. They own shops, restaurants, factories and hotels throughout the regency, and in Kebumen and Gombong control some large market stalls. Most are Indonesian citizens, but in 1981 there were 821

Chinese and twenty-five Arabs in the *kabupaten* registered as foreign citizens. Gombong is by far the largest Chinese centre, with 241 Chinese nationals.

Only one of the seventeen Chinese households in Prembun contains foreign nationals. Prembun Chinese own shops selling shoes, clothing, gold and groceries. Two families have businesses bulking agricultural produce and coconut sugar. All these households are well integrated into the community, though the stereotypical view of Chinese among Javanese is that they are aggressive and rude. Some resentment of their generally greater wealth prevails among the community, but among those with whom they trade they have a reputation for honesty and straight-dealing (see also Dewey 1962a:44). The only Arab family in Prembun owns a furniture store.

FAMILY, HOUSEHOLD AND NEIGHBOURHOOD

The Javanese kinship system has been comprehensively analysed in Hildred Geertz's *The Javanese Family* and I can add little to her account. Perhaps the most notable characteristic of the system is its simplicity. The nuclear family is the basic kinship unit and there are no other corporate kin groups. Kinship terminology is of the Hawaiian type with distinctions based on generation, seniority and sex. Inheritance is bilateral, but there is some tendency for males to receive a bigger share of their parents' resources, especially productive land.

Javanese distinguish between near and distant kin, but the boundaries are situational rather than stipulative. There is a notion of a kindred (Geertz 1961:25; cf. Geertz 1961:24; Jay 1969:117) and all members of the kindred (*sedulur*) should be invited to important ceremonies such as weddings, but on such occasions *sedulur* is a collective term for a number of dyadic relationships, rather than a bounded category.

Kinship terms used within the nuclear family are also widely used as terms of address for people in corresponding age and sex categories. *Mas* (elder brother) is a term of address for men about the same age as the speaker; *pak* (father) for older men; and *dik* (young sibling) for younger persons. Similarly *mbak* and *'yu* are used for women about the same age, and *bu* for older women.

Javanese dislike referring to persons by name alone (*njangkar*) and I have identified my informants by a combination of given names and kin terms which indicate their relative status to me.

For the purposes of this study some of the economic implications of the kinship system require further discussion. Geertz (1961:78–9) describes the kinship system as 'matrifocal'. She points out that the emotional ties of children to their mothers are far closer and warmer than those to the father. Divorces are frequent, and because of their participation in the labour force, women are well placed both to care for their children and to arrange subsequent marriages to their own satisfaction. In emotional terms, and to some degree in economic terms, fathers become almost peripheral to the household.

This description is broadly congruent with my own experience, but some modifications are needed. The most important difference is that divorce is far less frequent in Kebumen. Geertz (1961:69) describes 47% of marriages as ending in divorce, but in Kebumen very few women have been married more than twice. While it remains true that some first marriages, arranged by parents with only the grudging consent of the daughter, quickly end, second marriages and first marriages where the girl is more enthusiastic are stable. Some of this may be due to new marriage laws[10] which make divorce difficult, but my impression is that the relative stability of marriages in Kebumen pre-dates these laws.

A consequence of stable marriages is that households are more stable economic units in Kebumen than is apparently true of other areas of Java. Women are expected to make economic contributions to the household income, as well as care for the children and do household chores, and in cases where the husband is old or unable to find work, may contribute more income than the men. In theory, women have full control over their own income as well as full rights to property acquired during their marriages, but too much should not be made of this, for it is the women's economic responsibility to carry the household through bad periods. If a woman is a successful trader, she may well meet all the daily household expenses, with her husband's income being used for larger items. The effect is that even women with relatively large incomes have far less disposable incomes than their husbands. But despite the high labour force participation by women, and despite their relatively high and critically important economic contributions to household incomes, men provide most of the income of most households. In economic terms at least, the nuclear family is a unit, and the husband is not peripheral to it.

The other point which needs to be stressed is the economic consequences of the close ties between siblings. It is common for the incomes of unmarried children to be used to provide finance for a sibling's business and to pay for school fees. Persons who become successful traders or obtain well-paid jobs are expected to reciprocate with help for their siblings, or more likely, their siblings' children. Many girls get their initial training in the market place by working with their mother's sisters and, not unusually, living in their households. Fosterage is very common and children around ten years old often live in other households to care for younger children while their mother works. Among the wealthier villagers, kinship links of this sort are very important with respect to education. More than twenty children in Babadsari were living with parents' siblings because their own parents had transmigrated to Sumatra. Similarly, numerous Babadsari children were attending high school in the larger urban centres. Occasionally other kinship relationships may be utilized in similar ways. Young children often live with their aged grandparents, for example, but it is the ties between siblings, carried over to their children, which are the most important.

While the nuclear family household is the basic consumption and production unit, agricultural families rely on reciprocal labour for many tasks such as rice harvesting and house building. The high shares which neighbours receive when they participate in rice harvesting is a very important economic asset (Alexander and Alexander 1982; Stoler 1975). Reciprocal labour involves kin and, more particularly, neighbours. The ritual and social expression of neighbourhood ties is the *slametan*, a ritual feast to which men in the immediate neighbourhood are invited (Geertz 1960; Jay 1969). Neighbouring women and close kin prepare the special foods, which are either consumed on the spot or carried home to be shared. Major *slametan*, often involving a theatrical performance as well as a feast, are occasionally held on important occasions such as weddings. But minor *slametan*, where gifts of food are sent out to neighbours, mark all important stages of the life cycle (five, thirty-five and 245 days after birth, for example) and their frequency reinforces links among neighbours. In the course of daily life, visits between neighbouring households are frequent and many small gifts of food are exchanged. Occasionally very poor families receive gifts of food from wealthier families, but they are usually the first to be called upon to help with *slametan* preparations. Neighbours also purchase goods for each other on visits to the market towns.

THE VILLAGE: BABADSARI

In 1982 Babadsari's population was 3000 and the area of land was 248 hectares, of which seventy-six were under irrigation (*sawah*). There were fifty-one hectares of non-irrigated lands; irrigation canals, roads and graveyards accounted for four hectares; and the remainder was household compounds. Nineteen hectares of *sawah* were allocated to officials in lieu of salary (*bengkok*),[11] so that village officials held a quarter of the most fertile land. Three hundred and seventy individuals owned *sawah* assessable for taxes and 940 owned dry land. Only fourteen landowners possessed a hectare or more of dry land and only four a hectare or more of *sawah*. This land is all privately owned and freely alienable.

As yet there is no electricity in the village, although it is expected to be installed within the next five years. Villagers rely on oil or pressure lamps for lighting, and on wood, or occasionally kerosene, for cooking. A high percentage of households have wells within their compounds with a fenced-off section for bathing. Only the richer households have a bathing shed with a tub for storing water, and many villagers use the canal for bathing, washing and defecation. Latrines are fairly widespread, but most are primitive.

Rice is the staple food. The two rice crops grown annually use mainly traditional seeds rather than the high-yielding varieties introduced in the last decade, and almost all rice is consumed within the village. In the last ten years an increasing amount of *sawah* (and also dry land) has been set aside for citrus cultivation. In the first few years of growth the orange trees are merely planted in raised mounds, but after perhaps four years the whole area is built up and the soil beneath planted with vegetables. Sections of *sawah* are often temporarily raised and drained during the dry season for crops such as spinach, corn, eggplants and long beans. Coconut palms are grown along the ridges of *sawah* and most household compounds have a number of coconut palms as well as considerable numbers of banana and other fruit trees. Household compounds are a popular place for planting cassava, sweet potato and arrowroot.

While most households produce some of the food they require, they rely heavily on village stalls (*warung*) and markets for food supplies as well as basic necessities such as soap, kerosene and clothing. The village census lists a total of forty-five *warung*, which vary remarkably in size and the range of commodities they sell. The more substantial establishments are located in the front part of a house or in an adjacent building and their stock includes a range of durable foodstuffs, rice, fertilizer, spices, hardware, stationery, medicinal needs and haberdashery. Some *warung* stock a few vegetables and fruits, but the perishable nature of these commodities precludes large stocks and they are more commonly purchased from the market or from travelling vendors. Two *warung* provide meals for workers on an irrigation improvement scheme being carried out by the government, and wealthier villagers often buy items of prepared food for variety and have the odd drink of coffee or tea. *Warung* are scattered throughout the village (most households would be within fifty metres of one), but clusters are formed at strategic points: near the school or crossroads. All *warung* buy most of their supplies in the nearby market town, both in shops and the market place, but staples such as fermented bean cake (*tempe*) and coconut oil are bought from village producers.

Two small markets, one in the northern hamlet of Blawong and the other in the neighbouring village of Ungaran, are important sources of fresh vegetables and other foodstuffs. Both have bi-weekly markets but a few sellers congregate at these sites on other days. Some villagers buy goods other than foodstuffs at these two markets, but most consumers prefer to buy at the more distant markets of Prembun and Kutowinangun.

Buses and minibuses run regular services along the main highway, and minibuses run services to all marketing centres within the regency. *Colt*, a Japanese-made small pick-up truck has become the generic term for the latter. It usually has a covered rear end with rows of benches on both sides of the vehicle, but is often loaded with goods rather than people. In more recent years a more sophisticated version has grown in popularity. This is the *colt sestasiun* with four rows of comfortable seats used almost exclusively for passengers. Both types of vehicle are owned by wealthier villagers as well as townspeople and are hired out to drivers on a

commission basis. Minibuses are available for private hire, although the area they serve is restricted by the type of licence
acquired by the owner.

Horse- and ox-drawn carts are still important transport for
goods and people from villages to market centres, even though
their numbers are rapidly declining. In Babadsari between 1980
and 1982, *grobag* (a very large cart for heavy goods such as bricks
or coconuts) declined from thirteen to four, and *dokar* (a small
pony trap for passengers and light goods) from twenty-two to ten,
while three new minibuses bought the total to seven. The people
of Babadsari rely on buses and *colt* for travelling long distances,
but have to walk two kilometres to the main road for these cheaper
and faster means of transport. Many villagers, both traders and
shoppers, prefer to use horse-drawn transport directly from the
village to the market place. Currently ten *dokar* ply the Babadsari–Prembun and Babadsari–Kutowinangun routes on market days.

SOCIAL STRATIFICATION

The obvious contrast between the enormous wealth of some
sectors of urban Java and the poverty of most rural areas, disguises
the fact that rural villages are highly stratified. While no households in Babadsari are wealthy, or even comfortably off, compared
to the middle class of an industrialized society, the proportionate
range of incomes and wealth is at least as great. Despite relatively
equal distribution of land among landholders, the disparity in
access to economic resources is the major determinant of the
range, scale and returns to labour of a household's economic
activities.

Babadsari households can be divided into three broad social
groups: the elite, middle peasants and poor peasants.[12] The elite
group comprises village officials (*pamong desa*), civil servants
(*pegawai negeri*), retired government servants on pensions, and
landowners with at least 350 *ubin* (half a hectare of *sawah*). The
middle peasants are households with access to between 100 and
300 *ubin*.[13] The occupations of the female and male heads of these
households are tabulated in Table 1.1. The elite consists of twenty-
nine persons living in fifteen households, one of which is headed by a
widower; the thirty-two middle peasant household heads live in
seventeen households, one headed by a widower and one by a
widow; and the thirty-four poor peasants occupy eighteen house-

TABLE 1.1

MAIN OCCUPATIONS OF HOUSEHOLD HEADS

Occupational Category	Elite				Middle Peasants				Poor Peasants			
	m	f	t	%	m	f	t	%	m	f	t	%
Farmer	3	9	12	41%	7	4	11	34%	4	3	7	21%
Trader	2	3	5	17%	3	8	11	34%	2	10	12	35%
Petty commodity producer	—	—	—	—	3	2	5	16%	—	1	1	3%
Artisan	—	—	—	—	2	1	3	9%	3	—	3	9%
Labourer	—	—	—	—	1	1	2	6%	7	4	11	32%
Civil servant	10	1	11	38%	—	—	—	—	—	—	—	—
Household work	—	1	1	3%	—	—	—	—	—	—	—	—
	15	14	29	99%	16	16	32	99%	16	18	34	100%

holds including two headed by women. Twenty-seven of the households are nuclear families, and twenty-three include additional persons, mainly daughters-in-law and foster children.

About 10% of the households belong to the elite and are clustered in two hamlets. Two-thirds of the men have a regular income from a salaried job or pension, and a similar proportion of the women manage agricultural activities on at least half a hectare of *sawah*. They live in superior houses with concrete or tile floors and masonry walls and some of the older houses are of the *joglo* style with a pitched roof traditionally associated with the elite. Half the male household heads are village officials. Each is entitled to *bengkok* lands ranging from 175 to 500 *ubin* in return for their services to the village. Most village officials in Babadsari are men of mature years who have considerable prestige. Their jobs are not arduous but do involve numerous meetings and guard duties. Most work their land with wage labour or lease the land to others and live off the rents. The fact that the only household head who leases out all his land is a widower, hints at the important role of elite women in supervising agricultural activities, especially planting and harvesting rice.

Wealth in Babadsari village is in large part a function of government employment. The payments received by pensioners and the salaries of civil servants are substantial by village standards and their recipients do not have the problem of irregular incomes faced by other villagers. The two pensioners in the sample receive Rp 85 000 and Rp 45 000 each month. The first also receives payment for work in the village bank. His energetic wife earns money from trading and administrative work in the village office, which is used to finance their children's education. The second pensioner inherited 300 *ubin* of *sawah* shortly after retirement, and he and his wife supervise its cultivation.

The remaining five *pegawai negeri* are teachers or clerks. One woman and four men earn salaries between Rp 30 000 and Rp 50 000 per month, plus a rice ration. The husband of the woman and the wives of the three men are farmers, cultivating cash crops such as spinach, as well as rice. The wife of the fourth, as yet childless, is a full-time cloth trader who operates a village *warung* with her husband in the afternoon and early evening. The five elite households without government stipends have a lower standard of living. Three gain most of their income from about a hectare of inherited land. The other two are successful traders who later acquired land, but still maintain their trading activities and derive most of their income from this source.

All the women in the elite group take an active role in economic activities, generally in co-operation with their husbands. Nine women are farmers. They are mainly involved with supervising and feeding the labour force required to work their landholdings, but they also participate in reciprocal rice harvesting and frequently cultivate cash crops for sale. Three women work independently of their husbands: two cloth traders and a school teacher. Like their husbands, women among the elite are active participants in village affairs and spend a considerable amount of time at village meetings.

The middle peasant group in my survey numbers seventeen, or 34%, which is probably about 10% more than in the village as a whole. They describe themselves as *cukupan*: 'those who have sufficient'.[14] Most households are included in this category because they own more than 100 *ubin* of *sawah*, but a few gain a reasonable income from another source—for example, a minibus driver earns about Rp 7000 a week. While 100 *ubin* of irrigated rice land provides both rice and a cash income, it is not sufficient to meet all the average household's needs in rice, let alone the other requirements for survival. In all but one household, which is female headed, the men are actively involved in farming, and in three the women are also full-time farmers, although most women do some agricultural work at harvesting and planting. Eleven households include traders as well as farmers, and six further supplement their income with petty manufacturing. Wives in this middle peasant category play as great a part in income-earning activities as their husbands, and in many cases work far longer hours.

Eighteen households, or 36% of the total, are poor peasants: households with few productive resources and without regular or reasonably paid employment. Ten households own no *sawah*, and the holdings of the remainder range from thirty-five to seventy-five *ubin*. Such small holdings are not viable rice plots, so the *sawah* is either planted with cash crops or farmed in rotation with the owners of adjoining plots. All but one household also own garden land or dry land,[15] with holdings ranging from twenty to 100 *ubin*. This provides some welcome additions to the table in the form of greens, fruits, sweet potato and cassava, but even the largest farms cannot provide full-time employment for an adult. Apart from one elderly man, all the male household heads are engaged in off-farm employment as traders, labourers and artisans. Two of the women combine work on household land with care of their children, but most are small traders and agricultural labourers.

In addition to the household heads, some attention has to be given to other members over twelve years old, for such persons make a considerable contribution to household income. Many surveys[16] have pointed to the critical economic contribution of women and children. Among thirteen to fifteen year olds, for example, girls spend an average of 4.6 hours per day in income-producing work as opposed to 4.4 hours for boys (White 1975:141). But the most important economic contribution of children is as a substitute for adult labour in household maintenance but non-income producing activities. In the same age group, girls spend a further 4.3 hours and boys 1.4 hours in labour of this type (ibid:141). The labour force of the Javanese household is certainly not limited to the conventional adult male; it includes all persons over the age of ten or so.

The elite households include twenty-two children aged over twelve years, and five resident daughters-in-law. Ten are students (three at tertiary institutions), five are traders and four are civil servants (see Table 1.2). The middle peasant households include twenty-nine children, and two daughters-in-law. Nine are engaged in small factories and nine are high school students. Four work as

TABLE 1.2

MAIN OCCUPATIONS OF CHILDREN TWELVE YEARS AND ABOVE LIVING AT HOME

Occupational Category	Elite				Middle Peasants				Poor Peasants			
	m	f	t	%	m	f	t	%	m	f	t	%
Farmer	3	3	6	22%	1	1	2	6%	—	1	1	4%
Trader	2	3	5	19%	2	2	4	13%	4	4	8	30%
Petty commodity producer	—	—	—	—	4	5	9	29%	—	—	—	—
Artisan	—	—	—	—	—	—	—	—	4	—	4	15%
Labourer	1	—	1	4%	1	1	2	6%	2	3	5	19%
Civil servant	3	1	4	15%	1	—	1	3%	—	—	—	—
Household work	—	1	1	4%	—	4	4	13%	3	2	5	19%
Student	9	1	10	37%	6	3	9	29%	3	1	4	15%
	18	9	27	101%	15	16	31	99%	16	11	27	102%

traders and about as many are engaged in full-time household work. Eight of the twenty-five children from poor peasant households are traders. Two daughters-in-law are occupied with household work; four children are at high school, four are artisans, five are labourers and one is a farmer.

These figures show that while members of the poor peasant group desperately need additional income, it is their children who have the greatest difficult in finding work, mainly because they lack finance for an industrial or trading career. Labourers and artisans, who are drawn mainly from this social class, are unemployed for most of the year, working only during the short peaks in the agricultural cycle. The eight traders among the poor peasants are all involved in low-finance enterprises, work irregularly and seldom make as much in a day as an agricultural labourer.

The economic life of Javanese peasants has little resemblance to the stereotype of the Asian rice-farming villager.[17] No household is fully engaged in rice cultivation, and only the richest have sufficient land to provide agricultural employment for all household members who desire it.[18] Rice farming remains an important source of food for home consumption, but it has long been replaced by other crops as a source of cash income and, in any case, farming provides the main income for only 30% of households. There is little difference in the participation of men and women in the labour force: all but a few women are employed in income-generating activities for as many hours as the men.[19] Similarly, most of the children over twelve also provide important additions to the household income, either directly or by substituting for the mother in childcare, cooking and household cleaning. The exception is the children of the village elite: a third are still at high school and few make an economic contribution. But while women and children work nearly as many hours as adult men, they receive far lower returns—about two-thirds of the adult male return for women, and half for children.

WOMEN'S WORK

In *The History of Java* Raffles remarked that:

> In the transaction of money concerns the women are universally considered superior to men, and from the common labourer to the chief of the province it is usual for the husband to entrust his pecuniary affairs entirely to his wife. The women alone attend the markets, and conduct all the business of buying and selling. It is proverbial to say the Javanese men are fools in money concerns. (1817:353)

More recent studies of Javanese women have continued to stress their active participation in both household management and income-producing activities. In general, women work longer hours than men, although men, particularly among the poor, are usually engaged in more arduous tasks (Hart 1978; Penny and Singarimbun 1972, 1973; White 1976a). But extra-household employment is not limited to women who are poor: although the types of enterprises in which they are involved differ, even women from the wealthiest village households are expected to contribute to household income (Hull 1979).

Only one female household head in my survey did not have an income. She is an elderly woman heading an extended household, caring for her grandchildren to free her daughter-in-law to work as a trader. Only seven other women over twelve were not employed outside the house, and in each case spent much of their time cooking, cleaning and caring for the children of women with regular work.

These high rates of participation in the labour force are often regarded as a product of women's high status *vis-à-vis* men (*Mindere Welvaart* IXb3:1; Peacock 1973). Although it is true that women control their own incomes, have the right to dispose of their own property and make the economic decisions in the businesses which they run, it is ethnocentric to assume that paid employment has the same implications for Javanese women as it has for middle-class women in industrialized societies. Because few Javanese women live in independent households, most of their income is immediately spent on daily requirements, and the household's disposable income is concentrated among the men. Nor is employment an alternative to housework: while employed women may have some household help, they also spend many hours in household duties in addition to paid employment. Javanese men certainly claim that women have greater expertise in household matters, but this stems, at least in part, from their desire to avoid the problems of organizing daily household expenditure on a limited budget, and women do not have the authority to make major household decisions alone (see Hatley 1984:4).

In my view an understanding of the high rates of female employment must begin, not with a discussion of relative male and female status, but with an appreciation of the poverty of Javanese rural society. Most village families live so close to the subsistence margin that they must seize any opportunity to increase their incomes—status considerations play little, if any, part in their decision to accept a job. More wealth and higher income do not lead to a withdrawal of village women from the labour force, but to their changing to more remunerative employment. Given the economic structure of Javanese rural society, the woman from an elite household supervising a rice harvest and paying the harvesters is as necessary to her household's reproduction as the poor peasant woman selling a dozen eggs by the roadside. Nevertheless the importance of women's work is appreciated by Javanese, and a woman's possession of an independent income, even where she has little practical control over its disposal, contributes to her self-esteem.

The main sources of employment for women are trading and farming. Forty percent of the women in my sample are traders, and a quarter regard farming as their main income source. The others work as farm and non-farm labourers, in small factories and as artisans and civil servants. Women who regard themselves as farmers are concentrated among the elite, so that trading is by far the most important source of income for the majority of Javanese rural women. If we add women who have been traders at some time in the past, nearly two-thirds of the women have had such experience: an especially remarkable figure when we remember that some of the young girls will probably take up this occupation later in their careers. The figures for men are much lower: 17% are currently traders and 18% have been traders.[20]

WOMEN AND TRADE

Given the importance of trading as employment for women, it is not surprising that markets are women's domains.[21] Women predominate among both vendors and customers, although many of the larger traders and all the market administrators are men. Javanese see trading as a legitimate means of livelihood and, within the villages at least, it is by no means the despised activity portrayed in some of the literature (Boeke 1954:24–5; Chandler 1982). Traders come from all social classes. In my sample, 18% of elite women, 24% of middle peasant women, and 33% of poor peasant women are traders, and similar figures were obtained in other village surveys (see Stoler 1977; White 1976b). The lower percentage of traders among the elite is not evidence of unwillingness to engage in trade—the village headman's wife is among the shrewdest businesspeople in the district—but of the greater opportunities for more remunerative employment. Aristocrats (*priyayi*) and civil servants (*pegawai negeri*) may affect contempt for traders, but *priyayi* women have been engaged in *batik* trading since the turn of the century (Palmier 1960) and the wives of *pegawai negeri* are prominent among the Kebumen market elite.

As with any other economic activity, however, trading reflects the class structure of Javanese society. A cloth trader with finance approaching Rp 2 000 000 has little in common with a cloth seller whose finance does not exceed Rp 20 000. The first woman works shorter hours, obtains far greater profits, and deals with different customers. Successful entry to the ranks of traders requires not only economic skills, such as the ability to judge commodities or to bargain successfully, but also access to finance. And it is the latter which is the major determinant of success.[22]

The more successful traders, those with sufficient finance to concentrate on profitable commodities, such as cloth sold in major markets, obtain their initial finance from close relatives and spouses. Less successful traders, such as those dealing in small quantities of agricultural products, obtain their very low initial finance from a much greater variety of sources, including their savings. Increments to the initial finance, however, indicate a reverse pattern. Successful traders increase their finance by obtaining credit from their suppliers. Less successful traders, who cannot obtain credit, rely on friends, relatives and spouses for finance increases.

Javanese regard trading as an individual pursuit and those who acquire initial experience by working with another person quickly establish their own businesses. Even in a highly skilled trade, such as *batik* selling, traders are usually independent within a year. Consequently most apparently joint ventures involve youngsters working with established traders to gain experience, although husbands and wives sometimes co-operate for long periods, especially in the cloth trade. Very recently, employer/employee relationships characteristic of the *toko* have entered the more profitable areas of the market, especially the cloth and textile trades. Previously these women and men would have used close relatives as assistants, providing some training in return, but they are now encouraging their children to remain at school and seek other employment.

Although women may have help from their children and foster children, household duties remain their responsibility and it is by no means an easy task to balance the demands of the *pasar* against those of the home. Women often abandon trading for shorter or longer periods, and, as the traders differ in their entry requirements and conditions of work, there is mobility between trades. A third of my sample, mainly poorer women, had spent at least a year in more than one trade. Short-term interruptions of trading concerns are mainly due to seasonal peaks in well-paid employment and to childbirth. Small-scale traders, in particular, often leave the *pasar* for more remunerative work in the agricultural harvests, and even successful traders curtail their activities to supervise harvesting or planting on their land. Young children (seldom seen in the *pasar*) are usually cared for by siblings or close relatives and may be brought to the *pasar* to be breastfed. Unless the birth was particularly difficult, however, women return to work at the end of forty days; in some cases within a week!

While a few women have been able to increase the scale of their enterprises by switching from one trade to another—Bu Samilah is a good example (see p. 124)—bankruptcy was the most commonly mentioned reason for abandoning a particular trade. Bu Suwuh has begun several enterprises. For three years, while her family of three children were still young, she produced soybean cake (*tempe*), selling it in Kutowinangun market two days of the week. When her husband, unable to find enough work, took over childminding, Bu Suwuh entered the rice trade using the crop from a small area of household land as her initial stock. But when mechanized rice hullers entered the village four years later, hand pounded rice became unprofitable so she began making *getuk* (a sweetmeat) from family rice stocks. This activity was both time-consuming and unremunerative, and after two years she switched to coconut trading. This is commonly regarded as a precarious occupation because of the skill needed to judge the quality of unhusked nuts, and she became bankrupt a year later. At the time I met her, she had been a basketware seller for four years, using a loan from a relative to provide initial finance. Although Bu Suwuh's initial occupation as a *tempe* producer enabled her to care for her young children, with this as with her other activities it was the barriers posed by finance and experience which determined her activities. As she was forced to acquire income from somewhere, the demands of childrearing became only one of a number of constraints on her choice of occupation (cf. Peluso 1981).

Bu Zainuddin, who has five young children, was forced into trading when her husband deserted her. Selling household rice stocks to acquire her initial funds, she began buying eggs in the village for resale to a Kebumen wholesaler. Finding sufficient eggs was a major problem as local production is largely consumed or sold to *warung*. She also had difficulties judging the quality of eggs, which were not shared by her Kebumen buyer. After six months without profits, she began purchasing coconuts which she shelled and prepared for copra production. Like Bu Suwuh, her many misjudgements in determining the quality of nuts bankrupted her within a year. For the last eighteen months she had had reasonable success retailing ready-made clothing, selling her gold ear-rings to provide the initial finance. The ear-rings had been purchased when gold was $US35 an ounce and were sold when it reached $US600; the connections between the international market and village trade are evidently quite remarkable.

1. In 1905 the population density was 523 per square kilometre, which even then was regarded as too great, and among the heaviest in Java (*Mindere Welvaart, Samentrekking . . . Kedoe* 1908:10, 89; IXc:351).

2. The most important *kecamatan* towns are Kebumen, Gombong, Karanganyar, Pejagoan, Kųtowinangun and Prembun, each formerly termed a *kawedanan*, but now given the status of *wilayah pembantu bupati*. *Kawedanan*, however, remains the term in common parlance.

3. The extension of the Yogyakarta–Cilacap railway line in 1888 had a positive influence on trade, and thirteen new markets were opened in Kebumen and Purworejo (*Mindere Welvaart* VIf:201). The numbers of traders increased and agricultural production was stimulated with more widespread planting of coconuts, areca nuts and *sirih* (*Mindere Welvaart* VIb:155, 199). Lime-burning, brick and tile as well as other small-scale industry also expanded as a result of the railway line extension (Abendanon 1904:44; *Koloniaal Verslag* 1892:1, 5).

4. In 1904/5 sugar was cultivated in the Prembun (350 *bouw*), Kutowinangun (350 *bouw*) and Kebumen (300 *bouw*) areas, with a further 500 *bouw* in the Pituruh and Kutoarjo areas of Purworejo regency (*Mindere Welvaart, Samentrekking . . . Kedoe* 1908:89).

5. *Sawah* is the Indonesian term for irrigated farm land, traditionally used for rice, but nowadays used for numerous other crops including tobacco, citrus, peanuts, soybean etc. Other important terms for agricultural land are *tegalan* (the unirrigated hilly areas used for cassava, chillies and tree crops) and *pekarangan* (areas around the houses planted with tree crops, vegetables and medicinal plants). See Ochse and Terra (1934); Penny and Singarimbun (1973); Stoler (1978) and Terra (1932) for discussions of the importance of *pekarangan* crops. Gelpke (1901:18ff) describes various kinds of *sawah* and dry lands.

6. Stoler (1975:59) states that recently, as a result of double-cropping and the introduction of rice hullers, there has been an increase in rice traders in Kali Loro. On my last field trip there were some similar developments in Kutowinangun. See Mears (1961; 1978) on marketing rice.

7. According to *Mindere Welvaart* (IXc:48) this was also true in the early 1900s. The report claimed that in normal times people ate twice a day, rice for one meal and cassava or corn for the other.

8. The word *aliran* literally means 'stream', but is more usefully defined as 'ideological orientation'.

9. The first positive mention of Chinese trade in Java is found in the annals of the Sung dynasty (920–1279) in the tenth century. Chinese traders acted as intermediaries between the great Chinese trading houses and the native people until the time of the V.O.C. (Dutch East Indies Company). During the V.O.C. period Chinese traders in Java acted as intermediaries between the V.O.C. and the native population, and after the fall of the V.O.C. they were intermediaries between European wholesalers and the Javanese (Liem Twan Djie 1947:16–24). Numerous sources have pointed to the important role of the Chinese in middleman/intermediate trade during the colonial period: buying up agricultural produce and selling imported articles (Burger n.d.:34–5; Burger 1939: 7, 27; Handbook of the Netherlands East Indies 1930:303–6; Liem Twan Djie 1947:7; *Mindere Welvaart* VIf:96). The Chinese have also had a very important role as toll collectors, bazaar holders and leaseholders from the seventh century onwards (van Deventer 1904:97). In Bagalen the linen trade was in the hands of the Chinese and Arab middlemen (ibid:102).

10. See Soewondo (1977) for a discussion of the Indonesian Marriage Law of 1973.

11. *Bengkok* lands are the shares reserved for village functionaries in lieu of salary. Each is assigned an area, in this case from 0.36 hectares (250 *ubin*) to 10.87

hectares (7160 *ubin*) of *sawah*. In Babadsari *bengkok* land is split between twenty-three village officials, with the Village Headman holding ten and a half hectares.

12. For details of the survey on which this is based see Alexander (1985:30–5). See also *Mindere Welvaart, Samentrekking . . . Kedoe* 1907 for a historical perspective.

13. Seven hundred *ubin* equals one hectare. Although 100 *ubin* does not make the average family self-sufficient in rice, most villagers regard it as the smallest viable unit. Stoler (1977:79) sees 0.2 hectares of double-cropped *sawah* as the minimum required to produce enough rice to feed a household of average size throughout the year in Kali Loro.

14. 'The accepted definition of a "cukup" level of income is 240 kilograms of milled rice equivalent per person per year, of which an average of 120 kilograms is estimated as average staple food needs in a rice-based diet' (Hart 1977:13). See also Penny and Singarimbun (1973:83) and Sajogyo (1975).

15. Of the 600 Babadsari households 409 have access to less than 0.25 hectares of agricultural land. Eighty-seven households have access to between 0.25 and 0.5 hectares and thirty-two have access to more than 0.5 hectares. Seventy-two households have no access to agricultural land (Kantor Sensus dan Statistik 1980). Those with access to agricultural land include landowners, sharecroppers and renters as well as village officials who receive *bengkok* land in return for service.

16. Gille and Pardoko (1965:503–4); Hart (1977); *Mindere Welvaart* (IXb3); Stoler (1975; 1977); White (1975).

17. In Stoler's (1975:55–6) Kali Loro sample, 42% of men over fifteen and 82.5% of women over fifteen quoted their major occupation as outside the agricultural sector. The breakdown is as follows:

Occupation	*Men* (603)	*Women* (737)
farming	54.2	16.3
farm labourer	3.8	1.2
trader	5.5	27.5
production of food for sale	2.5	9.5
crafts	2.5	23.5
pensioners,		
civil servants, etc.	12.4	0.9
student	10.9	4.6
other	2.0	2.2
none	6.1	14.2
	99.9	99.9

Sideline occupations were also an important source of income for most households.

18. Thirty-seven per cent of Stoler's (1977:79) Kali Loro sample were landless. In the Penny and Singarimbun (1972) sample 37% had no *sawah* and 22% had no land at all.

19. White (1976a:285) shows that the average daily work hours of adult males (15 and over) total 8.7 of which 7.6 are in directly productive work. The figures for adult females are 11.1 and 5.9. The equivalents for males aged eleven to fourteen are 4.8 and 3.3; and for females in the same age category 8.6 and 4.7. Average daily work hours of males nine to eleven years total 3.2 of which 1.9 are indirectly productive work. The figures for females of nine to eleven years are 5.4 and 3.1 hours daily.

20. These figures accord with those from other Central Javanese villages. Stoler (1977:83) states that 'In Kali Loro almost forty per cent of the adult women were engaged in some form of trade and probably another thirty per cent had traded at some point in their lives; only eight per cent of the men were traders'.

21. *Mindere Welvaart* (IXb3:16) points out that small-scale trade at the turn of the century was almost solely in women's hands. The same report (Appendix VI:26–9) also stresses the importance of women in *warung* trade and argues for increased education on basic economics for women.

22. As McGee (1973:167–9) notes, there is a persistent tendency to underestimate the barriers to becoming a trader.

2

The Pasar

MARKET PLACES

ANY early-morning traveller in Java quickly becomes aware of the importance of rural trade. Every few kilometres, hundreds of traders and their customers spill over from the official market places, clustering along the sides of the narrow roads which are blocked by trucks and buses, horse carts and bicycles.

There are 102 official market places in Kabupaten Kebumen:[1] thirty-three under *kabupaten* administration, and sixty-nine controlled by village councils. The *kabupaten* markets are divided into seven administrative areas, each with at least four markets; one for each of the constituent *kecamatan* located on the main road. All of the *kabupaten* markets, with their locations and tax receipts for the 1981/82 fiscal year, are listed in Table 2.1.

Market fees amounted to Rp 142 748 610 in 1981/82 and provided a considerable proportion of the *kabupaten* income. Receipts were distributed relatively evenly throughout the year, although 10% was taken during July, immediately before the celebration of Lebaran. While only indirectly related to the level of trade, the amount of the annual market fees directly reflects the number of traders in each market.[2] The two largest market places, Tumenggungan in the *kabupaten* capital and Wonokriyo near an army base, alone account for 65% of total fees. Then follow the market places in each *kawedanan*, most of them situated on the main road. The sixteen remaining markets are much smaller. Although there are twice as many market places controlled by village councils, sixty-nine as opposed to thirty-three, they are less significant than their *kabupaten* counterparts.

The number of traders in the markets ranges from the 4000-odd

TABLE 2.1

MARKETS UNDER *KABUPATEN* ADMINISTRATION:

Location and Tax Receipts for the 1981/82 Fiscal Year

Market	Kecamatan	Tax Receipts Rp
TUMENGGUNGAN	Kebumen	49 327 855
Taman Reja	Kebumen	2 544 040
Bocor	Buluspesantren	488 015
Sruni	Alian	1 013 435
Endrokilo	Alian	1 083 980
KUTOWINANGUN	Kutowinangun	6 333 730
Ungaran	Kutowinangun	436 690
Jatisari	Kebumen	1 822 540
Ambal	Ambal	1 243 590
PREMBUN	Prembun	4 428 095
Khewan Prembun	Prembun	534 415
Kabekelan	Prembun	1 933 490
Tlogopragota	Mirit	848 100
KARANGANYAR	Karanganyar	11 876 380
Giwangretna	Sruweng	692 525
Garuban	Sruweng	330 005
Sidomulyo	Klirong	301 730
Karangjambu	Klirong	445 970
WONOKRIYO	Gombong	43 216 125
Khewan Gombong	Gombong	908 400
Banyumudah	Buayan	78 760
Kuwarasan	Kuwarasan	503 390
Karangsari	Buayan	166 960
PETANAHAN	Petanahan	4 727 620
Puring	Puring	1 510 195
Jagasima	Petanahan	564 705
Kritik	Adimulyo	117 365
Tanjungsari	Adimulyo	465 935
Dorowati	Adimulyo	1 226 850
DEMANGSARI	Ayah	2 714 500
Candirenggo	Ayah	76 200
Rowokele	Rowokele	703 320
Jatiluhur	Rowokele	93 700
TOTAL		142 748 610

in the main Kebumen *pasar* to thirty-five in the unofficial village market of Babadsari. The *kecamatan* markets have at least 1500 vendors and even official village markets such as Krakal have between two and four hundred traders. These figures are considerably higher than those noted for other regions in Java which report a range from 100 to 3500 (Anderson 1980:767; Dewey 1962a; Peluso 1981). Indeed, the Kebumen markets seem to have more traders than peasant markets anywhere in the world.[3]

MARKET TOWNS

The distribution of markets is governed by both the sub-*kabupaten* administrative structure and the network of roads. Major market places are dotted at about ten kilometre intervals along the main southern Java highway, and are mainly situated in the major administrative centres. Similar markets fall at five kilometre intervals along the highway in the *kecamatan* towns or in *kecamatan* towns on the side roads.

Bigger towns have more than one market place. The largest market town is the *kabupaten* capital Kebumen, which encompasses about 650 shops (*toko*) and kiosks (*warung*) as well as a very large market place (*pasar*) which is open every day, and some smaller *pasar*. Gombong, the largest town in the western portion of the regency, is near an army base and has a large Chinese population. Its major market is the same size as Kebumen's, and it has a large number of modern shops and restaurants serving motor traffic between West and Central Java. The other major market towns are Prembun and Kutowinangun in the east, and Karanganyar in the west. Each has several market places, one of them open every day, and is a *kecamatan* capital. The other market towns include only one or two markets and are active on only two days a week.

An understanding of the structure of markets in the Kebumen region is enhanced by conceptualizing the system in terms of market towns rather than market places. Not only do many economic transactions take place outside the geographical limits of the official market places (*pasar*), but market days regulate economic activities throughout the town, not merely in the market places themselves. On non-market days many of the shops (other than specialized vendors such as gold sellers) are open and at least one *pasar* will be full of traders, but the scale of economic activity is very low because the buyers are limited to the town's inhabitants.

On market days, however, the whole town comes alive; the shops are thronged with customers, the markets hold more traders than would be thought possible, and hundreds of small sellers congregate along the narrow strips bordering the highway. Because market days heavily influence transport routes, they tend to regulate social as well as economic activities throughout the region. While there are frequent buses along the highway even on non-market days, they are often reluctant to accept passengers for short trips, and it is very difficult to get to towns off the highway without the expense of hiring an entire minibus (*colt*) or horse carriage (*dokar*). But on market days, as many as 200 *dokar*, as well as minibuses and trucks, run between the market towns and the interior towns and villages, making it easy to visit both these places and the points in between.

A study which concentrated on activities within the designated market places of each town would therefore give a misleading picture of the rural marketing system. Not only would it miss about a third of the transactions, including most of the wholesaling, but also it would underestimate the extent to which the economic activities of the 'modern' or 'formal' sector are constrained by the 'traditional' periodic market system.

PERIODIC MARKETS

Each market town has been allocated two market days each week. The market days are paired—Sunday/Wednesday, Monday/Thursday, Tuesday/Friday, with Saturday being used only in very small market places. In towns with several market places all *pasar* are open on the same day. The use of the national seven-day week, rather than the five-day Javanese week, to calculate market days sets Kebumen apart from Yogyakarta and East Java. I was unable to ascertain when this practice began but it at least pre-dates 1900. Market days are officially fixed by the *kabupaten* administration, but the pattern has remained the same in Kebumen for fifty years.

Taking Kebumen as the centre, the effect of market days is to distribute economic activities in a regular and equitable way throughout the regency. Kebumen, for example, is allocated Sunday and Wednesday. On the following days activity shifts to the major town in the west, Gombong, and then to the intermediate town of Karanganyar. Neighbouring towns have sequential days, which limits transport expenses and facilitates the collection of twenty-four hour credit. Market days within each *kecamatan* follow a similar pattern, with the *kecamatan* towns as the centre.

At least one *pasar* in each market town is open every day of the week, serving mainly local customers for five days and the wider hinterland on the two official market days. I use the term 'periodic market' for activities on the formal market days and 'daily market' to refer to activities during the rest of the week. Similarly I call sellers who work predominantly in the periodic markets 'cyclical traders' and use the term 'daily traders' for vendors who confine their activities to a single market near their house.

The hierarchy of market towns in the Kebumen regency is largely based on their respective importance as administrative centres. Kebumen market town is the central or principal market on the grounds that it provides the widest range of goods and services, although it cannot be seen as the centre of bulking and distribution chains. Gombong, a marginally smaller market, is the principal market for the western section of the regency, and provides goods and services on a similar scale to Kebumen. In both Kebumen and Gombong the periodic market system is superimposed on daily markets which offer a reasonable range of commodities. Karanganyar, Kutowinangun and Prembun on the main road, along with Petanahan and Demangsari in the south-west portion, rank as secondary markets. These differ from the primary markets in that although daily markets operate, their activities are on a much reduced scale and commodities are largely confined to foodstuffs. In the remaining markets under *kabupaten* administration, market place activity is mainly confined to the periodic market day.

The primary and secondary market towns perform an important role in the bulking of agricultural produce, and these seven markets are the focus of bulking local agricultural produce as well as distribution points for extra-regional produce. With a few exceptions, however, little agricultural produce is channelled upward from the secondary to primary market places and local agricultural products are transported directly from the secondary market places to extra-regional buyers. But Kebumen in particular is an important distribution point for many bulk-breaking activities which include both consumer durables and agricultural produce. Minor markets are frequently important in the upward bulking of local fruits and vegetables, but while some produce is resold in the primary and secondary markets, much is destined for more distant markets.

On any particular day a trader has the choice of several possible markets in which to sell her goods. Some of the factors governing the choice are obviously contingent on tradition, friendship, or a close relationship with a particular wholesaler, but four factors are important in all cases: residence, competition, transport and re-stocking. Transport is a heavy cost for most traders, often taking half their returns, and this encourages them to work in the closest markets. But the more distant and smaller markets have fewer traders, which means not merely less competition and higher profits but also, especially for fruit and vegetable sellers, the chance to restock perishables at lower prices. Small traders in non-perishable commodities, however, cannot limit themselves to the smaller and more distant markets; they must visit the larger markets to restock at reasonable prices. Whereas fruit and vegetable sellers mainly restock in small and distant markets, and retail in the larger ones, for small cloth, clothing and household commodity traders, the pattern is reversed. In either case small traders tend to work in both the largest market closest to their home base and a selection of smaller markets. Larger, established traders are able to concentrate on the main markets, relying on the higher volume of trade to balance lower prices.

PASAR, DEPOT, TOKO, WARUNG

Javanese distinguish four types of economic institutions connected with the buying and selling of commodities: *pasar, depot, toko* and *warung*. While there is some overlap, especially between the last pair, each institution has a particular economic function, deals with a discrete clientele, and to some extent has its own set of norms governing transactions.

The *pasar* is the large market place familiar from most studies of Asian markets. In the Javanese case the term *pasar* refers not only to trade located within the *pasar* in the narrow sense, the market place proper, but also to buying and selling in the streets nearby. For most rural Javanese, the *pasar* is a very exuberant (*rame*) place and a visit every couple of months or so is an exciting occasion. Purchases by such villagers are limited to the more expensive consumer items—cloth, ready-made clothing, copperware—or goods bought infrequently, ranging from household items to seedlings. The villagers who visit the market place more frequently are mainly *warung* owners buying vegetables, fruit, rice and noodles for resale when they return home, but traders and the people living in the town buy their daily requirements of foodstuffs in the *pasar* also. Within the *pasar*, prices are not marked or fixed and bargaining is normal for most purchases. Supplies to the *pasar* are provided mainly by wholesalers or agents purchasing direct in the villages, but vendors may purchase stock from another trader within the *pasar* or from a visiting farmer.

Although the numbers fluctuate with the season, Prembun contains about thirteen *depot* bulking agricultural produce. The major crops in approximate order of importance are: *bengkuwang* (yam beans), chillies, coconuts, citrus, peanuts, soybean, green gram and rice. While the *depot* will buy direct from the producer, and there are numerous small buyers situated in front of each *depot*, most produce is bought from other traders. The *depot* then resells in loads large enough for economic transport: 100 kilograms for a trader who proposes to wholesale in a regional *pasar* and will transport it by *colt*; truckloads of two and a half tonnes for clients in major cities. Within *depot*, produce is weighed and prices are relatively fixed. *Depot* do not, however, break down incoming goods into retail packages. This is the role of wholesalers, who are located within the *pasar* and resell to other vendors.

The separation of the *depot* from the *pasar* proper is a relatively recent development in Prembun—although in East Java in 1954 the Chinese wholesale establishments seem to have been outside the *pasar* (Dewey 1962a:50; Geertz 1963b:8)—and is mainly a response to changes in the transport system. Locating *depot* on the outskirts of town makes access easier for trucks and *colt*, without hindering farmer-sellers and small traders. The wholesalers who break down loads remain inside the *pasar* to avoid the evident problem of transporting small loads.

It is often difficult to distinguish physically between *toko* and *warung*, for while many *toko*, even in small towns, are housed in substantial buildings with plate glass windows, the smaller *toko* appear identical to the larger *warung*. A more useful basis for classification is in terms of economic functions. Whereas *toko* retail expensive consumer items which are mainly produced outside the region and wholesale factory-produced goods ranging from cigarettes to tinned fish, *warung* retail commodities of all types direct to the consumer.

There are sixty-seven *toko* in Prembun. Twenty-six of these are owned by Chinese, one by an Arab family, and another by a man from Tapanuli in North Sumatra. Only thirty-four are owned by Javanese.[4] Some of the *toko* are highly specialized and sell one major commodity: six deal in gold, three in steel furniture, eight in building supplies and fourteen in high quality manufactured cloth and expensive *batik*. Other *toko* are essentially wholesalers of factory-produced consumer items: cigarettes, coffee and tea; kerosene and spare parts for pressure lamps; simple drugs such as aspirins; powdered milk; and soft drinks and confectionary. Most customers in these stores are themselves *warung* owners or *pasar* traders who will make their profits by breaking down the commodities into smaller selling units, but the richest villagers and the townspeople buy items such as cigarettes in the *toko*. *Toko* prices are relatively fixed and it is normal to receive a receipt with all purchases.

The vast majority of *warung* are situated in the villages, but there are sixty-five *warung* in Prembun providing services for the urban population.[5] While they vary tremendously in size—the largest *warung* have turnovers rivalling the *toko*, while the stock of the smallest would not exceed Rp 3000 worth of prepared food—they share the economic function of selling direct to the consumer. The common unit of sale in a *warung* is minute: a single cigarette, two aspirin, forty grams of washing powder, or 100 grams of biscuits. Village *warung* often accumulate a bewildering variety of stock, and the biggest among them will stock every item that a villager might buy.[6] The largest village *warung* in Babadsari whose stock I counted had 212 separate items, including thirty-four Western medicines, forty toiletries, and twenty types of stationery. Some *warung*, particularly within towns, specialize in selling prepared food and drinks; a small plate of rice and vegetables costs Rp 90, with a further Rp 45 for some chicken-flavour curry containing miniscule pieces of flesh or bone. There are more than twenty-five eating *warung* in Prembun. Prices for many items in the *warung*, especially manufactured and prepared food, are fixed, but it is often possible to bargain for better quality. Most *warung* owners in the villages buy agricultural produce for resale or bulking. It is common for *warung* to extend credit to regular customers and sometimes the owners are money lenders.

Although many manufactured goods produced outside the region enter the local distribution network through the *toko*, it would not be useful to conceptualize the division between the *toko* and *depot*, on the one hand, and the *warung* and the *pasar*, on the other, in terms of 'formal' and 'informal' sectors.[7] Many of the goods sold in the *toko* will be resold in the *warung* or *pasar*, while agricultural produce first bought by a *warung* owner may later reach factories as far afield as Singapore. The *depot*, *toko*, *warung* and *pasar* must be seen as sectors within a unified market system.

Nevertheless, it should be emphasized that the four institutions serve separate economic functions and sell to different clientele. Although they often sell the same commodities, the selling unit is very different: large quantities in the *toko* and *depot*, small in the *pasar* and smaller again in the *warung*. It is worth pointing out that the failure to appreciate that few transactions in the *pasar* are to direct consumers (cf. Anderson 1978) often stems from a misapprehension of the minute quantities of final retail sales. A woman buying a single cabbage in the *pasar*, for example, may well resell it in as many as five or six portions.

Javanese conceptions of *toko*, *warung* and *pasar* differ with economic circumstances and social status. Many villagers, apart from the elite, prefer to buy in the *pasar* or *warung* because they are intimidated by the *toko*. They believe that shop goods are more expensive and that customers cannot bargain over prices. The elite, however, who have the wealth and social status to interact with shop owners on more or less equal terms, assume that shop goods are of a uniformly high quality and mistrust the market trader. They claim that it is better to buy quality goods in the *toko* than risk buying inferior goods for a similar price in the market. In fact, medium quality goods are often cheaper in the *toko* and it is possible to lower prices. Many villagers are also timid about using Chinese shops for, although most Chinese speak Javanese, they do not have the appropriate command of speech levels and appear rude. Conversely, villagers claim that the Javanese shop owner's superior command of Javanese idioms will manipulate them into paying high prices.

PREMBUN MARKET TOWN

Prembun town, the major site for my market research, is officially divided into three *desa* (Prembun, Bagung and Kabekelan), but the boundaries are ignored by the 4500 people who live there. Economic transactions in Prembun take place in four distinct geographical locations: in the shops and stalls lining the main road;

in *depot* for the bulking of agricultural produce; and in the two general and three specialized *pasar*. Small-scale sellers slip into any empty space. Each location involves a specific category of trader and a particular clientele, and transactions within each location are governed by different norms.

Entering the town from the west on the market days of Monday and Thursday, the first signs of economic activity are apparent at Jalan Wonosobo, a major crossroads and bus stop (see Map 3). A livestock market is situated about a kilometre down the side-road in the village of Sidogede. Although this market, Pasàr Khewan Prembun, is open both market days, Mondays are much busier, with some 200 male traders dealing in buffalo, cattle, goats and sheep. At the crossroads itself is a small poultry market, and it is a minor collection point for crops such as peanuts and chillies. Two hundred metres to the right along the main road is Pasar Bengku-wang. This comprises a large bamboo and corrugated iron shed, the locus of the wholesale *bengkuwang* trade (see Chapter 6), and a number of *depot* dealing in chillies and oranges. In the high season up to 400 tonnes of *bengkuwang* flow through the market each day, but in the low season the turnover is less than one tonne.

A further 500 metres to the east, abutting on a number of other *depot* specializing in ground-nuts, green gram and soybean, is Pasar Kulon. One of the two major markets in Prembun, Pasar Kulon (West Market) is also the main centre for *batik* and hard-ware traders, but other traders are scattered throughout its area. Two hundred and fifty metres further east is the wholesale coconut market and in front of this the bicycle market. Scores of small traders line the roadside bordering these markets. The largest of the official market areas, Pasar Wetan (East Market) is situated about 125 metres further east of the coconut market. This is the main food market, with fruit, vegetables, meat and dried-fish sellers figuring prominently. The town ends abruptly less than 100 metres to the east with a timber yard, a lime kiln, and a small *warung*. Shops, both large and small are distributed throughout the town, but the majority are concentrated along both sides of the road between Pasar Kulon and the coconut market.

PASAR WETAN

Pasar Wetan, as it is commonly known, is located in the *desa* of Kabekelan from which it takes its official name. It is bounded by a

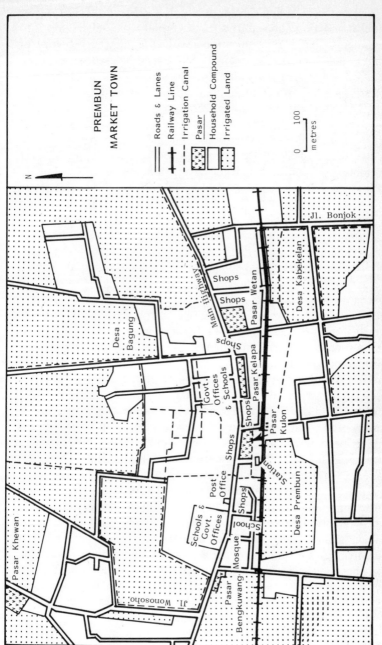

Map 3 Prembun Market Town

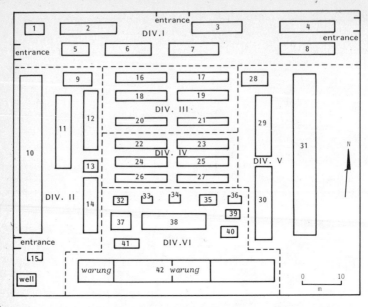

Map 4 Pasar Wetan

barbed-wire fence on three sides, but the southern boundary is formed by a small canal behind which is a thick stand of trees. The *pasar* (see Map 4) contains forty-two stands (*los*), twenty-five substantial structures of brick and tile, and seventeen sheds of bamboo and thatch. Not all traders have a position in the stands. In each alleyway, numerous poor traders sell the same types of goods as the nearby stands, from bamboo tables or pieces of burlap. Positions in the stands are allocated by market officials and daily fees for a selling position range from Rp 15 for a spot in the open to Rp 200 for a lockable section of a *los*.

A combination of geographical and functional criteria creates six divisions in Pasar Wetan. Division One (Stands One to Eight) which is normally the first section reached by customers, contains most of the artisans (*tukang*), with barbers, watch repairers and preparers of traditional herbal medicines most common. Expensive household items such as mats and copperware, and staples such as dried cereals and tobacco are also found here. The area between the sheds is the decorative bird market.

Division Two (Sheds Nine to Fifteen) is dominated by a very large stand occupied by traders selling a wide range of locally manufactured household and agricultural requirements such as rope, hats, hoes and knives. Other localized stands specialize in metal ware: solderers, tinsmiths, etc. On the border of this section a large number of traders sell cheap prepared food including iced drinks and roasted corn. Condiments, vegetables and tobacco can also be bought in very small lots at this location.

Division Three (Sheds Sixteen to Twenty-one) houses the cloth and clothing market, as well as tailors with hand sewing machines who will make clothes on the spot. Most of these traders would prefer to work in Pasar Kulon, the main selling point for these goods and services, but have been unable to obtain space. The vendors of Division Four (Sheds Twenty-two to Twenty-seven) deal in household staples such as bean curd, soybean cake, condiments, vegetables, salt and coconut sugar.

Division Five (Sheds Twenty-eight to Thirty-one) contains a very large stand, the top end of which is always busy. In the planting seasons, seedlings for clove and orange trees and chilli plants are bought here, and during the remainder of the year the occupants sell fruit. Fresh fish sellers are also found in this section of the market alongside the vendors of sweets, prepared foods and iced drinks. The larger traders are located in the shed, the smaller traders in the open space nearby.

Division Six (Stands Thirty-two to Forty-two), at the southern end of the market, contains all the meat sellers, as well as a mixture of cabbage, condiment, betel and dried-fish sellers. The two largest *warung* in the market are located at the southernmost point.

PASAR KULON

Pasar Kulon (see Map 5) is half the size of Pasar Wetan and consists of nineteen sheds, some of which are lockable. At the rear are a long row of houses, many of which are also eating places for traders and customers. To the east of the market office at the entrance are seven small shops. This market is divided into two sections, the core cloth market and the periphery. The market is open every day, however, and the structure on the official market days of Monday and Thursday differs from that during the rest of the week.

On periodic market days, the entrance next to the market office sets the tone for the market place: large numbers of women buying and selling second-hand cloth and clothing, which they carry in

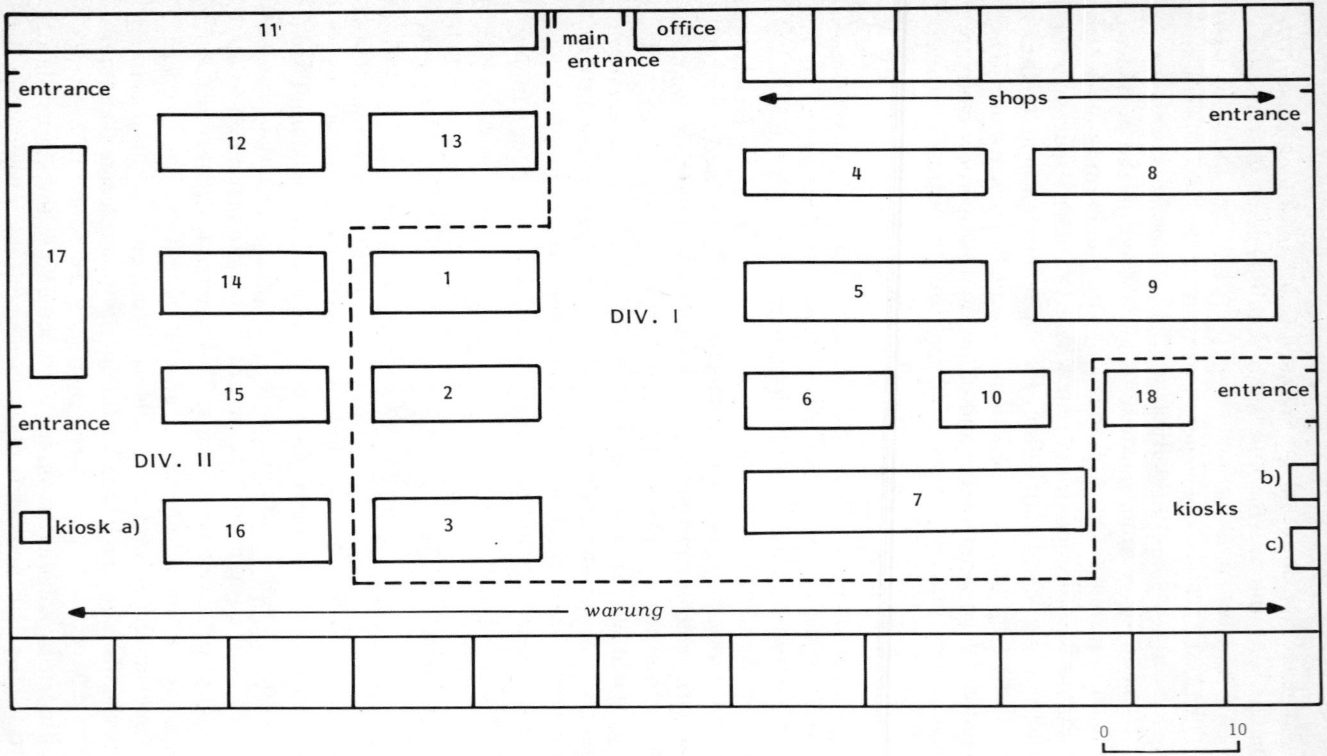

50

Map 5 Pasar Kulon

bundles on their hips, clutter the entrance. Division One (Stands One to Ten), the core block, is almost entirely concerned with the sale of cloth and clothing.

Division Two (the periphery) consists of Stands Eleven to Eighteen, plus three kiosks and a row of *warung* to the rear. Goods sold range from hardware and tobacco on the northern boundary, through rice, vegetables, prepared foods and sweets, to an almost empty stand at the rear where two sellers specialize in dried cassava, chips, dried fish etc. Shed Thirteen near the entrance contains mainly traders in manufactured kitchenware, soybean cake, prepared sweets and chips, as well as a few clothing traders.

LOCALIZATION

The geographical layout of the two markets provides important clues to their economic structure. Broadly speaking, traders performing similar services or selling similar goods are grouped together, giving the prospective customer the chance to look over all goods at once, which is a very important factor in an economic system which lacks advertising. One might expect newcomers to set up stands away from existing competition. They reason they do not, according to the traders, is that most people would not buy from such an isolated seller. An important exception to this general practice are sellers of haberdashery and odds and ends such as pencils and exercise books. They are generally scattered throughout the market, for they say that as most of their sales are unplanned and spontaneous, they are better off in non-localized positions. When the new Kutowinangun market was built, these traders were grouped towards the rear of the market. They complained bitterly that their sales had fallen, and within a month had dispersed throughout the market.

The costs of setting up a permanent stand in a market place are very high by Javanese standards. Consequently villagers selling their own produce, as well as the poorer traders, have to seek other locations. One possibility is to circulate within the market, avoiding the entrance fee by pretending to be a customer, another is to sell on the street. Even among these small-scale *bakul*, trading in a particular commodity is highly localized: in one place bird sellers, soybean traders in another, and women buying eggs in threes and fours in yet another. A narrow strip of twenty-five square metres alongside the road, for example, contains twenty-three wholesale tobacco sellers, selling in quantities of one kilogram and upwards. A similar area encompasses fifteen kapok traders, and for two weeks in December the roadside is covered with rice seedlings for sale. Linking these sub-markets are rows of retailers selling in extremely small units—single cigarettes, a few onions, bundles of cabbage leaves—and buyers of rural produce who will later resell.

NUMBERS OF TRADERS

It is not easy to calculate the number of traders in the Prembun market places, let alone in other areas of the town. Not only do many vendors move continuously throughout the market places, but some who sell mainly to other vendors may visit three or four markets in the course of a morning. My figures, therefore, should be regarded as the lower limit of the numbers of traders. I conducted each count over three market days, counting the traders in one-third of the market each day. Only by this means could I arrive at accurate figures for, without talking to participants, it is by no means easy to distinguish traders from their friends, relatives, bystanders and customers.

My enumeration of the traders in Pasar Wetan is based on January 1980. This was the busiest month during my fieldwork, although it is generally recognized that the busiest time in the market is the period before Lebaran. There were 1038 traders in Pasar Wetan, 76% of them female. A second count during the month of the rice harvest in April, showed only slightly fewer traders (987), although there were obviously far fewer customers and the market finished earlier than usual. Most traders apparently preferred to work in the market during the busy period from about 6 to 9 a.m. and join the harvest later in the morning. The majority of traders came from within twenty kilometres of Prembun.

Pasar Kulon during a market day in January had a total of 413 traders, 69% of whom were women. Once again there was little difference in the number during the off-season. On non-market days when Pasar Wetan is closed, Pasar Kulon changes its character. Most of the larger cloth sellers work in other towns, and their places are taken by artisans and small vegetable sellers. Consequently, while the number of traders remains the same, the proportion of small traders increases and the proportion of women jumps to nearly 90%.

Two of the three specialized markets, the bicycle and livestock markets, are dominated by men: all traders are males and there are very few women customers. Most of the smaller coconut traders are women, but the larger buyers are mainly men. Two hundred and sixty traders are involved in these three markets.

It is difficult to survey the number of persons involved in trading outside the shops and the market places: a villager may bring a tray of chillies and depart when they are sold. On one day, however, I counted 449, 195 either buying or selling wholesale, and the remainder retailing.

These figures give some idea of the ways in which market days transform small towns such as Prembun and Kutowinangun. On a typical market day in January, more than 2000 people, three-quarters women, sell commodities in the streets and markets of Prembun. A further 636 people work in the shops, *warung* and *depot*. To this must be added the drivers and conductors of the *colt*, the grooms for the 200 *dokar* and *grobag*, and the *kuli* who carry and load purchases. There are also the market officials and bank personnel, as well as the beggars and buskers who follow the market circuit like any other trader. In all, a minimum of 3000 people are directly involved. Added to this, of course, are the customers whose numbers I was unable to survey or even to estimate with any degree of reliability. But it is probably reasonable to suggest that Prembun's normal population of 4500 more than triples at the height of the market. Between 4.30 a.m., when the first of the producers arrive, and 8:30 a.m., when most of the major trading has been concluded, it is almost impossible to move along the main road, and the town remains crowded until most traders have left around 11.30 a.m.

On a non-market day, Prembun is very quiet. Only Pasar Kulon is open, and while the number of traders is constant, the cloth traders have been replaced by retailers of vegetables and foodstuffs for the town community. The *pasar* takes on the function of a large *warung*. Indeed, the traders who remain describe their activities as *warungan* as opposed to *pasaran*: the activity centred on the periodic markets.

1. This is not a recent development; in the 1830s there were market places in all the major towns and larger villages and goods traded included rice, chillies, tobacco, linens, cotton, buffalo and cattle, opium and arak. Blacksmiths as well as silver- and goldsmiths were also found in the market places (ARA Bagalen 1832: 31–2). The silver- and goldsmiths along with the opium- and arak-sellers have long since disappeared.

2. Market fees are calculated according to the space occupied by the trader and the grade of market. The fee is also scaled according to whether the position is in a shed (*los*) or open space.

3. The Philippine city market studied by Davis (1973), for example, had 1521 stalls and an unspecified number of mobile traders serving a population of 50 000. The smaller Philippine town market Estancia, studied by Szanton (1972), was situated in a community of 14 000. Daily market traders averaged 250 people, with 600 in the periodic market. The city market of Oaxaca (Mexico) had only 2000 traders despite its population of two million, although a market in a small regional town had 750 traders among a population of 7000 (Beals 1975).

4. Burger (1948/49:243) noted that middle-class Javanese merchants in the *toko* trade only began to emerge at the beginning of the twentieth century. Early reports state that shops throughout Java and Madura were in the hands of Chinese and a few Arabs (see Droste 1921:203). The number of Javanese shop owners, particularly in small towns, has increased dramatically in the last thirty years.

5. Women have long dominated *warung* as well as *pasar* trade, and according to *Koloniaal Verslag* (1939) and *Mindere Welvaart* (VIa:24), *warung* trade in some divisions was almost exclusively in women's hands.

6. This is due, in part at least, to the *warung* owners' desire to build up a stable clientele (see Isaac 1981:363).

7. For a similar four-fold division in Brazil, see Forman and Riegelhaupt (1970:194–7). After toying with notions ranging from the dual economy to formal and informal sectors, scholars now seem agreed that such models reflect an unstated traditional–modern dichotomy and are of little value for analysis. See McGee (1978) and Forbes (1979).

3

The Traders

BAKUL, JURAGAN, AGEN

THE ubiquitous Javanese *bakul* was graphically described in an early proclamation from the Dutch colonizers:[1]

> Women who, instead of taking up some honest business by which to earn a living decently, seek to make a little money by sitting all day by the road-side selling a few vegetables and other little things of small value, and do this in such multitudes that they jostle each other and create great disorder in the market place, beside depriving one another of profit and the possibility of obtaining a sufficient living from this trafficking.

These disparaging remarks refer specifically to *bakul cilik-cilikan*, small-scale vendors, but the term *bakul* is used by the Javanese to refer to all traders, from retail market vendors to wholesalers buying agricultural produce in large quantities. The *bakul jalan* buys produce by the road-side. The *bakul keliling* vends her produce while moving through the market or visiting houses in the village, and the *bakul ngider* distributes goods wholesale, travelling from market to market. The *bakul dasaran* retails from a stall in the market place or some other fixed location, while the *bakul borongan* uses her stall in the market mainly to wholesale goods to retail *bakul*.

All traders, both male and female, are *bakul*, but the term is seldom applied to the large-scale traders uninvolved in retailing. Traders mainly concerned with bulking or bulk-breaking activities, wholesaling in some senses of the word, are called *juragan*, although the term has status connotations which make it unsuitable for self-reference. *Juragan* have larger amounts of finance and trade in larger quantities over longer distances than *bakul*, but apart from scale there are no clear distinctions between *juragan* and *bakul*. *Juragan* are also more likely to be men, although Chapter 6 discusses three very successful women *juragan*.

The term *juragan* may also be used for those traders who buy agricultural produce direct from the farmer and who are more precisely called *tengkulak* or *penebas*.[2] *Tengkulak* buy harvested crops in reasonably large quantities and pay directly in cash. *Penebas*, however, buy standing crops, especially tree crops but increasingly other agricultural produce as well. After reaching agreement on price, the *penebas* makes a small down-payment (*manjer*) and is then responsible for harvesting the crop. The arrangements for final payment are flexible. In theory the *penebas* agrees to pay a fixed price before harvest, but in most cases which I observed producer and buyer agreed on a final price after the *penebas* had resold the produce.

Agen also buy direct from the producer. The *agen* is a broker acting on behalf of a third party who, in the Kebumen region, is a *juragan* who runs a *depot* or warehouse (see pp. 42–5). *Agen* scout for produce and arrange deliveries to a *depot* when supplies are relatively scarce, but bulk produce within the village when quantities are large enough for direct sales from producer areas to urban centres. Occasionally the term *agen* is also applied to the *juragan* middleman who has stable relations with either suppliers or distributors. Such persons are, however, independent traders and the term is not often used in this sense.

Although producer/sellers are not as important in this region as in the peasant markets of Mexico (Beals 1975), Papua New Guinea (Epstein 1982) or the Philippines (Szanton 1972), they do have a role in market trade. Because of the part-time nature of their activities, they are usually referred to as *wong tani* (farmer), rather than *bakul*. Most *wong tani* are producer/sellers who buy a little extra from neighbours and sell it to a *depot* or to retail vendors in the *pasar*. But some produce specialized crops and take up full-time trading for a limited period: producers of rice seedlings and citrus stock are common examples. Another more common type of producer/seller is, however, always called a *bakul*. This is the vendor who prepares food and beverages in small quantities and retails them in the market or from house to house.

MARKETING STRUCTURE: AN EXAMPLE ·

The details of the marketing structure differ with the type of commodity, the season and the level of demand, and for that reason its complexity is best illustrated by the detailed case studies in later sections. But some broad features can be sketched by examining the marketing of cabbages, which are one of the most important foodstuffs bought into Kebumen from other regions. The marketing structure for this commodity is set out in Figure 3.1.

Cabbages sold in Kebumen are grown in the colder highland regions near Bandung and Wonosobo. The producer has four selling outlets. In some instances a *penebas* harvests and distributes the crop, and occasionally the farmer himself takes the crop to market for sale to a *bakul*, but most commonly the produce is sold to a *juragan* or his *agen*. Early in the morning the *juragan* or *agen* accompanies a truck driver directly to the fields. The cabbages are weighed, a price per kilogram is negotiated and paid, and the cabbages distributed to a *depot*. Late that afternoon the *juragan* and truck driver deliver quantities of cabbages to another *juragan* (occasionally termed an *agen*) in a large *kabupaten* market such as Kebumen. The recipient *juragan* is given a bill which is generally paid at the time of the next delivery.

The *agen* or *juragan* in the regional market then redistributes to *bakul* within the district markets, writing a 'ticket' for each sale and also making an entry in his account book. These *bakul* in turn sell the bulk of their produce to village market traders and *warung*, as well as serving urban consumers. But unless the urban consumer is buying cabbages for a special occasion such as a *slametan*, she seldom buys a whole cabbage, and is content with a bundle of leaves. The cabbages purchased by the village *bakul* or *warung* owner are also divided into bundles of leaves for resale. Occasionally a group of *bakul* from the smaller district markets will club together and buy directly from *depot* or *penebas* in the producer region.

This relatively simple example of a marketing structure indicates that the Javanese terms for traders are not entirely congruent with the hierarchy of functions, and that the distinction between wholesale (*borongan*) and retail (*eceran*) transactions is by no means clear.[3] Accounts of peasant marketing often confuse person and role, identifying wholesale and retail functions with different

58

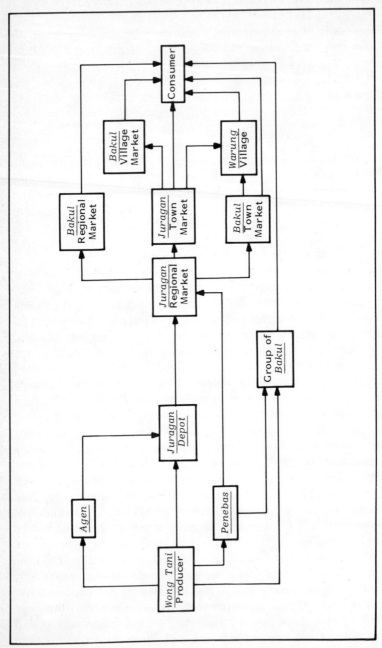

Fig. 3.1. The Marketing Structure

TABLE 3.1

THE RELATIONSHIP BETWEEN PRICE AND MARKETING LEVEL[a]

Market Level	Sale Price Per Kg. (Rp)
Producer (*wong tani*)	25
Agen	28
Depot	60
Regional Market (*kabupaten-juragan*)	65
District Market (*kecamatan-juragan*)	75
Bakul (district market)	85
Bakul (village market)/Urban *Warung*	90–110
Village *Warung*	95–115

[a] These prices are averages of three trips where I followed the commodity from the point of production to point of sale.

individuals, thereby disguising the complexity of trading relationships. But diversification of roles is an important survival strategy for traders and most *bakul* combine wholesale with retail functions, sometimes without knowing they are doing so. For this reason it is often very difficult to distinguish between wholesale and retail sales without detailed knowledge of the context of individual transactions, a problem made more difficult by the miniscule quantities in which commodities are sold to the final consumer. I use the term wholesaler very sparingly to refer to traders who sell on a large scale to other traders, without any implication that the buyers may not also be wholesalers in a strict sense.

The allocation of value at various points in the marketing structure is indicated in Table 3.1. In these cases prices increased more than three-fold between producer and final consumer. My impression is that this is common for foodstuffs sold between regions but that the prices do not increase so markedly for crops retailed in the areas in which they are produced. The variation in the prices paid by direct consumers reflects both the increased importance of bargaining and that at this stage the cabbages are not sold by weight. The biggest increase in prices is between the producer and the *depot*, with a pattern of small general increments until the cabbages are finally retailed. Once again I think that this is the usual pattern, although using averages obscures the large profits which are occasionally obtained on the distribution side of the system (see Chapter 6, pp. 154–8). It is also worth pointing out

TABLE 3.2

DISTRIBUTION OF TRADERS BETWEEN COMMODITIES:

Periodic and Daily Markets in Prembun[a]

Category	Periodic Market		Daily Market	
	No.	%	No.	%
Vegetables	264	14	122	31
Dry Goods	260	14	33	9
Fruit	62	3	29	7
Meat, Fish & Eggs	39	2	9	2
Seedlings	37	2	—	—
Livestock & Birds	50	3	—	—
Cloth & Clothing	270	14	8	2
Handicrafts	213	11	7	2
Manufactured Goods	107	6	4	1
Locally Manufactured Foodstuffs	199	10	73	19
Prepared Food & Drinks	151	8	64	16
Tobacco	102	5	16	4
Miscellaneous	36	2	9	2
Artisan	110	6	14	4
TOTAL	1900	100%	388	99%

[a] Traders in specialized markets—livestock, coconut, bicycle and bengkuwang—are not included.

that the initial transport costs for this commodity and the risks that it will perish if transport is not available are particularly great and that this reduced the apparently high profits of the *depot*. Hiring a truck to take two tonnes of cabbages from Bandung to Kebumen costs at least Rp 50 000, and all costs other than unloading are met by the *depot*.

THE PASAR TRADERS

Although, as I have indicated, the *pasar* proper is only one among several loci of transactions within the Kebumen marketing system, it is true that most *bakul* are concerned with transactions within the *pasar*. On a market day 1451 traders are crowded within the confines of two Prembun *pasar*, buying and selling both to each other and to the customers.

Table 3.2 shows the distribution of traders between various commodities in both periodic and daily markets. In the periodic

TABLE 3.3
SEXUAL DIVISION OF ALL PREMBUN TRADERS:
Periodic Market Day

Category	Women	%	Men	%	Total
Vegetables	255	97	9	3	264
Dry Goods	203	78	57	22	260
Fruit	60	97	2	3	62
Meat Fish & Eggs	39	100	—	—	39
Seedlings	9	24	28	76	37
Livestock & Birds	6	12	44	88	50
Cloth & Clothing	178	66	92	34	270
Handicrafts	92	43	121	57	213
Manufactured Goods	60	56	47	44	107
Locally Manufactured Foodstuffs	179	90	20	10	199
Prepared Food & Drinks	125	83	26	17	151
Tobacco	62	61	40	39	102
Miscellaneous	22	61	14	39	36
Artisan	45	41	65	59	110
TOTAL	1335	70%	565	30%	1900

market, the most important categories of commodities are vegetables, dry foodstuffs and cloth and clothing, each with 14% of
traders; and locally manufactured foodstuffs and handicrafts with
about 10% each. In the daily market, the more specialized commodities diminish in importance. Nearly a third of traders deal in
vegetables, with 20% selling locally manufactured foodstuffs and
16% of traders providing snacks and drinks. The changes in
commodities are complemented by a change in the sexual division
of labour: whereas 69% of traders in Pasar Kulon are women, this
rises to 88% in the daily market.

The sexual division of traders in the main commodity groups is
shown in Table 3.3. Overall, 70% of traders are women. Women
dominate the sale of vegetables, meat, fish and eggs, fruit, prepared food and drinks. These are also the commodities which
provide work for the greatest number of small traders. Men
predominate in the livestock and seedling markets, and more than
the usual proportion deal in manufactured goods and handicrafts,
and work as artisans. Thus, although women dominate the market
as a whole, there are strong clusters of men dealing in particular
commodities or providing particular services. My impression is

that, in those commodities with reasonable numbers of both male and female participants, males are represented more heavily than average among the larger-scale traders, but except for the specialized commodities listed earlier, most of the biggest traders are women.

The very large numbers of traders in the Prembun market pose considerable problems for both research and exposition. It is difficult to indicate the range of commodities and the conditions under which they are sold without becoming mired in a surfeit of empirical detail which interests no one but the writer. Rigid categorization runs the opposite risk of imposing inappropriate generalizations which inhibit detailed analysis and which may direct attention away from the larger traders who exercise a disproportionate influence on the structure of the marketing system. I have therefore undertaken a simple empirical classification of commodities, and discuss traders in terms of the commodities with which they deal. My intention is to give an idea, not only of the range of commodities available in the market, but also of the means by which they are bought and sold. I should stress that this is intended only as a preliminary discussion and that detailed analyses are reserved for later chapters. Because of the analytical difficulties with the use of terms such as 'profit' and 'capital', which are discussed later, I mention only the selling value of the trader's stock and the 'return': i.e. the difference between the buying and selling prices.

Any account of the activities in the market place, however, must pay attention to a major distinction between what I have called 'cyclical' and 'daily' traders. Cyclical traders work in a particular location only during official market days and trade in several towns during a week. Daily traders concentrate on one town, visiting other *pasar* to restock rather than sell. Not surprisingly, the cyclical traders come from a wider area, have greater finance, deal in the more expensive commodities, and are more likely to combine wholesale and retail functions. This in turn leads to considerable differences between the periodic and daily markets in Prembun. The daily market has fewer traders, proportionately far fewer sellers of expensive commodities, higher proportions of female traders and a smaller and more homogeneous group of customers.

AGRICULTURAL PRODUCE

Vegetables

Each periodic market day 264 traders sell vegetables, as do 122 in the daily market. Vegetable sellers can be subdivided into four categories. The 118 *bumbon* sellers deal in imported commodities such as onions, chillies, ginger, turmeric and garlic. Seventy-nine sell local vegetables such as water spinach, round-leafed spinach, and long beans. Imported perishables (cabbages, carrots, potatoes) are sold by twenty-four vendors in the periodic market, but by only four in the daily market. There are forty-two vendors of root crops such as cassava, sweet potato and corn. Some of these crops are grown locally, but others come from the more mountainous areas of the *kabupaten* and Wonosobo.

Bu Sri and her daughter are daily traders selling cassava. They normally sell small quantities from a piece of burlap next to a kiosk, but on market days share a section of a shed in Pasar Wetan with four other women, each of whom pays Rp 25. Bu Sri is about thirty-five and has been trading in cassava for fifteen years, while her fifteen-year-old daughter has been working with her for two years. Each day they buy about twenty kilograms from a roadside collector who has purchased it in Wonosobo and sell it as two qualities on the basis of size. They pay Rp 1000 and expect to resell it for Rp 1300. Bu Sri occasionally purchases ten kilograms of dried cassava for Rp 500, retailing it at Rp 65/kg.

A young vegetable seller who works on the Prembun, Kutowinangun and Ungaran market circuit as well as Butuh on Saturdays, describes herself as a spinach trader, although this is only one of the commodities she stocks. She also sells snacks and whatever fruits and other vegetables she can buy cheaply. On one occasion, her stock included forty bundles of spinach, ten bitter gourds, two papaws and three kilograms of oranges, plus 100 tiny packets of *krupuk pilos* (a savoury snack packed in small plastic bags, a favourite with children). Mbak Siti daily spends about Rp 300 on vegetables and a further Rp 1000 a week on a large bundle of the savoury snacks which she purchases from a small Javanese-owned workshop in Prembun. She retails her goods in units of Rp 5, the smallest coin in general use, and is therefore able to sell for 50–100% more than she paid. Her customers must buy more than the minimum unit to gain a discount.

Bu Wajibah, recently married, has been a *bakul bumbon* for three years. She is a small-scale cyclical trader who works the local market circuit of Prembun, Kutowinangun and Ambal and spends one day at a more distant market. Her stock, which typically consists of twelve kilograms of locally grown green chillies, ten kilograms of imported red chillies and thirty kilograms of onions from Brebes on the north Java coast, has a value of Rp 10 000. She hopes to make Rp 2000 to Rp 3000 from turning over her stock every five days. Her goods come from two sources: a wholesale agent who has a *depot* in Wates, seventy kilometres to the east, distributes chillies and onions to *bumbon* traders in Kebumen, usually consigning them to the market and collecting payment later in the morning; and a wholesale *bakul* located in the market from whom she buys chillies. In Pasar Wetan, for example, there are three large wholesalers with at least a quintal of each variety of *bumbon*, who sell both to traders within the market and traders and *warung* outside it.

Dry Goods

These commodities include rice, soybean, peanuts and dried beans. There are 260 dry goods traders, many of them essentially wholesalers, on a periodic market day, and only thirty-three in the daily market. As I mentioned above, most rice is channelled through government agencies. Within the *pasar*, rice (*beras*=hulled rice) is sold by two types of vendor: the small-scale trader specializing in rice, and owners of permanent kiosks who sell rice along with other goods.

Bakul beras buy rice direct from the farmer both in the market place and in the village, either hulled or unhulled. It is displayed in baskets, and Bu Harti, a small-scale rice vendor, has three to four baskets (20 kg. per basket worth Rp 12 000 to Rp 16 000 retail) of various types of rice in front of her. These always include *beras jahir*, the best quality long grain rice, and *beras ketan*, glutinous rice. Half a coconut shell is used as a retail measure and contains about one and a half kilograms. She trades in Prembun every day, making about Rp 15 per kilogram or Rp 2100 in the course of a week.

Kiosk holders are considerably more prosperous than the other traders. Bu Arjasumitra, the wife of a local *Carik* (secretary to the village headman) has stock worth more than Rp 200 000, including six quintal of the cheaper high yielding rice and five quintal of *beras jahir*. This rice is mostly the production surplus to her household's needs from the four and a half hectares of *bengkok* land and three hectares of privately owned *sawah* farmed by her husband. Her other goods, including chillies, cassava, noodles, sugar and tea are delivered to her on various credit arrangements. She sells both wholesale and retail and numerous civil servants pay monthly accounts (*bon*). This type of kiosk is found in most markets. Although she was unwilling to discuss her returns, they would exceed Rp 2000 per day on the non-rice stocks alone.

Fruit

On a periodic market day in Prembun there are sixty-two fruit sellers, mainly located in Pasar Wetan. Fruit sellers have small stocks worth between Rp 3000 and Rp 10 000. Turnover is rapid to avoid spoilage and what is unsold one day should be sold the next. Cyclical traders often buy fruit in one market to sell in another.

Bu Manis, a middle-aged spritely lady has sold fruit for more than thirty-five years. As is typical of seasonal fruit sellers, she buys in the market place from both farmers and collector *bakul*, including *penebas* who buy fruit on the tree and harvest it themselves. Bu Manis spends three days in the small village market of Kenayan ten kilometres north of Prembun, works in Pasar Wetan on market days, and in Pasar Kulon for the rest of the week. She occasionally transports fruit from one market to another, but usually stores unsold fruit in Prembun for sale on the following day. Her average daily investment is Rp 3000, occasionally as much as Rp 10 000 if buying a quantity of oranges. On a typical market day her early morning stock consists of twenty-five hands of bananas of various kinds and about one basket (twenty kilograms) of oranges. She usually sells bananas by the hand, but sells other fruit such as oranges and guava by metric weight using the scale of a neighbouring *bakul*. She expects to make Rp 400 to Rp 500 above expenses each day.

Bu Sukardiy is among the largest fruit sellers, specializing in imported fruits such as *salak* (a fruit with a snakelike skin), which she buys in Magelang and Purworejo. She and her husband operate a joint enterprise and spend about Rp 25 000 to restock twice a week. Her husband mainly sells to other traders, while she retails in Prembun and Kutowinangun markets. She makes far more on each sale than Bu Manis, but, as her overheads are considerably higher, her nett returns are much the same, although her turnover and thus her income is much greater.

Meat, Fish and Eggs

One indication of the high cost of animal protein is that the thirty-nine traders on a market day fall to nine in the daily market. The twenty Prembun meat traders all acquire their meat from one of the three slaughter houses in their home village of Jlegiwinangun, picking up the meat early in the morning and paying for it on their return. Their equipment is simple. A basket contains the three to fifteen kilograms of meat they have acquired, scales, knife and chopper boards, and this is covered with a bamboo tray. Refrigeration facilities are non-existent and meat traders constantly whisk the meat to keep off flies.

Although there is a heavy demand, the supply of fresh fish is sparse and irregular. Salted fish, however, is widely available. Three specialist wholesalers are located in each of the main markets and a large number of *bumbon* sellers also include salted fish among their stock. Egg sellers are few and far between: one is located in Pasar Wetan while two of the rice kiosks in Pasar Kulon usually have a few eggs (duck and hen) for sale.

Mbok Wir is a forty-five year old mother of six who initially sold cassava, but who for the last eighteen years has been selling cattle, buffalo, goat and horse meat butchered in her home village of Jlegiwinangun. Her husband, a farmer, takes care of the younger children and her two eldest daughters help with her stall. Sales of meat are relatively stable, but higher sales are recorded during three periods of major religious celebrations in the Javanese months of Mulud, Sawal and Lebaran. Most buyers purchase very small quantities, frequently asking for a fixed amount such as Rp 25 worth. The meat sellers spend a long time in the *pasar* and must sell out their stock each day. The Jlegiwinangun meat traders are often seen trekking home from the market about five in the evening, and if they have been particularly unlucky, trying to sell leftover meat on the way. Unlike many other traders, meat sellers have a clear notion of their costs and returns, and the price of meat available to them fluctuates very little. Meat traders often describe their return as a *komisi* (commission) of Rp 200 for each Rp 2000 invested on a stock of ten kilograms, although most are clever enough to raise this a little. Rp 1000 covers their market expenses and household shopping, and the remaining Rp 1000 is set aside for clothing and school expenses. Most meat traders sell a proportion of their meat to civil servants on credit, charging a higher price and collecting payment monthly.

Mbak Nariya, a young girl of eighteen, intelligent, alert and very perky, is a trader praised by others for her industriousness and success.[4] Her mother runs a permanent mixed dry goods stall in Pasar Kulon where Mbak gained her early experience, but for the last three years she has been working independently in Prembun, Butuh and Pituruh, the latter two markets in the neighbouring *kabupaten* of Purworejo.

The dried salted fish sold in the Kebumen region comes from two sources, Cilacap to the west and Semarang to the north. Although Semarang is slightly further away, fish from that source is marginally cheaper and therefore more popular.[5] Traders specializing in dried fish are mainly wholesalers: Mbak Nariya sells mostly to small-scale *bakul* and *warung*, although some of her sales are retail. She purchases fish in Semarang for herself, her older sister who is also an independent dried fish seller, and her mother. She travels by bus to Semarang once a fortnight (occasionally once a week) and, depending on current stocks, purchases between five quintal and three tonnes of dried fish from one or more of three large-scale fish wholesalers. The Rp 300 000 to pay for these purchases is hidden beneath her clothing. If the load is small it is transported by shared chartered *colt*, but amounts approaching a tonne are later delivered by truck. She has also established close contacts with drivers carrying coconuts from Prembun to Semarang who often backload some dried fish for her and other traders. Rather than make the trip to Semarang herself, she occasionally leaves an order in charge of one of the truck drivers and later makes payment through them also. In return her family often feeds and provides overnight accommodation for the drivers.

Her three suppliers in Semarang, one Javanese woman and two Chinese men, give her goods on credit, but expect one lot to be paid for before collecting the next, and give her a small discount if she has done so. But occasionally debts overlap and, if she has arranged a consignment through the coconut truck drivers, she is presented with a bill and makes payment later.

At any one time she has about two quintal of dried fish in her

stall, with the remainder stored at home. Her stock consists of six
to eight different varieties of dried fish which she has bought
wholesale for between Rp 400 and Rp 800 a kilogram. Selling
wholesale she hopes to make between Rp 50 and Rp 200 per kilogram. Her daily returns range from Rp 500 to Rp 3000, but she sells
about seven quintal a week for around Rp 10 000 over the purchase
price. She sells to *bakul* and *warung* outside the market only for
cash, but ten *bakul* in Pasar Wetan obtain one day credit.

Seedlings

Seedling vendors are usually farmers who grow their stock, and for
whom trading is a seasonal occupation. At the height of the 1980
season there were thirty-seven, twenty-eight of them men, selling
only in the periodic market. The range of seedlings includes rice,
clove and citrus trees, several spinaches, eggplant, chillies, tom-
atoes and corn. It is very difficult to determine the costs of production and therefore returns, but a packet of twelve birds-eye chilli
seedlings wrapped in banana leaves, or a packet of twenty-four
round-leafed spinach seedlings, is sold for between Rp 10 and
Rp 25. A typical trader has 300 packets in stock.

Livestock and Birds

According to the official in charge of this market there are 200
livestock traders on a Monday, but on a Thursday there are only
fifty. All are men, and as this market is strictly a male domain I
visited it only twice. The sale of livestock (cattle, buffalo, goats
and sheep) is confined to this market. Decorative birds are sold
within Pasar Wetan while ducks, largely bred for their eggs, and
chickens, used for both eggs and meat, are sold in restricted areas
at various sites along the main road. There are about fifty traders
in these birds. Mas Payan is a young man who works on the
Kutowinangun, Prembun and Kebumen market circuit buying
most of his stock for cash at the roadside or from neighbours. He
usually has about six fowl which he carries in his bicycle's paniers.
Prices are extremely variable, but he aims to make Rp 300 to
Rp 500 on each of one or two daily sales. The livestock of traders in
the Pasar Khewan sells even more slowly: one goat seller with four
goats sold only one for Rp 20 000 in three weeks. Livestock is
expensive, a small to medium buffalo costs around Rp 175 000 and

a cow for use as a draught animal around Rp 300 000, so that these sellers rely on making high returns on a low turnover.

MANUFACTURED GOODS

Cloth and Clothing

Vendors of *batik* cloth, clothing, textiles and hats number 270 in the periodic market, but only eight in the daily market. On periodic market days Pasar Kulon is essentially a cloth market.[6] Although there are considerable differences in the value of their stock, the more successful cloth and clothing traders are the market elite. Not surprisingly, in view of the finance required, these women are often drawn from the village elite and many are married to village officials, civil servants and teachers. As the cloth trade is discussed in some detail in Chapter 5, this section concentrates on a seller of ready-made clothing (*bakul sandangan*), an occupation which is structurally similar to cloth trading but is regarded as more lucrative.

Bu Siti, who is twenty-six, and her school teacher husband reside with her parents, but her three young children are cared for by a servant. Bu Siti began work with her mother who sold both cloth and clothing. After marriage she started her own business, pawning some gold jewellery given to her by her husband. Unlike the majority of cloth and clothing traders, she works only in Prembun, but as with many cloth traders Bu Siti has a clear idea of the economic structure of her business. She estimates the value of her stock, which includes a wide range of babies', children's and adults' clothing, at Rp 400 000. Overheads amount to about Rp 400 daily: Rp 50 for market fees, Rp 100 for transport, Rp 50 for storage and Rp 200 for a porter. Over the course of a year her gross daily return after expenses ranges from Rp 370 to Rp 3000, climbing to Rp 6000 at Lebaran, and on most days she acquires the Rp 1000 she needs for household expenses. Cloth and clothing traders replace their stock regularly, obtaining new stock from travelling wholesalers almost as soon as the old is sold. Most goods are purchased by the process known as *ngalap-nyaur*: the goods are taken on credit, and paid for when sold (see Chapter 5). If they remain unsold they are returned. Most clothing traders have a series of debts of this nature with about ten traders, who in turn buy the goods in the shops and *pasar* in the large towns of Solo and Yogyakarta.[7]

The *pasar* also includes traders in the manufactured textiles which are preferred for both custom tailored articles and locally manufactured clothes. Fifteen of the textile traders in Prembun are mainly retailers, but three others supply both the retail traders and local workshops. The stocks of each of these vendors are worth well above Rp 2 000 000.

Handicrafts

A vast range of products is manufactured in household workshops and other local industries. These include fish nets/traps, hats, baskets, rope, mats, knives, agricultural equipment, graters, buckets, furniture, brooms, copperware, lamps/tinware, and pottery (see Chapter 4). There are 213 vendors of these items in the periodic market but only seven in the daily market. Each of these handicrafts has a specialized pattern of production and distribution, and I have selected two examples which emphasize this diversity.

Bu Tutor's village, Mrinen, has been producing items from disused tinware and bottles since the 1820s and Bu Tutor learnt the skills of soldering and manufacture from her mother. Bu Tutor, who is at least sixty years old, spends four days selling in the periodic markets of Prembun and Kutowinangun. The remaining three days she manufactures goods at home, although she also makes the odd bottle lamp during slack periods in the market.[8] Using wire, pliers, a glass jar and a prefabricated wick holder, she makes a bottle lamp in about ten minutes.

Bu Tutor stocks twelve different items including household lamps, watering cans and drainers, with a total retail value of approximately Rp 30 000. She makes all her goods herself, with the exception of a lantern which she buys from another producer in the village for Rp 110 and retails for Rp 150. Some of her bottle lamps are wholesaled, but most are retailed. Her returns, less the cost of material, are between 25 and 50% of the retail price and she reckons on a complete turnover of stock every six weeks. Her daily overheads amount to Rp 270: porterage Rp 100, market fee Rp 30, rent of bench and roofing Rp 20, and Rp 60 for her return by ponycart, which she takes to minimize damage to her goods. On a good day she clears about Rp 300.

Her raw materials come from two sources. Off-cuts of tin, and glass and wire are purchased from a shop in Kebumen, while the disused bottles, jars, electric light bulbs, tin lids and tin cans are bought from itinerant traders who buy in bulk in the large cities of Bandung and Jakarta. On one of her train trips to Jakarta a typical *bakul* of this type took fifty kilograms of oranges. On her return, she sold 200 bottles for Rp 1400 and seven Indomilk tins for Rp 316 to Bu Tutor, and also supplied others.

Bu Tugirah, a young woman with three children, is strictly a market trader, who learnt the skills of selling mats from her mother who still works alongside her. She stocks mats made of sedge and pandanus grasses which are used for bed, floor and bench coverings. The mats comes from four sources: local centres in Kabupaten Kebumen, the Malang/Surabaya region, Tasikmalaya, and Yogyakarta. The locally made mats are generally very coarse, but those from Yogyakarta, while also of pandanus grass, are finely hand woven, sometimes plain, sometimes with interwoven sections dyed green and pink. The Malang/Surabaya mats are striped in bright colours from sedge grass, machine interwoven with nylon and edged with plastic. The finest quality mats are generally acknowledged to come from Tasikmalaya in West Java. They are made of finely woven sedge grass, in subdued greens, purples and pinks with interwoven cotton thread. Nylon wool pompons decorate the ends. Bu Tugirah has about 100 mats, keeping roughly a *kodi* (a bundle of twenty) of each type always in stock, with a retail value of at least Rp 80 000.

Bu Tugirah purchases her supplies in the *pasar*. *Bakul* from Surabaya/Malang and Tasikmalaya, all men, regularly travel through the market and supply a *kodi* of mats at a time. They are often willing to extend credit to regular customers until their next trip. A woman *bakul* provides Yogyakarta mats in the same way. Locally produced mats are generally sold in pairs by their weavers.

There is little bargaining over mat prices, although there is considerable discussion of quality. Returns on individual mats range from Rp 50 to Rp 100 and Bu Tugirah sells about ten in a normal day for a gross return of around Rp 800 daily. She pays her husband, who is a porter and *grobag* driver, to transport her goods from market to market but receives a discount. She spends about Rp 100 on travel and a further Rp 50 for market fees.

Manufactured Goods

The 107 sellers of manufactured goods in the periodic market fall
to four in the daily market. The most common articles include
sandals, belts, bags, costume jewellery, household equipment,
nylon rope, calendars, books, cassettes, plastic goods, notions and
haberdashery. These consumer durables are mainly manufactured
in the large cities, and those freely available in the market are
generally regarded as inferior in quality to similar goods in the
shops. Market sellers certainly concentrate their stocks at the
lowest end of the price range for each type of article.

Bu Maryati, a widow and sole support for her family of three, is
a *bakul klitikan*: a vendor of notions and haberdashery. She has
worked in the Kebumen, Kutowinangun and Prembun market
circuit for more than ten years. Her stock, which is among the
largest for this type of trader, is incredibly varied—face powder,
cotton thread, pins, needles, hairnets and costume jewellery—
items which individually cost little, but overall are worth about
Rp 30 000. Bu Maryati buys most of her stock from shops in the
nearby town of Kutoarjo, and although she gets a small discount
when paying cash, she usually has an unpaid debt with the shop-
keeper. She calculates that she makes about Rp 500 a day, but
expenses, including Rp 50 market fee, Rp 75 transport and Rp 100
for the porter who carries her goods to the bus, cut heavily into
returns.

Locally Manufactured Foodstuffs

Javanese pride themselves on their ingenuity in processing unlikely raw materials into foodstuffs and each region has its own
speciality. No trip is complete without *jajan*, small packages of
special food taken home for relatives and neighbours. In Kebumen
the favoured item is *emping*, a crisp cracker made from the *mlinjo*
fruit. Other locally manufactured foodstuffs such as arrowroot
noodles (*su'un*), soybean cake (*tempe*), soybean curd (*tahu*), dried
crisps (*krupuk*) and soybean sauce are more regular items in the
diet and are processed in small household industries (see Chapter
4). There are 199 traders of locally manufactured foodstuffs in the
periodic market and seventy-three in the daily market.

Bu Warsinum has been selling *tahu* for three years, working in

Pasar Ungaran on Wednesdays and Sundays, and in Prembun for the remainder of the week. Every day she buys three to four kilograms of *tahu* at Rp 900/kg. on twenty-four hour credit from a small factory in Kutowinangun. The *tahu* is of three kinds: small and large pre-fried pieces, and large unfried pieces. Demand is constant, prices are relatively fixed, and she remains in the market only until her goods are sold. Her gross daily return is only Rp 300, but her overheads are minimal: Rp 70 for transport, and Rp 25 for market fees.

Almost all of the vendors of manufactured foodstuffs operate on a similar scale to Bu Warsinum. Mainly older women with little finance, they rely on establishing a regular group of customers to provide a small daily livelihood.

Prepared Food and Drinks

No one with money goes hungry in the *pasar*. An enormous variety of prepared foods and drinks is available from both itinerant and stationary traders: anything from a quick snack or iced drink to a full rice meal.[9] The *bakul* themselves are major customers of both the *warung* and itinerant vendors, being supplied with drinks during the course of the day and paying at the end, but they also buy snacks from other vendors, both for immediate and home consumption. There are 151 vendors of this type in the periodic market and sixty-four in the daily market.

Bu Karsotaman is a small-scale sweetmeat trader who largely sells to customers purchasing *jajan*. She works in Pasar Wetan on periodic market days and in Pasar Kulon on other days. Her stock is restricted to *lapisan* (a rice-flour layered cake coloured pink and white with a thick, jelly-like texture) which she makes herself, and *apem* (a pink rice-flour cake with a spongy texture), which she buys from another trader. The *lapisan* is manufactured from household rice stocks and sells for about Rp 125 a plate, but is more frequently sold in quarters of Rp 35 each. Bu pounds the rice and prepares the *lapisan* each evening, leaving the sweet to set in a flat round enamel plate. On daily market days Bu produces twelve plates of *lapisan*, double on periodic market days. Each day she purchases twenty rounds of *apem*, selling for Rp 150.

Her return is about Rp 400 a day, roughly half from each type of sweetmeat, with an extra Rp 200 on market days. Her overheads are limited to the Rp 25–35 market fee, for she walks the two kilometres to and from the *pasar* carrying the sweetmeats in a basket wrapped up in a sash.

Tobacco and Betel Supplies

These traders number 102 in the periodic market and sixteen in the daily market. Tobacco sellers stock various qualities of tobacco, cigarettes, papers, cloves, *klembak*, *kemenyan* and *gambir*.[10] The tobacco is also used as part of a betel chew, along with *suruh* leaves, betel nut, lime and chalk which are usually sold by separate vendors. The 102 traders include equal numbers of men and women but many of the women are young and/or attractive which is regarded as a selling advantage. When I discussed with some friends in the market the love affair recounted in Hildred Geertz's (1961:128–30) study of the Javanese family, they were quick to remark that the protagonist was a tobacco seller.

Pak Rusti is an elderly man who has been a tobacco trader on and off for many years. His household is self-sufficient in rice and he obtains most of his cash income from tobacco trading. He started trading in 1936 and worked until the Japanese occupation. Cholera among his five children ate up his finance and when he re-established himself as a trader in 1957 he had to sell part of his small holding of rice land. Part of this paid his debts and the remainder was used for trading stock. A close friend originally taught him his trade.

Pak Rusti obtains his stock from a variety of sources. Once every two or three months he buys supplies of the *klembak* spice on credit in the Magelang area where he has five regular suppliers. He maintains links with each, as not all necessarily have supplies available at reasonable prices. He buys *kemenyan* spice from a regular source in the Kutowinangun market and most of his tobacco on credit from a grower in Jlegiwinangun. He also buys imported varieties of tobacco from a wholesaler in Prembun for cash. It is easy for the consumer to distinguish locally grown from non-local tobacco. Locally grown tobacco is sold in rolls, whereas non-local tobacco is loosely packed in baskets. Pak Rusti's stock is worth around Rp 30 000 and on a typical market day he sells about Rp 10 000 worth on which his gross return is 10%. His overheads, market fees of Rp 35, and rent of a stool at Rp 30, amount to Rp 65.

He regards his net profit as the Rp 100 he takes home after spending Rp 900 on food for his family.

The typical betel (*suruh*) seller is a very small-scale trader whose stock has a selling value around Rp 2500. One seller's stock includes bundles of *suruh* leaves with a retail value of between Rp 10 and Rp 200, fifty *gambir* knobs (Rp 10 each), five bundles of lime (Rp 25–35 each) and fifty betel nuts (Rp 5 each). This seller, an elderly lady, makes only Rp 100 a day.

Miscellaneous

There are about thirty-six vendors who do not fit easily into the above categories. Among these are sellers of kapok, kerosene, firewood, flour sacks, horse feed, children's toys and flower offerings. I have singled out a kerosene seller, for although she is in no way typical of the others, kerosene is an important household item with a special method of distribution.[11]

Bu Pringoatmaja is an elderly widow who has been selling kerosene for the last twenty-five years. She sells from a spot outside her house opposite Pasar Kulon, but regards herself as very much part of the *pasar* scene. She obtains her kerosene on order from a nephew, the local agent for the government-controlled petrol and kerosene company. He supplies the kerosene at irregular intervals and Bu pays him for the previous delivery when she orders the new. Weekly consumption averages about five and half drums with demand three times as heavy on market days. A drum contains a nominal 200 litres, but when filled to the brim holds up to ten litres more. As payment is calculated by the drum, this is a windfall profit. Her son-in-law, a retired civil servant, provided the deposit of Rp 5000 per drum.

Bu Pringoatmaja pays Rp 10 000 for each drum of kerosene and makes an official profit of Rp 200 per drum and a windfall of up to Rp 500; in all about Rp 3000 each week. Customers buy from half a litre to six litres and pay a set price of Rp 50 a litre. Many customers leave their bottle or plastic container and are given a number. Those who have paid have a full container on their return, whereas others must wait until cash customers are served, and supplies are often exhausted. Kerosene is also delivered by trucks to vendors in the villagers, but the basic price is higher and supplies irregular.

Artisans

The remaining *pasar* participants are artisans (*tukang*), who provide services of one sort or another: 110 in the periodic market and fourteen in the daily market. *Tukang* provide a wide variety of services: barbers (*tukang cukur*), tailors and dressmakers (*tukang jahit*), watch repairers (*tukang jam*), shoe repairers (*tukang sepatu*), tinsmiths (*tukang soldir*) and herbal medicine suppliers (*tukang jamu jawa*). Equipment varies, but is usually simple. Barbers carry scissors, combs and mirror in a wooden box; tailors and seamstresses must have a portable sewing machine, scissors and thread; while the traditional medicine suppliers carry a large range of roots and spices ready to be mixed into a wide variety of potions.

The sellers of indigenous medicines and tonics (*tukang jamu jawa*) are the most diverse and numerous of the *tukang* and require further clarification. One type of *tukang jamu* are itinerant peddlers, all women, who carry a series of bottles in a basket and shoulder sash. The various herbal medicines are prepared at home and they travel a regular route through the markets and villages. They usually stock about seven different remedies, one to cleanse the blood after menstruation, others to increase the appetite, to reduce weight, and to relieve headache and pains. Many villagers take some of these foul tasting remedies every day, especially during seasons of heavy work. A second group of *jamu* sellers are mainly male, and sell *jamu* prepared by the large urban manufacturers, such as Jago and Air Mancur. These traders are flashy and exuberant, and their stalls are often equipped with loudspeakers, radio and cassettes. They usually travel between periodic markets by van and are paid a commission on sales.[12]

The third and largest group of *tukang jamu jawa* are those who make up *jamu* on the spot using natural products. They are always women. Bu Turah has a large range of roots, herbs and spices arranged in a series of little wooden boxes in front of her stall, as well as little plastic bags filled with mixtures she has prepared at home. She was unable to cost her stock as it is so varied and was compiled over a very long period of time. She buys her goods in the periodic market place from farmers and wholesale *bakul*, paying farmers in cash but maintaining debts with some of the traders. A typical *jamu, galian singset*, which is a slenderizing potion, costs about Rp 30 to prepare and sells for Rp 50. Sales remain much the same throughout the year and she makes about Rp 400 each day. Most Javanese have some knowledge of the types of medicinal preparations available and their major contents, but generally buy rather than make them themselves. Bu Turah worked alongside her sister for a year until she was able to recognize the various roots and memorize the range of preparations.

In sharp contrast to the purchase of goods, there is little haggling over the price of services. In many cases the customer pays without asking the price: if insufficient is offered the *tukang* will request and usually receive more. But occasionally the *tukang* states the charge before accepting the job. This is particularly true of tailors and seamstresses, and of those who repair torches and cigarette lighters. A *tukang jahit*, for example, might charge Rp 200–300 for making a blouse, Rp 400 for a dress, and Rp 25 for a pillow case. Watch repairs may cost anywhere between Rp 500 and Rp 7000.

OTHER MARKET PLACE PARTICIPANTS

Not all the thousands of people bustling about the *pasar* are sellers of goods and services and their customers; porters, market administrators, beggars and buskers also have important roles in marketing activities.

Porters

The most surprising feature of the porters (*kuli*) in the Kebumen markets is that they are all male, in contrast to markets of Yogyakarta and Magelang where one frequently sees women bearing heavy loads from one part of the market to another. A common comment from traders is that the only finance a porter needs is his native strength, unlike themselves who have to pay for their stalls and stock. In addition to carrying goods for traders between the stalls and transport, loading trucks with vegetable products, and guarding goods overnight, porters may negotiate transport. They receive a fee for each service and, like traders in some commodities, try to establish a regular clientele by working predominantly in one section of the market. There is a pool of porters associated with the coconut and *bengkuwang* markets, for example. The coconut porters receive Rp 500 for loading 1000 coconuts on to a truck, while *kuli* in the Pasar Bengkuwang receive about Rp 100 for each bag they pack and carry to a vehicle.

Pak Midi works in the Prembun and Kutowinangun market towns where he has established close working relationships with traders in the cloth market. He meets mobile wholesale cloth traders arriving by bus, carries their goods into the market and, when they wish to move on to the next market, carries them out again. He generally receives a payment of Rp 100 for the two-way carriage. He also fetches food and drinks, particularly for cloth traders, and stores traders' goods with a street-front shop owner while they wait for transport. As with most payments for services, *kuli* get a set and widely recognized fee, although occasionally a porter and trader haggle over the amount. While there is a wide range of motor and animal transport, human labour is the cheapest form of transport, and bulky but cheap commodities are often carried considerable distances to selling points. Every morning, for example, men from the mountain villages carry forty- to fifty-kilogram loads of bamboo or firewood at least five kilometres to the main road. The *kuli*'s black shorts and naked, scarred back and shoulders denote his hard and, in Javanese eyes, somewhat demeaning occupation, but many of them make over Rp 1500 per day, which is considerably more than most traders.

Market Administrators

Administration of the markets in Kebumen is the responsibility of the Department of Public Works situated in the *kabupaten* office. Most policy directives comes from this central body, and local market administrators mainly collect market fees and maintain order. The Mantri Pasar Prembun is responsible for four official market areas: Pasar Kulon, Pasar Wetan, Pasar Khewan and Pasar Tlogopragota at Mirit. The other market areas, Pasar Bengku-wang, Pasar Kelapa and Pasar Sepeda, and the *koplak* (area where horse carts and other vehicles park) are attached to one of the divisions. The *mantri pasar* supervises office staff, including a secretary, twelve ticket collectors and numerous sweepers respon-sible for cleaning the market place. The *mantri pasar* is responsible for remitting fees to the Department of Public Works (Departmen Pekerjaan Umum) once a week and maintains detailed records of all income earned by his administration.

The market administrators permeate the whole town on market

days, with each ticket collector expected to obtain fees from all
traders within his allocated area. Fees range from the Rp 10 paid
by the itinerant trader selling a tray of goods, to the Rp 100
charged for a complete section (*plong*) of a shed which is split
between traders sharing it. Small-scale traders pay up to Rp 25 in
fees and larger traders Rp 50–100. The charge for a lock-up kiosk
in Pasar Kulon is Rp 200 per day, paid monthly.

In the Pasar Khewan traders are charged for each animal: Rp 50
for small animals such as goats, and Rp 200 for large animals such
as buffalo. In the Coconut Market small traders are charged Rp 25
and the larger buyers from Semarang Rp 200. A fee of Rp 25 is also
collected from each horse driver, and large trucks pay a fee of
Rp 100, although the constant movement of the horse drivers
means they frequently escape charges. Upon payment of the fee a
ticket is attached to the appropriate stall or vehicle, but not
infrequently a trader pleads insolvency and asks the collector to
return later in the morning. The lenient collector will come back
later only to discover that the trader has left. On completing his
task the ticket collector submits a report, his cash funds and ticket
book to the office.

The Mantri Pasar Prembun, a relatively minor official in the
local hierarchy, started his career cleaning the market and worked
his way up through the ranks of ticket collector, secretary to
mantri pasar. His wife and children are all traders. Nowadays,
however, high school graduates would normally be appointed.

Beggars and Buskers

Like the customers, buskers and beggars tend to be ignored in
market surveys. But a considerable number of people earn their
living in this way and they, like the traders, travel a market circuit
contributing considerably to the excitement of the *pasar*. Some
beggars have severe physical deformities which deny them normal
sources of income, but in most cases there is little obvious difference between beggars and buskers. Most display little talent in
their singing or playing, and traders frequently toss them a coin
just to get rid of them. The few with talent—generally comics or
transvestites—travel much wider circuits than the less well-
endowed and make considerable incomes. The normal gift to a
beggar is Rp 5, the smallest coin, though some traders will offer a
few chillies or onions.

About ten beggars or buskers may pass by a substantial stall-holding trader in the course of a day and she will probably give them Rp 5 each, regarding it as one of the overheads of her business. She will refuse particular individuals on the grounds that she is too busy, business is slack, or she finds the beggar particularly objectionable. Small traders, in particular, resent beggars, suspecting that they make greater incomes than themselves.

CREDIT SUPPLIERS

The final, but by no means the least important, group in the *pasar* are the formal and informal credit suppliers. These people are found in both the periodic and daily markets and offer a wide range of credit, and credit/savings schemes.

Bank Officers—Formal Credit Facilities

The most important formal credit facility in the Prembun periodic market is the Pemerintah Daerah Bank Pasar, a department of the *kabupaten* government. The six other formal lending institutions are all private companies; KOSIPA, KOVERI, Koperasi Mekar Jaya, Yayasan Guna Sarjuna, Koperasi Mes and KOPAS operate similar lending schemes to the official Bank Pasar. Many traders are unaware of the specific differences between the various lending schemes but regard them as minor and continually take loans from one source. Official interest rates for each bank are usually expressed as a percentage of the principal not on a per annum basis, and details of the loans obscure the interest rates charged.

Some banks, like the Bank Pasar and Koperasi Mes, operate only on market days; others such as KOSIPA operate daily. This affects the methods and periods of repayment. Bank Pasar and Koperasi Mes collect loan repayments weekly (or bi-weekly) over three months, while KOSIPA collects them daily over thirty days. It is only when interest charges on a per annum basis are calculated that the wide variation in interest rates becomes apparent: Bank Pasar 56%, Koperasi Mes 70%, and KOSIPA 167%.

The Bank Pasar was originally established as a regional autonomous project in 1956 and reorganized as the P.D. Bank Pasar in 1970. There are 120 employees who service 165 separate offices. The bank itself is split into four divisions serving forty-six markets (*unit pasar*); 181 villages (*unit desa*); government officials (*unit pegawai*); and industry, handicrafts, development and contractors (*unit industri*). The main office of the Bank Pasar is located in Kebumen with a branch office in Gombong. Representatives from these two offices set up temporary offices in the local periodic markets. Prembun, for instance, is serviced by a young man who also works in Kutowinangun and Tlogopragota.

The Bank Pasar services mainly local market traders, but shops and kiosk owners located near the market are eligible for credit on the condition that they work regularly in the market where the loan is requested, have an identity card, and have no current loans with other banking institutions. The minimum loan, which is usually for a three month term, is Rp 5000 and the maximum Rp 50 000. It takes three to five days to process an application so that traders are informed on the following market day. Some borrowers take their installments in person to the market office so as to avoid advertising that they have a loan, but most wait for the officer to collect their installments. Immediately a loan is paid off, most traders seek another.

The interest and other costs of a typical three-month loan of Rp 10 000 are as follows:

Basic Loan	Rp 10 000
Deductions: Expenses 2.5%	250
Stamp Duty	25
Amount Received	Rp 9 725
Repayments: Principal	10 000
Interest (56% p.a.)	1 300
Savings (7% of value of loan)	700
	Rp 12 000

Rp 275 is deducted for expenses and stamp duty so that the trader receives Rp 9725. The Rp 12 000 is paid back in installments of Rp 1000 a week. The Rp 700 which is regarded as savings is returned to the borrower at Lebaran and is designed to educate the trader in saving. Most market banks set aside about 5% of the loan as compulsory savings which are returned to the borrower once a year at a major religious festival, e.g. Lebaran or Christmas.[13]

In December 1982 there were sixty debtors in Prembun market, 110 in Kutowinangun and twenty-five in Tlogoprogota. Of the sixty debtors in Prembun, fifty-eight had had previous loans. The range of borrowers included five vegetable sellers with small loans of Rp 5000, and fifteen with loans of Rp 10 000 (they included a *bakul klitikan*). Nineteen people including a coconut oil seller and a meat seller had loans of Rp 15 000–20 000. Two people, one a *bakul tahu*, had loans of Rp 30 000, while a kiosk owner in Pasar Kulon had the largest loan of Rp 40 000.

Loans are relatively easy to obtain, but the repayment criteria are strict and relatively few traders could meet the repayment schedule on even a small loan. Repayments on Rp 10 000, for example, are Rp 1000 per week and many relatively successful traders such as those dealing in clothing would find it difficult to guarantee that amount every week. But for the traders who can afford the repayments, this is a flexible source of credit especially as the regulation against other current loans is relatively easily transgressed. *Bakul* quite frequently have loans in different markets with different institutions and pay installments on both.

Bakul also borrow through formal credit institutions in the village. Babadsari, for example, has two: Bank Kredit Desa established in 1956 has more than 400 borrowers currently listed in its books; Lembaga Pembiayaan Pembangunan Desa established in 1969 has more than 200. According to the Village Headman, in 1982 more than half the loans were taken out by traders. Both charge a basic rate of 10% of the principal (25–56% p.a.).

Tukang Kredit Ngider—Informal Credit Facilities

The major reasons given by informants for their use of more costly informal credit was that they preferred to deal with women, and if they were short of cash they could, with a little pressure, delay their repayments. *Tukang kredit ngider* are of two types: those who lend cash and those who sell goods on time payment, though a single person may do both. In either case, repayment is by regular installment (*nicil*).[14] A large proportion of *tukang kredit ngider* are from the Tasikmalaya region of West Java. Mas Harto is a young married man whose wife and child still live there, but he works from a base in Purworejo where he purchases his goods, mainly pots, pans, thermoses and cloth. When I interviewed him he claimed to have 150 debtors in the Prembun market place and collected the installments every day. Although his prices are subject to bargaining and interest is not mentioned, I once saw him sell a thermos which he had purchased for Rp 3000 for Rp 5000 in daily installments of Rp 150. Very few transactions in the *pasar* produce profits at this rate.

Bu Siti is one of the local people, mainly women, who earn a living by providing credit. She comes from a relatively prosperous family in the nearby village of Sidogede and has been a *tukang kredit ngider* since 1967. She buys goods in Purworejo or Kebumen, generally after a customer has made an order, although occasionally she buys first and seeks a buyer later. She deals mainly in expensive consumer items, such as furniture and kitchenware, and usually requires a large deposit at the time the order is placed. For example, on a wardrobe costing the customer Rp 70 000, she demanded a deposit of Rp 15 000 and was to receive weekly installments of Rp 2000. Apart from providing credit, she also profits from her customers' belief that her experience and her command of high Javanese will enable her to negotiate lower prices. Her market customers pay each periodic market day, but she also deals with *pegawai negeri*, who pay installments on a monthly basis. At the time of the interview she had fifty customers in Pasar Khewan Prembun, located near her home, and a further 150 in Pasar Wetan, the periodic market. I was unable to ascertain what profit she made on individual transactions, for she was naturally reluctant to reveal the prices at which she had bought. Bu Siti's sister is also a *tukang kredit ngider*, selling gold jewellery and making cash loans to market traders. For a typical cash loan of Rp 10 000 the debtor pays back Rp 12 000 or Rp 700 each periodic market day! This is the same overall interest, but a faster rate of repayment than the Bank Pasar, although few of her customers stick strictly to the schedule.

Borrowing from 'friends' is also common among traders. Borrower and lender are careful to establish whether interest is charged. In fact it is quite common for a flat rate of 10% irrespective of the period of repayment to be charged and repayment is usually irregular. Even among relatives there is an expectation that something extra in cash or kind will be returned on top of the principal.

Arisan

Very few traders use any of the formal banking institutions for saving or stock replacement, but rely on the *arisan*, a rotating credit association (see Ardener 1964; Chandler 1982; Geertz 1962).

Those *bakul* who do not belong to a market *arisan* almost invariably belong to one in their home villages and many belong to several. Traders use *arisan* so that their finance is not fragmented by daily expenses and so that they occasionally have a reasonably large sum to invest in stock, or in some cases, an expensive household commodity. But one cloth trader complained that whenever she drew the *arisan* her creditors came flocking around her for payment. Most market *arisan* have sizeable contributions: either Rp 500 or Rp 1000. In some *arisan* each participant is assigned a number before the round and collects in numerical order. In other cases the names of those who have not collected are deposited in a jar, and the winner drawn.

The major problem with *arisan* is to ensure that those who have collected will continue to contribute.[15] This is achieved either by keeping the number of participants small so that a round is quickly completed, or by limiting participants to those who have other ties with each other. One of the largest market *arisan* involves sixty-eight cloth traders who pay Rp 1000 each Tuesday and Friday. The organizer of the *arisan*, who keeps the books and collects the contributions, has first draw, and every market day two people collect Rp 34 000. In this *arisan* Rp 200 is deducted from the fund as a contribution to 'Aisyiyah, the women's branch of the reformist Islamic organization Muhammadiyah, although only a few of the participants are members.

1. An edict dated March 1683 (de Vries and Cohen 1937:264).

2. According to Wiradi (1978:32) 'the Javanese word *tebas* means "to cut away". To sell agricultural crops by way of letting the buyers to *tebas* or harvest the crops themselves is called *tebasan*. In the past, it was a "cash and carry" transaction, but in recent times, the payment may be made a few days after the harvest, though a certain amount of the down payment may be necessary just to confirm or guarantee that the transaction has been agreed by both the buyer (*penebas*) and the farmer. In pure *tebasan* practice the transaction takes place just before harvest'. Cf. Alexander and Alexander (1982:613–14).

3. For example, see Dewey's (1962a) account of first and second stage carriers.

4. But her savings were wiped out in a single night when she and her family were victims of a robbery, which was attributed to a group of young thugs who had watched her buy some gold jewellery a few weeks previously. They raided her home, beat up her parents and stole all valuables including gold and a bicycle. Such events are common enough for most people to exercise extreme caution. Mbak Nariya travels to Semarang to buy stock and, like many women, carries cash in a bag under her clothing. Men wear a money belt or, like the *juragan* in Chapter 6, have an escort carrying an unobtrusive parcel. Thefts commonly occur on crowded public transport, and less frequently in the market place itself. Many traders' handbags bear the scars of attempted snatches.

5. Semarang has traditionally been a source of salted fish for the Kebumen region (*Mindere Welvaart* IXc:352).

6. There are fifty-six cloth traders, 194 clothing traders, eighteen textile traders and two *peci* sellers in the periodic market places.

7. See Chandler (1984) for a description of cloth manufacturing and selling in the Yogyakarta region.

8. By my last trip Bu Tutor had ceased production, preferring to purchase goods made by others. She still works four days a week in the market, but now also runs a foodstall in her village.

9. Adam (1916:1604–5) has an interesting account of how a small-scale *bakul nasi* financed her trade in 1905. She borrowed some raw rice (*beras*), half of which she sold, and used this money to buy side-dishes. She cooked the other half of the rice and sold it with the prepared side-dishes in the market. From this activity she acquired sufficient income to pay for the loan of rice after three days! Profits were evidently higher eighty years ago.

10. *Klembak* is a root from a tree of the same name; *kemenyan/menyan* is incense; *gambir* is produced from a vine whose leaves when boiled produce a thick brown sediment which, after cooling off, hardens and is diced. All three are used as flavouring for tobacco, and *gambir* is also an ingredient for a betel chew.

11. The marketing system for kerosene seems to have changed little since the 1900s when it was dominated by the Chinese. Adam (1916:1604–5) states that kerosene sellers need no starting finance as they obtain the kerosene on credit from a Chinese trader on the condition that they pay for it the following market day (*ngalap-nyaur*). The Chinese buys and sells the kerosene tins for the same price and makes his profit by pouring off some kerosene from each tin.

12. Daumont (1977) discusses these two types of *tukang jamu*. In contrast to the female monopoly of the itinerant trade, male traders dominate the sale of industrially prepared *jamu*.

13. De Vries and Cohen (1937:27–31) note that a market bank was established in Sragen in 1937 with the aim of making loans to *bakul*. The maximum loan was fl.5, the interest charged at a flat rate of 20% and the debt had to be paid in forty daily installments. Five percent of every loan was set aside as compulsory savings to be returned at the end of the year. As with many other aspects of Javanese life, the pattern established by the Dutch is still in force. See also Dewey (1962a:101–3, 1964, 249–50) and Fruin (1938:114–18).

14. See Burger (1930:396 ff.); Adam (1929:46) and van Gutem (1919) for accounts of the Chinese *tukang mindering* who toured the markets and villages of Pati by bicycle and gave credit in cash or goods, especially printed cloth (*cita*). Many women *bakul* who were reliable in the payments became regular customers.

15. That this is always a problem was dramatically demonstrated in 1981 when the Chinese cloth traders' *arisan* in the main *batik* market in Solo collapsed. Weekly contributions for this *arisan* were Rp 250 000 and the newspapers estimated that some Rp 30 000 000 was due. The associated violence and arson led to several deaths and the destruction of part of the market.

4

Petty Commodity Production

IN an oft-cited passage, Chayanov (1931:144–5) asserted that the organization of the peasant economy

> is determined by the size and composition of the peasant family and by the co-ordination of its consumptive demands with the number of its working hands . . . the principal object of peasant economy is the satisfaction of the yearly consumption budget of the family.

Although subsequent studies have entered numerous caveats, the kernel of truth in the statement is as applicable to the rural Javanese as to the Russian peasants from which it was derived. For poor households in particular, labour is the major economic resource and, as returns to labour differ greatly in various avenues of employment, economic success is contingent upon seeking out and holding relatively well-paid employment. When such employment is not available the survival of the household requires its members to seek whatever work they can obtain, no matter how poor the returns.

In rural Java, where most families hold too little land to provide full-time employment for even a single household member, trading and household factories are not peripheral employment for a few families, but are major components of many households' endeavours for economic survival. Petty commodity production is an integral part of Javanese rural society and, together with the cultivation of market crops and petty trade, epitomizes most of what can be described as the 'peasant' features of the economy. As with *warung*, small factories spring up with amazing regularity, only to subside just as quickly, for while the finance required is low, it is the total wealth of most households, and even a minor hiccup in the cash flow becomes an economic disaster.

The defining feature of petty commodity producers is individual ownership and appropriation by direct producers (Kahn 1980:133). In each case the owner of an enterprise is also a worker within it, and the predominant form of the division of the proceeds is as shares to all participants.

Since at least the end of the nineteenth century, petty commodity production has been an important component of the Javanese rural economy.[1] An investigation carried out in 1903 noted:

> an examination of the budgets of 5 000 000 farmers in Central Java shows that, from cottage industry, trade in these products and earnings from cultivation in their own gardens of the raw materials used in this kind of industry an average of seventeen percent accrued to the budget. (Sitsen n.d.:15)

In fact, given the difficulty of obtaining data on these sources of income compared to farming, the contribution to the average budget was probably well above 17%. The Dutch scholars, however, described petty commodity production as cottage industry (*huisvlijt*), domestic industries (*huiselijke bedrijven*) or as sideline occupations (*nevenbedrijven*) (see Does 1893; Sitsen n.d.).[2] The danger with such terms is that they disguise the significance of petty commodity production: conceptualizing it as activities which household members undertake in their spare time from agricultural work in order to obtain additional income, rather than as a major source of the income which households need to survive.

Two features of the small factories of rural Java should be emphasized. Firstly, such factories are as typical of the contemporary Javanese economy as the familiar irrigated rice fields. And secondly, such factories are operated within a particular set of economic constraints: maximizing the household's total income is the major economic goal. Unlike capitalist firms, where the goal of maximizing profit often reduces employment, Javanese petty commodity producers aim to maximize employment for household members and will tolerate reductions in both marginal labour productivity and profit, as long as the total household income is increased.

THE ORGANIZATION OF PRODUCTION

Amongst the easiest forms of production to finance is the manufacture of *tempe*, a cake made of fermented whole soybeans which Javanese like to eat with most rice meals.[3] The simple equipment (a steamer and a few utensils) costs less than Rp 5000, and a further Rp 3800 buys the nine kilograms of soybeans for a day's production. This produces 900 pieces of *tempe*, which sell at ten for Rp 45, giving a daily return of about Rp 250 for seven to eight hours' work.

But although an established *tempe* concern requires very little finance, most people begin with even less: the basic equipment can be substituted by household utensils; soybeans might be obtained on credit; while the teak leaves and some, if not all, of the firewood may come from one's own or a neighbour's compound. Only the banana leaves required for the outer wrapping usually have to be bought.

Producing *tempe* is a relatively easy but time-consuming and low return occupation, which normally engages two or three household members. The soybeans are boiled and then soaked to soften overnight. The skins are removed and the beans placed in a deep bamboo container and trampled for about thirty minutes. The crushed beans are steamed once more for about an hour, strained and spread out on a bamboo tray. They are then rubbed with teak leaves coated with a mould from the previous batch. Once fermentation is established, the mixture is formed into small cakes, wrapped with banana leaves and tied with a strip of rice stalk. The cakes are left to ferment for two to three days until they are permeated with a light grey mould (see also Adam 1929:67–8).

Bu Sartina is the largest and longest established of the 36 *tempe* producers in Babadsari. Bu Sartina acquired her initial finance from her parents, who themselves ran both *tempe* and coconut oil businesses. Before her marriage she helped her parents in both activities and was given a small amount of money in return. These savings financed her entry to rice trading after her marriage, but as this was both unprofitable and incompatible with caring for her young family, she switched to *tempe* production. She usually obtains a week's supply of soybeans on credit from a *toko* in Kutowinangun. One of her daughters does most of the preparation, while another daughter counts the individual pieces, delivers them to the *warung* they supply and collects payment from the previous delivery.

Su'un (Chinese vermicelli or arrowroot noodles) production is among the most capital intensive of village industries. A full complement of equipment costs about Rp 400 000 and raw materials for one week's production around Rp 200 000. But a potential manufacturer can begin with far less: small quantities of arrowroot can be obtained on credit, and manufacturing might start with finance as low as Rp 40 000, although this will not maintain production at a viable level. Production on a reasonable scale requires a press, a large number of tin trays, bamboo trestles and a gas pump, as well as far more arrowroot flour than a neophyte producer can obtain on credit.

Successful *su'un* producers regard Rp 500 000 as the minimum financial investment. Some have painstakingly acquired this by working as labourers in *su'un* factories, while others have been successful traders. Additional sources of finance include pawning gold or property, and loans from relatives. In fact, most producers finance the basic enterprise from a variety of sources: selling gold jewellery, leasing or selling land, and using savings accumulated very slowly from wage labour, trade or farm income.

The organization of *su'un* production is relatively complex and an efficient *su'un* factory requires at least six workers, two of whom are capable of heavy work. The first task is to sieve, soak and strain the flour. Chlorine is added and the mixture left to whiten. It is then cooked to a porridge and a starter is added. Next morning, an adult male blends parts of the prepared mixture with hot water in a copper basin and transfers it to the press, in which he thumps the dough down with a pestle. He then prepares a second batch while another adult male turns the press. Two people are required to place a series of trays beneath the press so as to collect the noodles: they are usually young boys or teenage girls. The full trays are passed to another couple who stack them outside on bamboo trestles. Once a run of fifteen to twenty trays is completed, the coagulated dough is scraped from the sides of the press and the process starts again. It takes up to three hours to dry the noodles. The final task is to collect, tie and weigh the dried noodles in bundles of fifty grams and then in ten kilogram lots. The first two tasks—blending the mixture and turning the press—require some strength and are almost invariably work for the owner of the business and another adult male. The other tasks are all within the capabilities of teenage children and young males, although the work is tiring and repetitive. While as much labour as possible is drawn from the household, most *su'un* factories use at least two non-household workers.

The finance required for most other forms of petty commodity production approximates the *tempe* rather than the *su'un* end of the continuum.

MAXIMIZING EMPLOYMENT

While the level of finance required for entry to petty commodity production is low, the amount of finance restricts the size and type of enterprise and thus severely limits economies of scale. Potential producers are often faced with a choice between entering a potentially rewarding industry with finance which is insufficient for long-term viability, or adequately financing a small factory with few chances of long-term expansion.

A second constraint on entry, which is explored in this section, is the nature of the labour process. Producers often attempt to make up for their low finance by 'self-exploitation' of household labour: working for low initial returns in the hope that a viable business might be established and returns will improve. Types of petty commodity production, however, differ considerably in the level, form and scheduling of labour demands, forcing potential producers to select an avenue of production which matches the quantity and quality of their labour force at various points in the developmental cycle of their households.

There is a reasonably clear-cut sexual division of labour in petty commodity production: men carry out the heavier production tasks, young women the lighter, and mature women market the product. This division, however, owes more to the economic organization of the enterprise and the availability of relatively highly paid employment in other sectors of the economy than to Javanese notions of appropriate labour for men and women. On occasion, almost any household member will carry out almost any task.

An examination of the economic strategies of households with differing labour forces engaged in differing forms of production illustrates the interaction between the developmental cycle of the household and the labour process. Thus, to begin with the familiar, *tempe* production requires only a limited and unskilled labour force. While returns to labour are so low that no one apart from a family member could participate, it is one of the few occupations open to women with young families and no alternative caretakers. Bu Sartina started manufacturing *tempe* when her young family made rice trading difficult. Initially she did most of the work (though her husband assisted with the wrapping) but, as her children grew older, they gradually participated and by their early teens had taken over production and distribution. Bu Sartina is now mainly a farmer, planting and tending spinach and harvesting rice in season, but she still buys the raw materials for *tempe*. Bu Lasira agreed to produce *tempe* for her brother's *warung* because her second son, a recent junior high school graduate, could not find work. The son does most of the production work, occasionally helped by his nine-year-old sister, while Bu Lasira continues trading in rice, as well as buying raw materials and arranging sales. *Tempe* production, therefore, is a possible venture for households with young unskilled labour and little finance, even though returns are very low. But, as I demonstrate below, problems of buying raw materials at low prices and, particularly, creating stable outlets, quickly bankrupt most concerns.

The manufacture of coconut graters (*parud*) from wooden planks and wire is slightly more complex than *tempe* production. Four sizes of graters are manufactured for domestic use, and an unusually large one, a metre long, is made on order from coconut oil producers. Men fetch the trees used for *parud* from the hillier regions of the district, and after they have been sawn into planks and planed, young women tap a series of wire pins in a diagonal pattern on the board. It takes approximately two hours for a skilled woman to complete one grater. Although young women are invariably much quicker, mature women also made the graters and have complete control of their distribution.

Older women sell their household's production in the periodic market in Kutowinangun to both retail and wholesale traders. In this market three elderly women from Suwaran limit their stock to *parud*, and about six other retail traders stock basketware and kitchenware (also petty commodity products), as well as graters. The main buyers, however, are eight large-scale traders in kitchenware who bulk produce for sale in distant centres. Two of the elderly *bakul* also work in the Prembun market, where they both retail goods and bulk them for onward transmission.

Grater production is centred on the hamlet of Suwaran in the village of Kepedek where, although most households have access to some land, very few have sufficient for full-time cultivation. The pattern of production and distribution illustrates the ways in which the scheduling of petty commodity production is adapted to maxi-, mize access to more remunerative activities.

One Suwaran household has an almost optimum labour structure. The father and his two teenage sons purchase and prepare the boards. Three daughters use some of these boards to manufacture graters and the surplus is sold to other producers. The mother is the major retailer of graters in the Kutowinangun market. Most households, however, are faced with labour problems: either they have insufficient male labour to prepare the boards or insufficient female labour to make the graters. Wage labour cannot normally be used to meet these deficiencies because returns to labour are too low. The usual solution is to concentrate on one aspect of the production process.

One of the major retail traders, who works four days a week, is the only woman in her household. Each week she produces only five of the graters she sells, and obtains most of her stock from other producers in the hamlet. Her husband and her fifteen-year-old son, in addition to growing rice and cashcropping oranges, purchase and prepare wood which they sell to grater manufacturers in exchange for the finished product. The second son is a relatively well-paid labourer in a brick factory.

A third household has a shortage of male labour. The household consists of a widow, an unmarried daughter, and a married daughter with her husband and child. The son-in-law is a full-time farmer, while his wife does the household work and makes the occasional grater. The unmarried daughter, probably the quickest worker in the village, makes ten graters a day and her mother, four. All of the graters are made from the highest quality *sawo* (*Achras zapota L*) wood: the wooden boards are purchased for Rp 250 each and the mother wholesales the finished product for Rp 400–450.

These examples are clear illustrations of the minute division of labour which characterizes rural Javanese production: an item as simple as a grater may have been resold five times before reaching the consumer. Each of the main tasks—preparing the wood, making the grater, and selling it—provides special opportunities for a particular category of labour. Wood preparation is well suited to a man whose main occupation is farming, because the work need not be continuous and the product can be stockpiled or sold. Similarly, while only young women are quick enough to make graters full-time, older women can contribute, and are more effective at selling.

Su'un manufacturing is a more complex operation and no household has a sufficiently large labour force of the required age and sex distribution to staff a viable factory. All *su'un* factories employ between two and five wage labourers, who are normally assigned to the heaviest and most sustained work. All concerns pay the same wage, which at the time of fieldwork was Rp 400 for men and Rp 300 for women, about two-thirds of the rate for agricultural labourers. But *su'un* labourers are given two meals—one at midday and the other at the end of work—which, in addition to its regularity, gives labourers in a *su'un* factory among the highest annual wages in the village. Adult full-time labour obtained from outside the household is always paid wages rather than a share of the profits, but there may be some additional gifts at holiday times.

Because the returns to labour are relatively high, all members of *su'un* manufacturing households are normally engaged in production. Adult men carry out the heavy work, younger women are responsible for the lighter tasks and adult women take care of the marketing. Children within the households do much of the cleaning up, although commonly other children help in return for a meal.

There are other forms of petty commodity production which employ rather more wage labour: brick manufacturing and coconut oil production, for example. But even here the schedule of production is closely tied to opportunities for better-paid employment. Brickmakers close down during the heaviest agricultural seasons to allow their workers to till their fields or seek wage employment on other's land. Coconut oil is a more stable industry, in which the main labour component is splitting the nuts and grating the flesh, tasks normally, but not exclusively, carried out by men.[4] During the peak agricultural season, one of the small Babadsari producers gets his coconuts crushed mechanically at the largest factory in the village, because his normal workers are otherwise employed. Although the extra costs mean little return he must maintain continuous supplies to his retailers.

The organization of petty commodity production, therefore, is characterized by considerable flexibility in the organization of labour to maximize the income of the household. Seasonality of production, the type and scale of the enterprise, the use of extra-household labour and wage labour, and the extent to which tasks are subdivided are all variables which can be manipulated to provide more highly paid employment for household members. But the overreaching determinant of household income is the availability of finance, and it is precisely those industries requiring little finance that give few opportunities for alternative labour strategies. On the other hand, finance can overcome deficiencies in the household labour force. An enterprising woman with six young children began the first *krupuk*[5] factory in Suwaran. Borrowing Rp 40 000 from her grandmother and working alongside two wage labourers, she gradually built up production to a quintal a day. She now obtains Rp 2 000 000 of cassava on credit, and is able to pay eight labourers a daily wage of Rp 500 plus food and lodging, while she concentrates on managing the business.

RETURNS TO LABOUR

Following White (1976a), I calculate 'returns to labour' as income less direct production costs (e.g., raw materials and transport) but not including such factors as interest on investments or deprecia-tion. This is more useful than profit as a measure of the financial value of various forms of employment, not only because it ap-proximates the calculations made by the Javanese, but because variables such as depreciation cannot be calculated with any accu-racy.[6] As the preceding discussion suggests, there are considerable differences in the returns to labour derived from various forms of petty commodity production and the ways in which these are distributed among the participants.

In the two *tempe* concerns which I observed in some detail, most of the production tasks were undertaken by teenagers. Bu Sarti-na's household produces 900 pieces of *tempe* each day from nine kilograms of soybeans. The simple return to labour, without taking depreciation or fuel costs into account, is Rp 290, about the cost of one kilogram of rice.[7] Production each day requires about eight hours' labour, not including purchasing raw materials or distributing the *tempe*. The daughter who does the heaviest work receives Rp 150 each day and the other daughter Rp 100. Bu Sartina takes Rp 40 for general household expenses. The second household produces 500 pieces for a daily return of Rp 220. The son, who does most of the work takes Rp 100, and the remaining Rp 120 is used to buy food.

Su'un factories have far greater returns to labour, and two examples are tabulated in Table 4.1. These figures refer to full capacity weeks with eight hours' work each day: very hot weather halves production and during the rainy season production may stop completely for several days. Whereas one of the more successful *su'un* producers told me that he made Rp 5000 net profit per quintal of *su'un*, the figures calculated from the tables for both households are about Rp 7000 per quintal. This gives an overall return to labour of Rp 700 per hour, which is far higher than most other forms of employment available to rural Javanese.[8]

But indigenous calculations, as befit an economic system in which the household is both the production and consumption unit, do not differentiate between production costs and household maintenance costs. Bu Warso is probably typical in describing her gross profit as Rp 28 000 a quintal of *su'un* and Rp 1800 as her net profit. The latter figure is what remains after household costs have been deducted. When in full production, she reckons her net monthly profit as Rp 54 000.

Adults other than households members who work in the *su'un* factories are always paid set wages, even when they are relatives. Children are given meals and the occasional present. Apart from these sums, there is no set division of the income, which becomes part of the general household income. Children helping with production are seen as providing their services in return for support from the parents and receive no direct payment. Their education and clothing costs are regarded as adequate recompense for their labour, much of which is part-time, wedged between school and other activities. The work of adults and older children no longer at school is more time-consuming and regular, but even here no formal share-profit or wage system applies. Labour is provided in return for support, although parents occasionally give money upon request for new clothing or a trip to the movies. The return for labour is derived when the children marry and become independent. Families are regarded as working together to provide their young members with an education which might gain them access to secure jobs or rich spouses. Rarely, parents give their children pocket money or savings (*celengan*), which might amount to Rp 100 for a day's labour.

TABLE 4.1

WEEKLY PRODUCTION COSTS OF TWO *SU'UN* CONCERNS

	BU WARSO		PAK KUDRAT	
	Quantity	Price (Rp)	Quantity	Price (Rp)
COSTS				
Arrowroot flour	10.5 qu. @ Rp 19 000/qu.	199 500	14 qu. @ Rp 21 000/qu.	294 000
Chlorine	10.5 kg. @ Rp 1 000/kg.	10 500	21 kg. @ Rp 925/kg.	19 450
Kerosene	84 litres @ Rp 80/litre	6 720	110 litres @ Rp 80/litre	8 800
Coconut oil	5 kg. @ Rp 420/kg.	2 100	5 kg. @ Rp 420/kg.	2 100
Labour	4 labourers @ Rp 400/day	11 200	5 labourers @ Rp 400/day	14 000
Transport	Rp 77 × 6.2 qu.	4 340	3 trips @ Rp 750 (charter minibus)	2 250
Bus fares (to Magelang)	2 × Rp 500	1 000	—	
Local fares		200	Rp 150 × 2 × 3	900
Coolies	Rp 75 × 15 (Magelang)	1 125	Rp 75 × 24 (Kebumen)	1 800
Food for labourers	4 × 7 × Rp 200	5 600	5 × 7 × Rp 200	7 000
TOTAL		242 285		350 300

SALES	8.4 qu. @ Rp 360/kg.	302 400
	11 qu.	404 600
	(1.2 qu. @ Rp 350/kg.)	42 000
	(9.8 qu. @ Rp 370/kg.)	362 600
RETURN TO OWNER	60 115	54 300
DAILY RETURN TO OWNER	8 588	7 757
PROFIT (per qu. of *su'un*)	7 157	4 936

MARKETING

Organizing production is one problem, while selling the goods at a profit is another. The marketing of *tempe* and *su'un* illustrates the problems of petty commodity producers in gaining access to a market. In both cases a viable business requires a steady clientele, but the nature of the clientele differs. *Tempe*, a staple which spoils quickly and is produced in small quantities, is sold daily in the local community. *Su'un*, which seems to last for ever, must be produced on a considerable scale to be profitable, and is sold in large quantities at irregular intervals over a wide area.

As was noted earlier, there are few constraints on producing *tempe*: the finance is low and the knowledge widespread. There is also considerable demand for this staple of the Javanese diet. But the easy entry requirements make competition fierce and it is very difficult to establish the stable clientele which a successful business requires. One possibility is to become a regular supplier to a *warung*, for any newly established *warung* anxious to attract customers stocks *tempe* as a matter of course. Kinship and neighbourhood ties are the usual means of arranging such clientele. One Babadsari producer, Bu Sartina, sells 800 of the 900 pieces she produces to a *warung* owned by her brother, and sells the remainder to neighbours who buy directly from her house. Another supplies half her production to two *warung* owned by neighbours, but must sell the other 250 pieces directly to consumers and consequently sometimes has problems in disposing of her stock.[9] This second producer actually makes a higher return per kilogram than Bu Sartina, but her restricted clientele limits her production. A second possibility is to sell in the *pasar*. One elderly Ungaran woman works in two periodic markets, Prembun and Kutowinangun, and has established a clientele amongst the traders who regard her *tempe* as particularly tasty. She trades four days a week and produces *tempe* on the remaining three.

With a product as cheap as *tempe*, cutting prices is seldom possible without producing an inferior product, and as *tempe* is often the sole side-dish, taste is of prime importance. When one *warung* Bu Sartina supplied went bankrupt, a second *warung* sought her product, unceremoniously dumping their previous supplier who had been attempting to reduce her costs. *Tempe* is normally sold on credit, with most *warung* paying for the previous day's purchases when they receive new supplies.

Producers attempting to build a clientele for a *su'un* factory can seldom rely on kinship and neighbourhood ties. *Su'un* is bulky, it is not a staple item of diet, and there are more intermediaries between producer and consumer. Pak Kudrat, one of the *su'un* producers discussed above, initially retailed a considerable proportion of his produce in the local periodic markets. His wife, his daughter and two other relatives took about ten kilograms each market day, carrying it three kilometres to the main road and then travelling by bus. Over the years Bu Kudrat slowly established a supplier relationship with other traders and she now wholesales about 150 kilograms each day in the Kebumen market. Her major asset in building up this clientele was her knowledge of the traders and her provision of credit: some of her clientele must pay cash on delivery, others pay at the end of the market day, and a few are allowed debts of up to Rp 10 000.

The Warso family, *su'un* producers for nearly twenty-five years, established their main clientele in the district market of Magelang, some sixty kilometres from home. As this required travelling at night, Pak Warso took charge of marketing although this is usually a women's role. Once a week he hired a truck, selling a tonne in a single lot to a Chinese wholesaler, who in turn distributed it to retailers within the market. When the wholesaler established an egg noodle factory, and minibuses became more accessible, Bu Warso took over the marketing. She established a permanent arrangement with a minibus owner in Magelang, and over seven years built up a clientele of eleven traders in the Magelang market. Bu Warso travels two or three times a week, usually sharing the minibus with a fellow *su'un* producer. She also delivers to a fixed clientele in Prembun, Kutoarjo and Kutowinangun markets who are all large-scale market traders selling a variety of dry goods. The remainder of their produce is retailed by three girls who pick up the goods (and frequently bundle them also) from the factory, but only one of these, a relative, takes a load of twenty kilograms every day. Sporadic, but occasionally large, sales are also made to traders who visit the factory.

Establishing a clientele was a laborious business for Pak Kudrat. Initially his wife visited *warung*, and sellers of cooked food, offering short-term credit as an inducement to buy, while relying on female relatives to sell the rest. Later, as the factory became established and finance increased, she was able to move into a wholesaling role because she could provide extensive long-term

TABLE 4.2

AMBAL AND KUTOWINANGUN VILLAGES ASSOCIATED WITH PARTICULAR
FORMS OF PETTY COMMODITY PRODUCTION

Village	Specialization
KUTOWINANGUN DISTRICT	
Ungaran	terracotta pottery, bamboo containers
Mrinen	tinware, soldered goods
Kepedek	bricks, graters
Jlegiwinangun	arrowroot noodles (*su'un*)
AMBAL DISTRICT	
Ambalresmi	coconut sugar, *emping*, fishnets
Ambalkebrek	*emping*, coconut oil, copra
Pagedangan	brass spoons, cane baskets
Kembangsawit	bamboo trays
Dukuhrejasari	bamboo sieves, hornwork
Kradenan	bamboo fans, bamboo rice steamers
Ambarwinangun	bamboo rice steamers
Surabayan	small cane baskets

credit. But the process took many years and production expanded very slowly. Although Pak Warso began production on a larger scale because of an assured market, he too increased the size of his clientele only slowly, with his ability to provide credit being the critical factor in the acquisition of new customers.

VILLAGE SPECIALIZATION

The localization of the manufacture of particular products in specific hamlets or villages is a striking feature of the Javanese rural economy and has a long history.[10] While exact figures are not available, a considerable proportion of the goods sold in the Kebumen market circuit are produced in household concerns.[11] Some indication of the ubiquity of this method of production is that 412 of the 2106 traders in the Prembun periodic market sell local manufactures other than textiles, and locally produced items comprise the bulk of 350 traders' stock.

Table 4.2 lists some of the villages in the Kutowinangun and Ambal *kecamatan* which are closely associated with particular industries. At least four of the nineteen villages in the district of Kutowinangun specialize in a particular form of petty commodity production. The fact that these four villages are located near my field site, Babadsari, suggests that the list is by no means definitive. There is remarkably little overlap in production between villages, with the exception of brick manufacturing which, while centred on two hamlets of Kepedek, spills over into the contingent hamlet in Babadsari. Manufacturing appears a little less specialized in the Ambal district, but a quarter of the villages are identified with particular forms of production, either of an agricultural or handicraft nature. The villages around Ambalresmi where *mlinjo* and coconut trees are ubiquitous concentrate on *emping* (a chip made from *mlinjo* kernels), coconut sugar, coconut oil and copra manufacture. The villages south of Kutowinangun, in the northernmost part of Ambal, are mainly concerned with the manufacture of basketware from split bamboo: Kembangsawit, Kradenan, Pagedangan, Dukuhrejasari, Surabayan and Ambarwinangun all manufacture bamboo goods of various sorts.[12] Within these villages, there is further sub-specialization—Kembangsawit is known for its bamboo trays while Kradenan produces bamboo fans—but this is less obvious because young women, who make most of the goods, often move from their village after marriage.[13]

In the 1930s, a hamlet within my field-site of Babadsari was known throughout the region for the large quantities of high quality coconut oil which it produced (Ochse and Terra 1934:36). Today the numerous concerns mentioned in the report have disappeared and the current producer, established seventeen years ago, has no connections with the earlier enterprises. The development of relatively cheap motor transport and the spread of housing at the expense of coconut palms have apparently concentrated coconut oil manufacturing in the district towns, where large factories can take advantage of economies of scale. In Babadsari today there is approximately one coconut oil production unit per hamlet. All are small, apart from one which uses machinery to speed up the manufacturing process. Most coconut oil manufacturers in Babadsari buy coconuts from their neighbours, selling coconut oil back to them or the local *warung*, and nearly all their product is consumed within the village. Babadsari is not now associated with any particular form of petty commodity production, but is well-known for its cloth traders. A neighbouring village, Ungaran, specializes in pottery and bamboo containers (*tombong*), while its many traders deal in bicycles and ready-made clothing. Jlegiwinangun, to the north, manufactures *su'un* and slaughters livestock, so that its traders are naturally associated with these two products.

The percentage of households within a particular hamlet which derive income from its specialized form of petty commodity production is difficult to establish, but it is clearly very high. My own survey of the grater-producing hamlet of Suwaran indicated that two-thirds of households gained income from grater production and it was the major source of income for most of these households. Employment statistics compiled by village officials, the only source for a wider comparison, are an uncertain guide because they tend to disguise the extent of multiple employment. One of my informants, for example, is listed as a farmer (*petani*) on her identity card and therefore in village statistics. But although her husband owns land and she helps him at some times during the year, she herself is a full-time trader (six days a week) and spends considerable time in *tempe* production. On the other hand, Kepedek village statistics list only thirty-five persons engaged in petty commodity production, yet the village has at least twelve flourishing brickworks.

For these reasons only limited inferences can be drawn from the data on village occupations (see Alexander 1985:282). They do indicate, however, that the four petty commodity specializing villages in Kutowinangun have lower percentages of full-time farmers than Babadsari which I use as a bench-mark. Also, unlike Babadsari, in each of the four villages farm labourers outnumber independent farmers, which suggests that wage labour is more prevalent in these villages.

One, rather obvious, hypothesis for the concentration of petty commodity production in some villages is the extent of population pressure on land, especially the highly productive *sawah*. There is some statistical support for the land pressure hypothesis (Alexander 1985:283–84). In Kutowinangun district the average population density is 1284 per square kilometre and the average *sawah* holding per head is 0.04 hectares. Of the four villages heavily involved in petty commodity production, Kepedek and Ungaran have higher than average population densities, and all apart from Mrinen have less than average *sawah* holdings. In Ambal the average population density is 906 per square kilometre and the average holding of *sawah* is 0.05 hectares. Here the distribution is less significant, with two of the seven villages having lower than average population densities, and none having below average per capita holdings of *sawah*. In both areas, however, there are numerous other heavily populated villages which are not strongly involved in village manufacturing. Indeed, the average population density is so high throughout the area that most villagers have incentives to seek other avenues of employment.

The availability of transport seems a more important consideration. Villages in the more mountainous, isolated regions which have little or no wet rice land, such as Lumbu and Korowelang, also lack manufacturing industries. The poverty-striken coastal area of Ambal faces the same problem. On the other hand, Kepedek, Mrinen and Ungaran are located near market centres and main roads. Although Jlegiwinangun is some ten kilometres from the market, it has a good access road, unlike its neighbour Lumbu, where no industry has been established. The Ambal manufacturing centres are in two clusters: one group lies immediately south of Kutowinangun town, close to the main road, and the other is located near the Ambal market and a minor road.

The availability of restricted raw materials, such as clay, has facilitated the growth of industries centred around pottery, bricks and tiles. Ungaran has a hamlet close to the river which is heavily involved in pottery production, two hamlets of Kepedek are centres of brick production, and Pejagoan, a village near Kebumen with a mere seven hectares of *sawah*, is an important tile manufacturing centre.

But while the ecology and access to transport suggest why some villages are heavily involved in manufacturing, they tell us little about village specialization: about why so many households in Suwaran make graters, or those in Jlegiwinangun manufacture *su'un*. Understanding village specialization requires an investigation of other factors: the questions of skill, kinship and neighbourhood ties, and the structure of the market.

Although most petty commodity production involves relatively simple tasks, it takes skill and practice to achieve the output levels which make a factory viable. People who have participated as children are therefore probably well placed to establish businesses, for kinship and neighbourhood ties are important in acquiring early skills. Moreover successful entrepreneurs often lend equipment or finance to enable relatives and neighbours to begin manufacturing themselves. I discovered no attempts to restrict newcomers on the grounds that it would increase competition, and established producers appear willing to give many forms of non-financial aid to other households in the village. Indeed, there appears to be a positive belief that increasing the numbers of households specializing in a particular form of production will benefit all producers. In other words, new producers are seen as increasing the overall size of the market, not as additional competitors for a limited number of sales.

Understanding this apparently paradoxical view requires an appreciation of the structure of the market. In an economic system which lacks advertising other than by word of mouth, industries are grouped together for the same reasons that stalls selling similar products are grouped in the market places: grouping makes it easier for buyers to find the goods they wish to purchase. This is particularly true of items such as bricks or tiles, which are too expensive to transport to local market centres for sale. Persons wanting to buy tiles or bricks for a house know they will find a large range and will be able to compare prices in Pejagoan or Kepedek. Although many other villages have suitable clay, a tile manufacturer in such a village could sell only to fellow villagers and even they would probably visit the specialized sites to compare prices before buying. Similar points also hold for less bulky items. While manufacturers of *su'un*, graters and *krupuk* sell much of their production in the *pasar*, they also occasionally sell large quantities to visiting traders from other regions. Moreover, their concentration in particular villages enables them to share transport and thus reduce costs.

A CASE STUDY OF VILLAGE SPECIALIZATION

Jlegiwinangun, the village immediately north of Babadsari, is widely known throughout the Kebumen region for its production of *su'un*. This is an interesting commodity through which to investigate the process of village specialization for there are no obvious reasons why production should be localized. The raw material of arrowroot flour is grown widely, the product does not spoil quickly and, although bulky, it is relatively light. Moreover, although they require considerable finance, *su'un* factories are among the most profitable form of petty commodity production. The village's specialization developed fairly recently: the first *su'un* factory was established in 1946 but now nearly a fifth of the households are involved. Eighteen households are engaged in full-time production; a further ninety people are engaged as full- or part-time workers; and a considerable number of women, at least thirty, are *su'un* traders. Jlegiwinangun with a population of 2400 has a severe shortage of good land. There is very little *sawah* (fifty-two hectares, 80% of which is only rain-irrigated) and most dry land (174 hectares) is used for tobacco, arrowroot and orange cultivation. Before the introduction of *su'un* most residents were farmers or engaged in the butchering and sale of meat. Before Independence many men left the village to work elsewhere: among them were the entrepreneurs who opened the first *su'un* factories.

Pak Suyud and Pak Siswoyo had worked as wage labourers in a Chinese-owned *su'un* factory in Kutoarjo. Pak Suyud opened his *su'un* factory in 1946 using his savings and some finance acquired on marriage to buy equipment. His former employer supplied him with raw materials on credit. Initially he employed seven young people from Kutoarjo, paying them Rp 2.5 per month. His first wife took no part in either production or distribution, largely because they were keen to have children, although Pak Suyud had to wait till his third marriage before he succeeded. In the early period Pak Suyud spent at least two days a week seeking markets and regularly visited the periodic markets in the Kebumen region, selling off his produce (a quintal a day) in small amounts. By 1948 he was selling most of his *su'un* to a trader in the Karanganyar market. This arrangement worked amicably enough for two years until the trader decided to establish his own factory. Pak Suyud was placed in a quandary. He had lost his major client, his health was declining, he had no children, and conditions were hard in 1950. He therefore abandoned his factory and took up farming. Today his landholdings, 300 *ubin* of paddy land and 300 *ubin* of dry land planted with corn, peanuts and oranges, indicate that he is reasonably prosperous.

Pak Suyud's difficulties did not deter Pak Siswoyo from following a similar route, because he saw Pak Suyud's failure as due to marketing problems. As a bachelor, Pak Siswoyo had had five years' experience in the same Chinese *su'un* factory in Kutoarjo and set up a factory himself in 1952 after he married. He initially employed five local people who had work experience, paying them Rp 25 a day plus food and cigarettes. His wife has always been in charge of sales. In the early days she sold the *su'un* twice a week in

Kebumen, ferrying the produce by ponycart. By 1970 the *su'un* factory was well established and, as his wife was finding the task exhausting, they changed their marketing practices, selling to local *bakul* who resold their goods at markets in Prembun, Pituruh and Kenayan. Only one of their children, a twenty-year-old son, helps in the business, which has been successful enough to provide the other seven children with a good education.

Pak Siswoyo's neighbour, Pak Parto, observed the working of the new factory and two years later (1954) established his own. It operated for over ten years, but eventually suffered the fate of many small businesses and became bankrupt. The mixed fortunes of these early entrepreneurs have not discouraged a further twenty-five persons establishing *su'un* factories over the past thirty years, a quarter of which have closed down. The closures were for three reasons. Some people retired as they grew old, others switched the funds they acquired into more profitable ventures, and the remainder were genuine bankrupts who lacked cash to continue in business.

In 1982 there were eighteen factories, the most recent of which was established in 1980. The owner, Pak Sruni, like many before him, had acquired work experience in a neighbour's factory and two of his daughters were experienced traders of *su'un* from the same factory. This new factory already produces about ninety kilograms of *su'un* a day. The daughters each sell thirty kilograms on the periodic market days in Kutowinangun and Prembun and a further ten kilograms each at Pasar Krakal where they carry it on foot. But the bulk of production is sold by Pak Sruni's wife who takes two quintal by chartered minibus to Kutoarjo market every Sunday and Thursday.

Perhaps the most typical of the present day producers in Jlegiwi-nangun is Pak Kudrat. At the time he established his business in 1972 he had no land apart from his household compound. He made a living selling *su'un* produced in a neighbour's factory owned by Pak Haji Nur, the largest in the village, which turned out three quintal a day. It took many years for Pak Kudrat to acquire sufficient finance and he was heavily dependent on his wife to help him with both production and sales, as his eldest child was only ten years old at the time he started.

A familiar pattern emerges from these brief histories of individual enterprises. Households with insufficient or no land painstakingly acquire finance through wage labour or trade and channel their funds into the establishment of a *su'un* factory. Equally painstakingly they acquire further finance which is ploughed back into the enterprise and this enables them to expand to a viable level. The example of earlier enterprises, and the chance to acquire skills in production and trading, further stimulate emulation. The expanding population which contributed to the pressure on land has, in a broad sense, provided them with the market for their product. The importance of village specialization in acquiring initial skills and finance, and, more importantly, in localizing marketing, is indicated by the fact that Jlegiwinangun is the only village in the Kebumen region of some million people which produces *su'un*.

PETTY COMMODITY PRODUCTION

Although a comprehensive account requires discussion of the relationship between petty commodity production and agriculture, the main features have been established. The most important characteristic is that all enterprises are owned by the direct producers and there is no capitalist ownership. Although there is some funding by merchants, in the form of providing raw materials on credit, this is balanced by the producers allowing credit to the purchasers of their products. While enterprises differ considerably in scale, the value of equipment is low, seldom exceeding one to two weeks' supply of raw materials, and as there is little use of energy other than human labour power, productivity is also low. Finally, the dominant form of labour relationship is household labour with little formal division of proceeds between household members. Some of the larger enterprises employ wage labour, but this is not the major source of labour.

In all these factors Java bears a close resemblance to the petty commodity economy analysed by Joel Kahn in *Minangkabau Social Formations*. Kahn (1980:130–50; cf. Kahn 1982) suggests that the basic contradiction inherent in petty commodity production is that higher productivity, through the development of the productive forces, has the consequence of diminishing the number of owners and concentrating the means of production in a few hands. Kahn sees this as mainly due to the increased demands for finance which each step in the development of the productive forces entails. As mechanization increases, setting the productive cycle in motion requires increasingly large 'lumps' of capital, and the inability to obtain additional finance forces small producers out of the industry.

My Javanese material suggests one reason why this contradiction has not been realized in many parts of Indonesia, and why independent owner-operators continue to dominate rural industry. The topic can be approached through two interconnected features of the Javanese case: the apparent unwillingness of Javanese producers to expand production beyond a certain level and the lack of employment of wage labour. If the discussion is limited to the simplest forms of petty commodity production—*tempe*, graters and mat weaving are examples—there is a simple reason why production is not expanded and wage labour is not employed: returns to labour are below the lowest wage rates in the rural economy. These forms of petty commodity production, along with the very small scale trading, are occupations of last resort. They provide full-time employment for households which lack the land to become farmers, the wealth to finance a viable business, or access to regular wage employment. They also provide part-time employment for household members who cannot become fully engaged in more remunerative activities. It is the ease of entry to these forms of petty commodity production which keeps returns to labour below wage rates, and even in a viable enterprise the marginal productivity of both labour and finance approaches zero.

But with other forms of petty commodity production, such as *su'un* factories or brick works, the reasons for the lack of expansion are not so obvious. Most *su'un* factories, for example, employ wage labour, and the figures in Table 4.1 show that wage rates are well below the labourers' contribution to the profits of the enterprise. As *su'un* factory owners are able to extract surplus value, it would appear open to owners of capital to establish *su'un* factories and operate them with wage labour.

Understanding why capitalist factories are rare in rural Java requires consideration of both the internal structure of petty commodity production and its relationship with other sectors of the rural economy. As was noted above, a major constraint on expanding production is the creation of a larger clientele and in most cases this is achieved by selling on credit. Increasing the scale of production, therefore, requires not only financing equipment, raw materials and wages, but also financing a distribution network. In other words, an increasingly large lump of capital. But the return on finance, as capital, in a *su'un* factory is not particularly high relative to other sectors of the rural economy. For persons with some millions of rupiah, investing in a minibus, a petrol or kerosene agency, a mechanized rice huller, or land, to take only some examples, gives far higher returns. And owners of successful *su'un* factories do transfer funds to these areas. Finance in petty commodity production gives high returns only when it is combined with the labour of household members. The motive for investment is to provide well-paid employment for household members, enabling otherwise unemployed or lowly paid persons to make a substantial contribution to the household's income.[14] It is simply not economically rational to increase investment (and thus expand production) past the point where all household labour is fully engaged. At that point there are far more lucrative uses for funds.

1. Geertz (1963b:32) notes:

> The *pasar* must not be seen simply as a distributive apparatus which adds little or no real value to the goods which flow through it. It is a manufacturing, productive apparatus as well, and the two elements, the movement of goods and their processing—insofar as this is accomplished in Modjokuto—are wholly intertwined. Production, distribution, and sales are fused into one comprehensive economic institution.

Geertz (1963b:66–73) describes petty commodity production in East Java thirty years ago, while Boeke (1926), van Doorn (1926), Loriaux and van Doorn (1923), and Ochse and Terra (1934) describe similar enterprises earlier in the century.

2. Stoler (1975:54) notes that the Javanese distinction between the main occupation (*pokok*) and sideline occupation (*sambilan*) does not necessarily reflect the proportion of total income or amount of time spent in them.

3. *Tempe* production has long been particularly important in the Kebumen region because of the absence of meat in the local diet (see *Koloniaal Verslag* 1892:5).

4. Dewey observed a similar pattern in the Modjokuto region of East Java for full-time producers, but noted that where producers are engaged in part-time or self-production, women did most of the work (1962a:171–2).

5. *Krupuk* are crisp dried chips fried before eating, and made from a wide variety of ingredients such as cassava, rice flour or shrimps.

6. For a comprehensive discussion of the problems which arise from the use of such concepts as 'profit' in an economy of individual producers and traders see Kahn (1980:120–2).

7. The profit margin in both these cases—7.5 and 9.5 respectively—compare very unfavourably with data from the 1930s. Ochse and Terra (1934) report an average profit of 55% in 1933 which was the height of the depression. But at that time also the 'profit' on processing 1.2 kilograms of *tempe* was sufficient to buy only one kilogram of rice.

8. Sajogyo (1977:65) tabulates the returns in kilograms of rice per day of labour for the most common forms of petty commodity production. The figures are broadly in accord with those in this chapter: producers of bamboo articles and processed foodstuffs seldom gain two kilograms or rice a day, while *su'un*, coconut oil and brick manufacturing often return more than five kilograms.

9. Stoler (1975:75, 79) stresses that *tempe* producers in Kali Loro obtain a steady income throughout the year and 'that it is a binding occupation as it involves more than one family member and they supply a regular clientele'.

10. See van Doorn (1926:119); *Verslag der Nijverheidscommissie* (1933:274). Loriaux and van Doorn (1923:15) noted that in one hamlet of Purworejo regency most households manufactured shorts. Geertz (1963b:21), in comparing Java with Bali, claimed that village-based industry was of only 'marginal importance'. Whatever the case in East Java, this is not true of Central and north Java, as he himself noted in an earlier work (1956b:97).

11. Anderson's (1978:26) claim that the 'largest group of traders are catering exclusively for the consumer needs of the local population by selling a range of products of modern factory industry' is not supported by his own data. See his Table 12.

12. The cane baskets have been produced in Pagedangan and Kradenan since at least 1880 (Rouffaer 1904:172).

13. Men split the bamboo, but basketweavers usually buy the bamboo split, rather than prepare it in their own homes.

14. Another factor telling against the expansion of petty commodity production is the widespread, but probably false, belief that money paid for children's education is a good investment because it opens the possibility of well-paid salaried employment. Owners of *su'un* factories with young children are apt to place investment in their children's education above investment in expanding their business.

5

Selling Cloth: The Supply–Credit Nexus

HAVING established the structure of the Kebumen markets and the social characteristics of the traders who work in them, we can now turn to the *bakul*'s activities within the *pasar*: to the process of trading itself. Making a living with limited finance in a very competitive market requires considerable skills in manipulating credit, in acquiring and withholding information, and in bargaining with customers and suppliers.

The discussion of petty commodity production stressed that the central problem of producers was establishing regular sales and noted the crucial role of producer credit in cultivating a stable clientele. Within the *pasar*, all traders obtain credit from their suppliers, but they do not all obtain it on the same terms. The form in which credit is acquired is the major constraint on the trader's marketing strategy and thus on her income. The substantive focus of this chapter is cloth trading, which has three features which make it particularly apposite for an investigation of credit. Cloth traders (*bakul jarik*), who comprise 15% of all traders, range from the very successful women who are among the market elite, to others constantly on the brink of bankruptcy. Sources of supply include both large urban factories producing hundreds of thousands of metres each month and household concerns producing less than 500 metres each year. And credit arrangements, while variations of three main forms, are remarkably complex.

Although the consequences of relationships between supplier and trader for the creation and maintenance of credit are obviously central to an understanding of the market, it is a difficult area to research. The subject of credit, debts and especially interest charges, are not freely discussed; indeed, the initial response of most participants in such transactions is to deny their existence. The charging of interest contravenes the tenets of Islam and this, to some degree, accounts for traders' reserve on the matter, although with the spread of government-financed savings banks the religious objection to interest-generating debts is diminishing. Perhaps a more important reason for the reluctance to discuss credit is that Javanese lose status by admitting they are indebted. This has added weight for market traders, who are in the paradoxical position of having to demonstrate that they do not require credit in order to obtain it. General knowledge of the extent of a *bakul*'s indebtedness, especially during the periods of the year when she is unable to repay on demand, obstruct her access to further credit. Most traders do not keep accounts which indicate the exact extent of their indebtedness at a particular time, for such questions are unimportant in the conduct of their businesses.

For these reasons I approached the analysis of supply in general and credit in particular through the detailed examination of particular enterprises. The two traders Bu Menik and Bu Samilah, whose activities I describe, arrange supplies and credit in very different ways and the contrast between them demonstrates that access to finance determines trading success.

BATIK

Batik traders stock three main items: *jarik, sarong* and *slendang*. *Jarik* is the ankle-length *batik* wrap-around skirt usually worn by mature women. The male version is sewn along one edge into a tube known as a *sarong*. A *slendang* is a shoulder scarf which ranges from a purely decorative scarf measuring 150 x 30 cm., to a functional sling which may be as large as half a metre by four metres used for carrying heavy goods. *Batik* traders generally enumerate their goods in *kodi*, a bundle of twenty assorted pieces.

In the Kebumen area many small businesses, both Chinese and Javanese, make *batik*. The most common styles include Slendang Jawa, Watubarut and Tanuraksan. Slendang Jawa, a style peculiar to the region, is a shoulder scarf which comes in two sizes. Both are particularly large with a hand-waxed (*tulis*) design dyed in red and black, but the larger has a fringed edge and uses a coarse hand-woven cloth. Watubarut *jarik* and *slendang* are stamped (*cap*) or hand-waxed on second quality (*mori prima*) or third quality (*mori biru*)[1] cambric and feature flamboyant designs incorporating geometrical, flower or bird motifs in reddish-browns, blues or greens. Tanuraksan is also produced on low quality cloth in *tulis* or *cap* with subdued geometrical patterns in indigo and brown.

The other major styles of *batik* popular in the Kebumen region are produced in the village of Baledono in the adjoining regency of Purworejo. The ten Baledono factories, all small concerns owned and operated by Javanese families, make three types of goods, *jarik*, *sarong* and a medium-sized *slendang*, in designs of Yogyakarta origin. Each type of cloth has about five basic patterns, mainly geometrical, and each factory produces its own variants of these. Most designs are printed on third quality cambric. Colours are limited to indigo, brown and black and a distinctive Baledono style has evolved over the eighty years these goods have been in production.[2]

Batik from the major centres of production in Solo and Yogyakarta normally reach Kebumen *pasar* through the large markets located in these towns. Because *batik* production in the ex-Principalities is often based on the 'putting-out' system and co-ordinated by sizeable concerns, there are several levels of distribution between the factory and traders.[3]

This is also true, to some extent, of the distinctive *batik* from Pekalongan, but more commonly it is produced and distributed by household concerns. In a typical *batik* factory run by a married couple, the wife supervises production, arranging for the waxing to be done by village women and supervising the dying in a backyard shed, while the husband takes charge of the selling, making ten-day trips from Pekalongan to markets in Madiun, Solo, Magelang and Kebumen. In the small *batik* enterprises of the Kebumen and Purworejo areas, however, the wife arranges distribution, while the husband supervises production. This difference in the division of labour appears to reflect the scale of the business. In the Kebumen concerns output is too low to provide full-time employment for the husband, and he is able to combine supervision of *batik* production with other work in the village. Moreover, the selling range is much narrower and therefore the wife seldom has to be away from home overnight. These *batik* producers normally sell directly to *bakul* in larger *pasar*. But the dominant source of locally produced *batik* is the numerous mobile traders, who are not necessarily associated with particular *batik* producers, do not have market stalls, and do not sell directly to consumers. These traders, mainly women, visit all the markets active on a particular day, carrying about three *kodi* which they purchase directly from the factories. To complete the picture, some *batik* is distributed on a part-time basis often by women employees of *batik* factories who sell a few pieces of cloth to local *bakul*.[4]

BU MENIK: A SUCCESSFUL CLOTH TRADER

Cloth traders are among the market elite. They need extensive finance for they maintain large stocks of a commodity which is highly valued, slow to sell and non-perishable. As befits their status, they generally begin trading later in the day. In contrast to the rapid sales of small quantities which characterize other trades, cloth trading has a rhythm of long periods of inactivity or uncompleted transactions, interspersed with sustained periods of intensive bargaining. Many cloth traders come from the richer village families and are consequently better educated: even the elderly women usually have two or three years of schooling. This is not surprising for, as we will see, cloth traders must manipulate more complex finance, stock and social relationships than their fellow *bakul*. Even among this group Bu Menik is exceptional, for she has a B.Sc. in economics from a regional university.

In the Prembun and Kutowinangun markets Bu Menik ranks among the medium-scale *bakul jarik*. The large-scale traders are mainly wholesalers (*bakul borongan*). In Kebumen there are ten of these and Prembun and Kutowinangun have three each. By village standards Bu Menik's household is rich, but it would not fall within the wealthiest 15% in the town in which she lives. They own an old but substantial house (inherited from her mother), a small area of dry land but no *sawah*, a TV set and a motorbike her husband rides to work. But a wholesale *bakul* in the stall alongside her has three times as much stock, 200 *ubin* of *sawah*, a TV set and a minibus. The wholesale *bakul* has a more extensive network of suppliers and sells to *bakul* within the market as well as retail customers. Most *bakul jarik* are married to men who have regular employment, have considerable areas of *sawah* by village standards, or who are village officials.

A slight, active woman in her mid-thirties, Bu Menik and her husband married according to their own preference, but with their parents' consent, in 1976, and now have two children, a four-year-old boy and a two-year-old girl. Her husband teaches religious studies in a local high school. Bu Menik explains her demanding work routine as necessary to save for the education of her children whom she leaves at home in the care of an elderly woman from a neighbouring village. Their occasional illnesses are the only interruption to her work. She stopped only a week before the birth of each child and began forty days later. She breastfed them for six months rather than the customary two years, because of tiredness and consequent ill-health.[5]

Bu Menik works every day of the week: on Wednesdays and Saturdays she teaches at the junior high school and other days sells cloth in the *pasar*. She trades at Kutowinangun on Tuesdays and Fridays and at Prembun on Mondays and Thursdays. On Sundays she visits both Ambal and Kebumen markets, spending a few hours in Ambal as a wholesale distributor before moving on to the *kabupaten* market at Kebumen, where she is both a wholesaler and retailer, for the remainder of the day.

Bu Menik took over her mother's business ten years ago. Since that time she has risen before five each morning, beginning the day with prayers, and cooking and bathing before leaving the house. She arrives at the market shortly before eight and eats her rice meal (previously prepared at home) about nine after the initial rush of customers is over. Generally she has a snack about midday, and returns home between one and two in the afternoon. On Sundays her day is longer: she arrives at Ambal by 9 a.m. and returns from Kebumen after 4 p.m. She has no servants so household tasks occupy her until early evening, but she usually manages to watch TV for an hour or two before accompanying the children to bed. Despite this demanding routine, Bu Menik enjoys working and prefers trading to teaching. In part, this is because trading is less restricting: as her children are still young, she likes to feel she can drop everything and care for them as required. In part it is because her income from trading, while fluctuating widely from week to week, is much greater than from teaching.

In addition to Bu Menik's earnings and her husband's salary, the household draws income from fruit trees grown on land they own near Ambal and from chickens he cares for at home after work. They have a savings account with a local bank and both belong to *arisan* groups. She belongs to the Muhammadiyah school *arisan* at the school where she teaches and also to the cloth traders' *arisan* in the Kutowinangun market. Unlike many other traders, she uses these savings to buy expensive consumer durables rather than new stock. She belongs to the Civil Servants' Wives Association (Pertiwi) and Family Welfare Education (Pendidikan Kesehatan Keluarga) as do most wives of civil servants, but she is not an active member because she is usually in the *pasar* when meetings are held.

As with many traders, Bu Menik and her elder sisters acquired their initial understanding of the *pasar* by assisting their mother during school breaks. After finishing her university education, she applied for a job in a bank but was not accepted. Disheartened and embarrassed by her failure, she did not seek other 'suitable' jobs but instead took an increasingly active role in the business of her ageing mother. This was despite an initial disinclination for trading which, she claimed, required too much patience. When her mother retired to a life of prayer, Bu Menik took over her stock and finance, as well as her network of suppliers and customers.

Bu Menik inherited eleven *kodi* (i.e. 220 pieces of cloth) from her mother, valued at about Rp 300 000, and in the intervening years her stock has increased by only two *kodi*. She has, however, increased the variety, adding different kinds of *batik*, and a small range of table cloths, blankets and babywear. The factors which limit her stock include space, storage and finance. Each *bakul* is allocated a stall (*plong*)[6] or a section and while most have sufficient space to increase their stock two-fold, to do so would inhibit ease of movement and, probably more importantly, their ability to display the goods to advantage. The *kodi* are stored at night in the market place and Bu Menik pays a porter Rp 200 a day to pack, store and transport her goods to the day's market. There is a constant risk of theft and every morning while setting up her display she carefully checks each *kodi*. Larger stocks would make this a more difficult and time-consuming task.

The most important factor limiting her stocks, however, is the difficulty of accumulating finance from trading. Even for members of the market elite such as Bu Menik, trade income is mainly used for daily necessities. While she recognizes that larger stocks might theoretically increase the volume of her business and make it possible for even normal margins to allow financial accumulation, she also recognizes the fiercely competitive nature of the market. The relatively small amount of finance required to begin trading means that as markets expand so do the numbers of traders. Bu

Menik claims that the number of traders has increased substantially over the past decade, in part reflecting a natural increase in population.[7] More importantly, her turnover is now lower, so that she replenishes her stock less frequently and has to obtain higher returns on each item to maintain her income. In her view the difficulties in accumulating finance and the large numbers of traders make seeking high returns on a limited turnover a more rewarding strategy than accepting lower returns on a higher turnover.

LANGGANAN TETEP

For Bu Menik, as with most successful cloth traders, the major source of stock is her *langganan tetep*. A literal translation of *langganan tetep* is 'regular customer', but among cloth traders the term refers to a debt relationship of a particular kind. Such a debt is called *utang pandemen*, a 'fixed debt'. The phrase *langganan tetep* may be used to refer to both creditor and debtor in such a relationship, so that Bu Menik refers to her Chinese supplier in Magelang as her *langganan tetep*, and he reciprocates.[8] Stripped to its essentials the relationship connotes a set line of credit. The creditor advances goods up to a fixed limit and the debt must be repaid in full at Lebaran. In most cases the credit line will then be extended for the next year. Stock replacement within the year is on a cash basis, so that the total debt does not exceed the fixed limit, but short-term credit outside this limit may occasionally be granted.

Bu Menik's *langganan tetep* relationship with a Chinese[9] merchant in the Magelang market was established eight years ago, and she now acquires 75% of her stock from this source. She initiated this relationship with the aid of her elder sister, who is also a cloth trader. The sister, who had been *langganan tetep* with this trader for about five years, introduced the two and Bu Menik began travelling to Magelang every Saturday. Initially she bought about three *kodi* of *jarik* and *slendang* each time. A year later, after she had demonstrated that she was a reliable customer, she was permitted credit up to Rp 100 000. Bu Menik had no wish to extend credit beyond this level, both because of the factors limiting her stock discussed above, and also because it would be too difficult to repay the loan in an emergency. She now visits Magelang only once a fortnight, even once a month, according to

demand, carrying between Rp 30 000 and Rp 60 000 in cash to pay
for the goods. If she cannot meet the *nota* (bill), she can carry the
debt, or part of it, over to her next visit, but usually she pays in full
because if payments are up to date, she is given a small discount on
her subsequent purchases. Occasionally, rather than make separate trips, she and her sister will purchase goods on the other's
behalf.

In addition to this major *langganan tetep*, Bu Menik is the
creditor in a series of *langganan tetep* relationships. Although the
debts (*utang pandemen*) are smaller, sometimes miniscule, the
principles of the relationships are essentially the same. Two such
langganan tetep (who buy goods from her in the Kebumen market)
were taken over from another of her sisters who moved to Jakarta.
These involve debts of Rp 50 000 and Rp 15 000, with weekly
purchases of Rp 15 000 and Rp 5000 respectively. She herself initiated seven *langganan tetep* relationships in the Ambal market,
where she operates solely as a wholesaler and does not rent a stall.
This market is some seven kilometres from the main highway and
is therefore less accessible to larger wholesaler *bakul* who usually
visit several markets in one day. Bu Menik took advantage of this
and actively sought potential customers among the Ambal *bakul*.
Most of the relationships began on the *ngalap-nyaur* system (see
below pp. 121–3), which entails little risk because goods are distributed early in the day and partial or full payment is received a few
hours later. But she wanted to trade in the larger Kebumen market
on Sundays, and this was not feasible if she had to wait until the
bakul had sufficient sales to finance their purchases. As she came
to trust her Ambal debtors, she changed their status to *langganan
tetep* with *utang pandemen* ranging from Rp 2000 to Rp 25 000.

When the credit and debt relationships centred on Bu Menik are
considered as a whole, it is clear that most of the Rp 100 000 credit
extended by the Magelang merchant has been further redistrib-
uted to small traders in the Ambal and Kebumen markets. The
weekly payments made by these traders in turn pay for her weekly
purchases from her Magelang supplier. In periods of normal trade
such a system is efficient, and it is easy for her to tailor her
purchases to current market conditions. As each stage in the
overall system is founded by personal dyadic ties, the risks of
default are lessened. Apart from the judgement of human character required to establish *langganan tetep* relationships, Bu Menik's
financial talent is most in evidence at the end of Lebaran when all

debts should be paid in full. It requires considerable personal skill (and probably access to additional finance) for her to pay off her major creditor and collect her own debts. For the first three years Bu Menik repaid the debt in full, but on the fourth occasion her supplier suggested she carry over the debt to the next year. This has continued in subsequent years when her evident ability to repay the debt has relieved her of the necessity of actually doing so. Bu Menik, however, has not extended this favour to her debtors. She claims the debt repayments each year, presenting the *bakul* with small gifts upon repayment.

INTEREST AND RENEGING

A feature of the *langganan tetep* relationship is that, despite long-term credit and considerable amounts of capital involved, there are no overt interest charges. In fact, stocks can often be replenished at a discount rate if payment is made in full for the week's purchase. It is more difficult to determine if there are hidden interest charges on the *utang pandemen*. Certainly neither partner to the deal acknowledges interest charges and the goods acquired on credit at the start of the cycle retain the same value at the time of payment. While it is impossible to be certain that an inflated rate has not been charged for the original goods, I doubt that this is the case, for both parties are aware of current values. More to the point, it is doubtful that charging interest, either overtly or covertly, would be of long-term value to the supplier. Traders, citing the Islamic prohibition against interest, would not accept such charges and, as there are more wholesalers willing to extend credit than established traders willing to accept it, would seek other suppliers.

One of the most important considerations in the extension of credit through *langganan tetep* is the extent of market experience. While a potential debtor is unlikely to desire such a relationship without some experience of the market place, relative newcomers often underestimate the skills required for long-term survival. Experienced traders with permanent stalls, however, probably have far more potential creditors than they require. Fine judgement, and the sense of economic opportunity which Bu Menik displayed in the Ambal case, is needed to choose debtors who will be able to pay. Traders are also very cautious: debtors must demonstrate that they are reliable for a considerable period before entering more complex relationships.

Langganan tetep are advantageous to suppliers because they ensure a regular cash income and a reliable outlet for goods, but against this must be balanced the risks of default. Cloth traders who have debts with their *langganan tetep* above Rp 100 000 tend to be younger, better educated and carry larger amounts of stock. This is particularly true among the traders in factory-produced textiles or clothing, who carry stock worth a great deal more than most *batik* cloth traders. By contrast, *langganan tetep* relationships within the regional markets involve much smaller debts, and personal characteristics rather than strict economic criteria play a larger part in their establishment.

In other parts of the world debtor-creditor relationships are often also social relationships and in many cases are clothed in kinship idioms (Davis 1973:234). One function of such ties is to provide insurance against reneging on debts. The absence of such ties between *langganan tetep* raises the question of what serves this purpose in Java. A critical feature of *langganan tetep* in this regard is that the debt has a fixed term: the *utang pandemen* must be paid in full at Lebaran, which for Javanese Muslims is the most important religious festival of the year.[10] Lebaran ends the fasting month of Ramadan and typically at this time of year Javanese Muslims buy new clothing and festive food. This generates considerable activity in the *pasar* and successful *bakul* will turn over their entire stock. Payment of the debt is followed by provision of new cloth and this establishes a further extension of credit.

While sanctions against non-payment are limited, they effectively prevent *bakul* from operating in the market, or at least limit the range of their activities. For instance, if Bu Menik failed to pay her Rp 100 000 in full she would be unable to restock after the festive season and, while she might well continue to buy from her *langganan tetep*, there would be no discounts. But traders can and do renege on debts. Bu Menik has faced this problem twice, once for a debt of Rp 10 000 and another of Rp 5000. The *bakul*, who she no longer calls *langganan tetep*, had paid cash for goods over a couple of months, but then ran up debts and finally disappeared from the market place. Bu attempted to collect payment by writing to them,[11] but her letters went unanswered, and as further action would have involved considerable expense, she had to regard the money as lost. Although the delinquent *bakul* did not have to pay their debts, the news spread quickly and they effectively lost the possibility of trading in the market.

Probably the most important reason why *bakul* seldom renege on their debts, however, is that there is a constant stream of cash transactions within the overreaching credit relationships. A failure to maintain these transactions thus provides an early warning of danger. Bu Menik's creditor expects sales of at least Rp 30 000 each month, and a longer absence would involve close questioning about her business. She in turn expects her debtors to buy when she visits them each week. It is very important therefore that traders such as Bu Menik maintain a regular schedule. On one occasion she was unable to go to Kebumen market (where she supplies two *langganan tetep*) on a Sunday because anti-Chinese riots disrupted transport. Her *langganan tetep* were forced to find alternative sources of supply (possibly under less favourable terms) or to allow their stocks to diminish. As a result the *bakul* avoided Bu Menik on the two following Sundays, providing a rather unsubtle hint that she had failed in her obligations. Bu Menik, anxious to maintain the links, chartered a minibus to the home villages of the two *bakul* concerned and, after explaining the cause of her absence, re-established normal relations.

ITINERANT TRADERS AND NGALAP-NYAUR

Bu Menik buys 75% of her stock from her *langganan tetep* in Magelang. She obtains the remaining quarter from ten mobile traders. Three of the ten distributors of Baledono cloth from Purworejo supply Bu Menik. A further five traders sell her other locally produced *batik*: mainly Watubarut, Slendang Jawa and Tanuraksan. The other two mobile traders from whom Bu Menik buys regularly supply higher quality cloth: a woman from Kutowinangun sells her Yogyakarta *batik* and a Pekalongan trader provides a special variety of *slendang*.

Relationships between mobile *bakul* and market stallholders develop very slowly and have a more personal basis than *langganan tetep*. When they visit a market, mobile *bakul* stop to chat with a wide variety of cloth traders, although they generally sell to only a few. In part these conversations are a means of filling the time between supplying cloth and collecting payment, but they also provide information (not always accurate) on market conditions.

Bu Menik had a particular friendship with one mobile trader, a young woman from Baledono who had studied at the Foreign Language Academy in Yogyakarta before marriage. As the friendship developed, she became Bu Menik's major supplier of Baledono *batik*. When the friend separated from her husband and returned to Yogyakarta, Bu Menik began buying heavily from another woman who had been selling small quantities for a long period. In this case the important connection is that both women are adherents of the Muhammadiyah movement and have been responsible for organizing the cloth traders' *arisan*. They now have such a close relationship that the trader occasionally gives a bill (*bon*), allowing a month to pay, thus establishing something resembling the *langganan tetep* relationship, although on a monthly rather than an annual basis. The creditor's knowledge that both Bu Menik and her husband receive monthly salaries is probably also an important consideration. The two other Baledono suppliers sell only small, but nevertheless regular, amounts to Bu Menik. One is a middle-aged woman who previously sold to Bu Menik's mother, and the other is a young woman of recent acquaintance whose similar background and household status appear to have laid the basis for a close friendship. Although there are numerous Baledono suppliers in the market, most of them are kinsmen and the established traders appear willing to relinquish some business to aid their younger relatives.

Personal relationships often lead to trading links. A *bakul* who shares a stall with Bu Menik in the Kebumen market introduced her to a seller of Watubarut *batik* which, although amongst the most expensive *batik* sold in the market, is always in great demand. Bu Menik took the opportunity to vary her stock and the two women created something approaching a *langganan tetep* relationship with a long-standing debt of Rp 6000. The mobile trader lives in Kebumen, selling goods locally on commission, travelling to Kutowinangun to supply *bakul*. Recently the relationship has become less cordial. The supplier invariably asks higher prices than Bu Menik thinks are justified and often engages in rather acrimonious bargaining before accepting Bu Menik's offer. But although the weekly sales are for cash, the *bakul* does not press Bu Menik for repayment of the debt: clearly she hopes to maintain regular sales and regards the debt as helping her in this regard. The request for higher prices may be an attempt at a covert interest payment, but Bu Menik is well aware of prices paid by other *bakul*.

Commodities distributed by mobile traders are usually sold under *ngalap-nyaur*. Other terms for this arrangement include *mlebu-metu* ('to enter, to emerge') and *utang-piutang* ('to keep borrowing and lending').[12] In a strict sense *ngalap-nyaur* is the provision of very short-term credit: goods are distributed in the morning and paid for about noon. In periods of slow sales, all or some of the goods may be returned in lieu of payment. *Ngalap nyaur* differs from commission selling in that a price is agreed, and the *bakul* sells for whatever she can obtain. In practice, credit arrangements which traders describe as *ngalap-nyaur* usually involve a longer period of credit than three or four hours, but in the initial stages most repayments closely approximate the ideal. Once trust has been established, a greater flexibility in both terms and means of payment may be allowed. One day Bu Menik took five pieces of cloth from a regular supplier in the morning, but paid for only the three she had sold at noon. She paid for the other two before the end of the week, but occasionally she takes further cloth and the *bakul* carries a small debt for some weeks. As with *langganan tetep*, *bakul* attempt to repay all debts at Lebaran when the volume of sales ensures that they have sufficient cash in hand.

BU SAMILAH: A SMALL-SCALE CLOTH TRADER

For relatively large traders such as Bu Menik *ngalap-nyaur* is not a major source of supplies but provides the variety which creates an attractive stall to entice customers. Small traders unable to enter *langganan tetep*, however, rely on *ngalap-nyaur* to obtain their stock. Among these is Bu Samilah, an extremely energetic, long-established but relatively unsuccessful, cloth trader.

Bu Samilah is a wiry, shrewd, fifty-year-old who lives in a village two kilometres from the main highway. Before his recent death, her husband, a clothes presser, looked after the household while she, her twenty-two-year-old son and a twenty-year-old daughter worked in the market. Rather unusually, the two children co-operate with their mother in a single enterprise, pooling finance and income. In the last months of my fieldwork the son began working on his own and sometimes visited new markets. After the death of her father, the daughter cared for the household and for Bu Samilah's aunt who lives with the family, and occasionally arranged sales within the village. There are eleven children in the family: some have transmigrated to Sumatra and another two have moved to Jakarta, one to assist in the maintenance of a school and the other to work as a cloth trader. The youngest child, a girl, attends junior high school in Prembun and the family makes considerable sacrifices to pay for her fees, uniform, transport and books.

Bu Samilah has been a trader for forty years, thirty-five of them as a *bakul jarik*. The daughter of a hoe seller and cabbage trader, she started in *suruh* leaves. She began with almost no finance, and after three years of diligent scrimping and saving she built up her stock to three kilograms worth Rp 400. Realizing that her small stocks meant very low returns, after marriage Bu Samilah pooled resources with her elder brother to sell cloth. Three years later she had saved sufficient funds to work alone. In contrast to Bu Menik, she had to create both her financial and her credit relationships through her own efforts. She finished her education at the age of twelve and, although literate and numerate, her knowledge of Indonesian is limited.

Although Bu Samilah carries a wider range of goods than Bu Menik, she has fewer pieces of cloth, about 100 in all. She stocks *jarik*, *slendang*, ready-made *kebaya* (the long-sleeved blouse traditionally worn with a *jarik*) and linen. Her son stocks both *batik* and woven *sarong*, while her daughter sells underwear and infant's clothing.

Bu Samilah trades every day of the week in the *pasar* of Prembun, Kutowinangun, Kebumen and Krakal. On Wednesdays and Saturdays she gets up at 3.30 a.m. to hike the seven kilometres to a small market in the mountain village of Krakal. Bu generally has two meals in the market place, a rice meal soon after she arrives and a snack just before leaving. Returning home shortly after 1 p.m., she spends the afternoon caring for the citrus and other crops grown on their miniscule holding. The family lives in a small, unpretentious, but very well-cared for wooden house with a beautiful garden, the object of considerable pride to the family and the envy of other villagers.

Bu Samilah has no *langganan tetep*. In large part this is due to the poverty of her household and her lack of education. Her slight command of Indonesian prevents her initiating *langganan tetep* relationships with Chinese who speak only colloquial Javanese and would be unwilling to use it with relative strangers.[13] This and her own lack of finance inhibit giving credit to the even poorer traders in the markets where she works. Her inability to establish a set line of credit imposes severe limits on the scale of her business, and requires her to work much harder for lower returns. She cannot, for example, rent the larger or better-placed market stalls, nor can she afford to store her goods in the market place. Even if she was able to increase her stock, she would not do so because she could not carry such a large bundle.

Bu Samilah obtains two-thirds of her stock through a variety of *ngalap-nyaur* arrangements. Although she shares a number of suppliers with Bu Menik, most of her suppliers are women of more mature years. And, unlike Bu Menik who pays most of her *ngalap-nyaur* creditors fairly promptly, Bu Samilah's creditors usually have to prod her a little before receiving amounts due. She also belongs to the cloth traders' *arisan* and complains that her creditors come flocking for payment as soon as she collects.

The remaining third of her stock she buys through an institution known as *nicil*. Perhaps the best gloss of *nicil* is 'time payment'. Bu Samilah is given several pieces of cloth and promises to pay a proportion of the debt at regular intervals. While she is in the process of paying off one piece of cloth, she obtains others and therefore her total indebtedness tends to rise through the year until Lebaran, when it is expected it will be paid in full. Bu Samilah's main *nicil* supplier is an elderly man who used his Navy pension to finance his business as a wholesale *bakul* dealing in cloth from a Purworejo outlet. He travels the market circuit most days of the week, some days handing out goods and collecting installments, and on others collecting installments alone. His large account book in which he records transactions distinguishes him from other *bakul* who are content to make casual notes in a notebook.

Bu Samilah purchases goods from three *nicil* suppliers, and in the small mountain market of Krakal where there are only six *bakul jarik*, sells cloth to small traders in other commodities under *nicil*. *Nicil* transactions with other *bakul* are usually very discrete. Buyer and seller shake hands and in the process pass over the installment. There is rarely any attempt to delay the payment or lower the amount.

In *nicil* the level of the debt diminishes from day to day to day and some records must be kept. In her *nicil* transactions at Krakal, Bu Samilah takes note of the person's name or title and records the transaction in the following manner:

bakul ceting   3250/3000/2750/2500/2250/1750/
                   1500/1250/1000/750/500/250/125

This particular purchaser[14] bought a *sarong* worth Rp 3500, making an initial payment of Rp 250. Payment of Rp 125 completed the transaction within fifteen market days, a period of two months.

Occasionally Bu Samilah also sells *nicil* to farmers and other frequenters of the Krakal *pasar*, but only if she knows and trusts them. Payments in this case tend to be less regular and of fluctuating amounts, as she has to rely on catching them on their occasional excursions to market to sell produce. Customers come up to her stall, shake hands and whisper '*nicil setitik*', paying over the amount and watching it noted down in the book. There is considerable risk of default in *nicil* transactions with non-*bakul*. For instance, one woman who had been to Mecca—it was for this reason that Bu extended credit—acquired goods worth Rp 5000, paid an installment of Rp 2000, and made no further payment for five months. Bu Samilah hopes that the remainder will be paid, although she has not seen her since. She claims that there are no interest charges for buying by this method, which is possibly true because the *nicil* arrangements are not overtly mentioned until the price is agreed upon. But the same method of payment is used by *tukang kredit ngider* (see Chapter 3), whom all traders acknowledge charge very high interest rates.

Bu Samilah feels that she is engaged in a constant struggle to maintain a reasonable livelihood and she uses some unorthodox, perhaps slightly devious, methods to gain an edge over other *bakul*. She is always in the market at least an hour before most other *bakul jarik*, hoping to capitalize on any early passing trade, while her willingness to enter *nicil* transactions with other traders, and especially with farmers and other customers, is also rather unusual. But her greatest trading skills emerge in other areas.

In addition to new cloth and clothing, Bu Samilah sells second-hand apparel, an activity which is conducted in an even more circumspect manner than the *nicil* payments. In the regency and district markets there are large numbers of *bakul* circulating through the market buying and selling second-hand cloth and clothing, some almost new and some very tatty. Bu buys regularly from three of these women, purchasing only cloth which, after her husband has pressed and perhaps mended it, might pass for new. They are offered for sale along with her other *jarik* and *kebaya* and, while she never points out that they are second-hand, most customers are probably shrewd enough to recognize this is the case.

Similar strategies characterize her debt and credit relationships, for Bu Samilah needs considerable skills as a haggler in order to survive in a highly competitive field. Her relationships with suppliers are more complex and perhaps less cordial than Bu Menik's. On Wednesdays, Bu trades in Krakal for a few hours before continuing on to Kebumen where she replenishes stock, but does not have a stall and does not sell retail. One day when I accompanied her to Krakal and Kebumen, Bu first approached a *bakul* who deals in linen. She selected seven pillowcases, bargained long but not very strenuously, and made a large proportion of the payment in cash. The *bakul* demanded full payment, but Bu just walked off, saying that she could not afford more at present. Bu Samilah then went to another section of the market and approached a wholesale *bakul* occupying a large and prestigious corner stall. Almost immediately, six mobile *bakul* surrounded her, all offering Watubarut, the same product as the stallholder. Bu ignored these women, although they continued to cajole her throughout the proceedings. For the next twenty minutes, Bu Samilah bargained with the stallholder for six *slendang* in the Watubarut style. The transfers of cloth were bewildering, not least because the mobile *bakul* continually thrust forward pieces of cloth and Bu occasionally feigned interest in these to persuade the wholesale *bakul* to lower her price. Eventually a price was agreed and Bu Samilah paid her money. It was Rp 200 short and the *bakul* complained bitterly. Unwillingly, Bu Samilah produced another Rp 200, handing it over Rp 50 at a time. Bu Samilah's next task was to buy Watubarut *jarik*, and she opened bargaining sessions with three traders before purchasing four for Rp 13 000 on credit from a fourth. The bargaining was much friendlier in this case, but took just about as long. After buying a head scarf from yet another *bakul* without bargaining, and paying cash, she then bought some Slendang Jawa from a *bakul* in a neighbouring booth. This was a credit transaction and no price was mentioned. Bu sorted out the four she wanted and told the stallholder how many she had taken while holding them up for display. Later the same week two of the *bakul* who had not been paid approached her in the Kutowinangun market. One was given a partial payment, and the other was reluctantly paid in full.

CREDIT IN THE CLOTH TRADE

The bewildering variety of credit arrangements in the cloth trade are variations on three institutions: *langganan tetep*, characterized by its relatively large and fixed period of debt; the limited short-term credit of *ngalap-nyaur*; and *nicil* or 'time payment'. All are slowly established over a considerable period, and successful *bakul* require not only the bargaining and market skills which produce reasonable returns, but also the personal skills to establish and maintain cordial social relationships, particularly in the cases of *ngalap-nyaur* and *nicil*. From the trader's point of view the critical difference between the three credit institutions is the constraints they impose on the scale of their businesses: *langganan tetep* are essential if traders are to maintain a reasonable turnover, and traders unable to establish such relationships must work far harder, and far longer, for a lower income.

The majority of cloth traders in the district market circuit purchase their stock from mobile *bakul* or from wholesale traders with stalls in the larger markets, under *ngalap-nyaur*. The small elite, less than a fifth of the traders, combine *ngalap-nyaur* with their *langganan tetep* in the larger centres of Magelang, Solo and Yogyakarta, or less commonly with one of the biggest stallholders in Kebumen. A small minority, perhaps 5% of the poorest cloth traders, buy their supplies on the *nicil* system.

Ngalap-nyaur and *langganan tetep* have several features in common. Each is based on dyadic personal ties between a particular trader and a particular supplier. Each involve credit extended for a fixed period, and although supposedly the period is one year for *langganan tetep* and only a few hours for *ngalap-nyaur*, well established *ngalap-nyaur* debts may be carried for as long as a year. In both cases, however, the debt must be repaid in full at Lebaran. And finally, in both cases the level of sales between the two parties is far higher than the credit line might suggest, because there is a constant flow of cash transactions.

The most important difference between the two is the scale. *Langganan tetep* are not worthwhile to the suppliers at levels below a debt of Rp 100 000, which implies annual sales of about Rp 360 000. The upper level of such debts, at least among the traders in the *kecamatan* markets, is about Rp 500 000 and a turnover of Rp 1 500 000. *Langganan tetep* where both participants are *bakul* seldom exceed a debt of Rp 20 000. The debt limits of

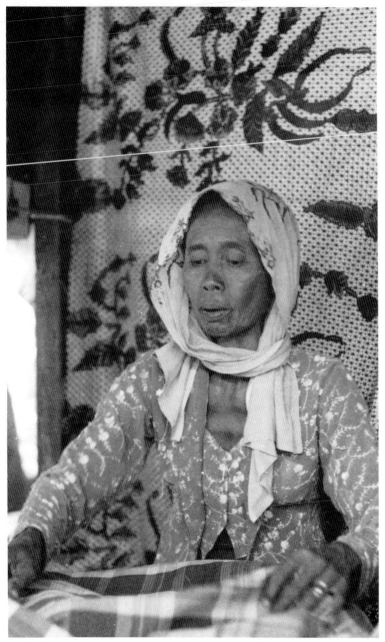

1. Bu Samilah, the most tenacious of cloth traders, displaying a woven tetron *sarong*.

2. Bu Bariyah with a selection of copper *dandang*: vessels used with a woven bamboo cone to steam rice.

3. Bu Menik bargaining with a customer for a printed *batik slendang*.

4. Bu Tutor, displaying a range of the oil lamps she has made from recycled bottles, tins and light bulbs.

5. Vegetable section of Pasar Wetan. All the vegetables on display are grown locally. Most leafy vegetables are sold in bundles.

6. Two fruit sellers in Pasar Wetan. The first is preparing citrus fruit for display and the second squatting nearby for a chat.

7. While a man sings the praises of his Javanese medicine over the microphone, his female partner prepares a mixture in a plastic bag for a customer.

8. The oldest of the copperware traders in Prembun market.

9. Two tobacco vendors in a village market. By repute tobacco traders are always attractive, and unusually for Javanese women enjoy a handrolled cigarette.

10. A vendor of expensive imported vegetables—cabbages, french beans and potatoes—mostly grown in the colder regions of Wonosobo and West Java.

11. The stock of a condiment seller (*bakul bumbon*), one of four mainly whole-sale vendors in Pasar Wetan, which includes chillies, onions and garlic. Note the preparation applied to her forehead to relieve pain, and the scales which are nowadays widely used in selling foodstuffs.

12. An itinerant tobacco seller (woman second from left) surrounded by women buying chewing tobacco in 50 gram lots. A solitary male looks on.

ngalap-nyaur are very much smaller, and at most a trader might acquire five pieces of cloth worth about Rp 10 000. She can, of course, enter several relationships simultaneously with different traders, but if they become aware that her total debt is approaching Rp 30 000 they will press for immediate payment in full.

The differences in scale have important implications for both the selling strategies of the *bakul*, and the quality of the links between supplier and trader. Although individual *bakul* specialize in particular types of cloth—Bu Menik carries a wide range of cheap *slendang* while Bu Samilah sells Watubarut *jarik*—it is important to carry as wide a variety of goods as possible, both to attract customers to the stall and also because comparing the quality and prices of goods is a major bargaining technique (see Chapter 7). *Bakul* such as Bu Menik use their *langganan tetep* to supply the bulk of their major sale items, and rely on *ngalap-nyaur* to generate variety. This enables them to experiment with new designs, for in the last resort unsold cloth can be returned. Smaller *bakul* relying on *ngalap-nyaur* for their major supplies have less ability to provide a wide range. Moreover, larger traders can seek a discount for bulk purchases when bargaining with their suppliers, and thus make higher profits in sales at the same price as small traders.

These differences in the supply structure affect relationships with other *bakul* in the *pasar*. Bu Menik, for example, often directs customers seeking Pekalongan *jarik*, which she does not sell, to a nearby stallholder, who in turn reciprocates. Bu Samilah, however, faced with a customer who is not satisfied with the cloth she is selling, will borrow a selection from another small trader, who indicates the price she wants. Often a sale is finalized, but generally it is Bu Samilah's cloth which changes hands because she has eventually persuaded the customer that hers is of superior quality.

The degree of bargaining and haggling over prices and payments also differs considerably between the two types of credit arrangements. There is little bargaining over prices between *langganan tetep*, for both parties are more interested in maintaining a regular flow of goods than in making a slightly higher profit on a particular item. Nor do *bakul* haggle over payments, for to do so would damage their credit reputation. The relationship between the two parties is economically particularistic, with neither an attempt nor a desire to initiate any social ties. With *ngalap-nyaur* the considerations are reversed. While it is true that bargaining between *bakul* is less extensive than in retail transactions, this owes more to the fact that both parties have equally accurate market information than to any concessions on price (see pp. 189–90). As the trader is often short of cash, particularly in the slow season, haggling over payments is very common. While some *bakul* regularly pay without argument or pleading, others make every effort to delay payment, and even regular payers often attempt a partial payment.

Finally, whereas with *langganan tetep* the economic context of the transaction provides the major sanction against reneging, *ngalap-nyaur* credit depends upon personal trust. The supplier therefore seeks every possibility to extend social ties, offering and reciprocating invitations to weddings and funerals, and visiting traders when they are ill. Small sums of money or other gifts are always part of these occasions and cement the relationships further. According to normal anthropological usage, the *langganan tetep* is not a patron–client relationship for it involves no social ties other than the market relationship and no social contacts outside the market. Despite the more personal links inherent in *ngalap-nyaur*, it also cannot be regarded as a patron–client relationship. It, too, is a largely economic relationship designed to strengthen and maintain trading networks, and any social links are always subsidiary to this goal.

As the *langganan tetep* provides obvious advantages for the *bakul*, the question arises as to why more traders do not acquire credit in this manner. The answer requires some understanding of *bakul*'s careers. Most traders begin work in a similar manner to Bu Samilah's children: participating as unpaid helpers in the business of an established trader and being repaid with small but regular gifts. It is here that they learn the basic skills such as the value of various types of cloth, bargaining techniques, and the source of credit and suppliers. Such 'apprenticeships' do not always involve close relatives. One middle-aged trader who now works full-time in the Prembun market worked with Bu Samilah for a number of years. Eventually she began buying goods *ngalap-nyaur* from suppliers introduced by Bu Samilah and acquired her own stand and about Rp 30 000 worth of cloth. She in turn taught her own daughter who, with a gift from her father-in-law, branched out into the sale of ready-made clothing.

Young *bakul* soon learn that the key to increasing incomes is to acquire a regular source of supply and credit. Not only does it make a larger stock possible, but also it alleviates the need for long bargaining sessions to acquire stock at a reasonable price. But, as was emphasized above, suppliers will not enter *langganan tetep* relationships unless they are certain both that the trader is skilful and trustworthy, and that she can maintain a reasonable turnover. Making the critical transition from *ngalap-nyaur* to *langganan tetep*, therefore, requires not merely trading ability but also access to enough finance to lift turnover to the base level. This initial finance is acquired from three sources: inheritance, savings or loans. The most common inheritance pattern is the one illustrated by Bu Menik, a daughter gradually taking over her mother's stock and credit relationships as the elder woman retires. Savings are mainly important in the case of what might be called 'middle class' traders: women married to civil servants who can use their husband's salaries and their own dowries to provide the capital for trading ventures. But the usual way to acquire capital is by borrowing: mortgaging household land, obtaining a loan from relatives, or pawning jewellery.

Few traders are as shrewd as Bu Samilah, but without capital she cannot increase her turnover and income. *Langganan tetep* relationships have become more common in recent years and it is noticeable that the women using such methods are younger than the average. Older women, such as Bu Samilah, have usually been traders for more than thirty years and have lived through very turbulent years of Indonesian history. Experience of the struggle for Independence, the inflation of the 1960s and killings of 1965 have had a critical influence on their lives, and it is not surprising that these women often stress the instability of prices and the inadvisability of long-term credit. No doubt this is an additional factor mitigating against *langganan tetep* relationships, but even if they attempted to establish them they would be unable to do so. Limited to small-scale trading, they must work far longer and far harder than the elite *bakul* for lower incomes.

The division between large traders using *langganan tetep* and the mass of traders whose stock is acquired through *ngalap-nyaur* is not a matter of individual differences in financial skills. It is a class relationship. Although an established trader using *langganan tetep* has very little of her own finance tied up in her enterprise, she must have access to considerable wealth to initiate credit relationships.

1. The highest quality cambric (*mori primissima*) is seldom found in the *pasar*.

2. Tanuraksan and Watubarut along with Karanganyar and Kutoarjo have long been prominent centres of local *batik* production (*Mindere Welvaart* VIa:35). *Batik* concerns in south Central Java in the 1920s were located along the railway line at Gombong, Karanganyar, Kebumen, Kutoarjo and Purworejo (Angelino 1930 Pt. II) and the goods they produced were imitated by *batik* concerns in Banjanegara (Does 1893:14).

3. Kertanegara (1958) has compiled a detailed report on the production and distribution of *batik* in Central Java. For histories and general descriptions of the *batik*-making process see Marzuki (1966), Rouffaer and Juynboll (1900), Veldhuizen-Djajasoebrata (1972), and Wieringa (1979).

4. The producer-sellers and mobile traders travelling from market to market are known as *bakul ngider* and the small-scale, usually part-time distributors as *bakul keliling*.

5. 'According to Islamic religious law, a mother is unclean and subject to a series of taboos for a period of forty days after childbirth' (Koentjaraningrat 1967:253).
'Mothers breastfeeding young children may be in the marketplace from early morning to early afternoon with someone bringing the baby to them for a mid-morning feed. In other cases breast-feeding may occur only twice a day, with supplementary feeds being given at other times' (White 1976b:342; see also Rens 1980).

6. Every shed (*los*) is divided into sections called *plong*, each of which is occupied by one or more usually independent *bakul*.

7. Although no one provides figures to support it, Chandler (1979), Peluso (1981), Stoler (1977) and White (1976b) all make the same point on the basis of statements by informants. Peluso (1981:79) attributes the rise to 'the standardization of measuring systems and the increase in general knowledge of village marketing and production procedures'. Stoler (1975:58–9), White (1976a) and Collier (1978) point out that the reduction of job opportunities in agriculture (including rice pounding) has led to an increase in the number of market traders.

8. The term *langganan* is also used in other Indonesian cultures. In Ujung Pandang trishaw drivers who have regular links with one person, refer to him as their *langganan* and he reciprocates. Forbes (1978:221) glosses *langganan* as 'lit. regular club member'. Cf. Forbes (1979). Siegel (1969:209), writing of Aceh, uses *langganan* in the sense of regular customer.

9. *Peranakan*, such as Bu Menik's supplier, are Chinese whose ancestors have been in Java for several generations and are to some degree integrated into Javanese culture. In contrast, the *Totok* or *Singkeh* remain largely Chinese in orientation.

10. In the month before Lebaran smaller-scale traders frequently enter into similar arrangements on a short-term basis. Obtaining cloth on credit and paying at the end of the month, they pay an extra Rp 50–100 for each piece of cloth.

11. It is probably worth pointing out that communications are very limited in Java. Telephones are extremely rare, telegrams expensive for both sender and recipient, and mail in general very slow. Such circumstances make alternative arrangements difficult.

12. An arrangement described by Geertz (1963b:38) appears to be a variety of *ngalap-nyaur*. A debtor takes Rp 30 worth of cloth on credit and repays half the debt after the cloth is sold. The debtor then takes another Rp 30 worth of cloth paying half in cash, thus raising the debt to Rp 30 again. Cf. Dewey (1962a:106–7). See also Kertanegara (1958:355–6) and Adam (1916:1606) for descriptions of the *ngalap-nyaur* system. Chandler (1981; 1984) also provides details of the supply-credit nexus in the clothing trade of the Yogyakarta region.

13. Bu Menik conducts her transactions with her Chinese supplier in Indonesian, occasionally in the familiar *ngoko* version of Javanese.

14. This *bakul* produces and sells toothpicks (*ceting*) used to fasten packages wrapped in banana or teak leaves.

6

Buying Chillies:
Information and Price Setting

A general model of peasant marketing systems, much favoured by geographers but also found in anthropology and economics, emphasizes a hierarchy of markets through which commodities move horizontally in space and vertically in bulk.[1] At each step up the market hierarchy, commodities are sold in larger quantities and are drawn from a wider area, with the extent of bulking at each step being determined by the characteristics of transport and economies of scale. In a reverse fashion, commodities intended for local markets are progressively broken into smaller packages. This hierarchy of markets is seen as an adaptation to four distinctive features of the peasant economy: the small scale of production and of individual purchases; the inefficient and expensive transport; the large number of individual traders who have relatively little finance; and 'the functional relationship between the market as an economic institution and the general, small-scale kinship-based patterning of social and economic relationships in peasant societies' (Anderson 1980:756). This last point is particularly important, for whereas the initial three features are empirical generalizations which can be tested, at least in theory, the last is an unsubstantiated assumption used to account for those features of peasant markets which are not reducible to simple economics or geography.

Dewey (1962a: xviii) described the paradigm case of this type of marketing system in her account of the small East Java town of Modjokuto thirty years ago:

> Its markets, like all Javanese markets, are tied into a network consisting of all markets, large and small, in a wide area. Through this

network goods produced within the peasant economy move from the rural areas and towns to the cities, and imported goods and goods from the cities move out to the towns and farming villages. Almost everything bought and sold by the average rural or town Javanese comes through this chain of markets.

She also described a series of Javanese trading practices which she regarded as particularly well adapted to such a marketing system. Modjokuto traders dealt in very small quantities, which they resold for very small profits. Rather than buy a consignment alone, they broke it down into small amounts both to spread the risk and to allow other traders the chance of profits. Credit was both limited and very short-term, and trading partnerships seldom survived individual transactions, although they might reform on later occasions. While these practices, which she saw as embedded in Javanese social structure, were well suited to the *pasar*, she argued that they were ill adapted to larger-scale trade. This was the major reason why the upper levels of the system—wholesaling in the simple sense—were controlled by the Chinese. Using a slightly more sophisticated version of the argument, Geertz (1963b) concluded that the structure of the Javanese *pasar* inhibited economic growth.

At first sight the data from my study of vegetable marketing neatly fit the conventional model of peasant markets. The marketing of agricultural produce involves very large numbers of traders, many of whom enter the trade only at the heart of the season. There is a hierarchy of functions as produce is bulked in ever-increasing amounts and later, to a lesser extent, broken down into small packages. Reported profits are low and are relatively similar at each point in the trading networks, many transactions are based on short-term credit, haggling is very vigorous, there is little bookkeeping and formal contracts are unknown. Personal links, occasionally kinship links, are the basis of most economic relationships. Finally, and perhaps most significantly, each trader operates a separate enterprise and there is very little wage labour.

But despite being embedded in the trading practices of the *pasar*, and despite considerable growth in the 'formal' sector of the rural economy, *depot* dealing in agricultural produce are clearly expanding in both numbers and scale. I initially became interested in the chilli *depot* which is the focus of this account because it was run by three women, but there were eight similar-sized businesses in Prembun in 1980 and by 1985 the numbers had doubled.

It should be stressed that while this chapter is written as an account of a particular *depot*, this is used as a convenient form of exposition of information gathered from a wide variety of sources including interviews, studies of other *depot* and, most importantly, months of observation in *pasar*. There is a widespread misapprehension of the role of anthropological accounts—'mere case studies'—in the understanding of rural economies. The value of such studies does not lie in the extent to which their empirical conclusions can be generalized: every village, every enterprise is to some extent unique, and the data needed to construct an adequate sample is seldom available. The value of anthropological accounts lies in the possibility of using the processes uncovered through the analysis of a limited range of relatively reliable and well-integrated information, to interpret more comprehensive but less-integrated and less-reliable data (see Alexander 1981; Hill 1984).

BU NYAI'S CHILLI DEPOT

The chilli *depot* is located in the Pasar Bengkuwang, a specialized point for bulking and distributing agricultural produce on the western extremity of Prembun. It encompasses a large, open shed which is the locus of the *bengkuwang* (yam bean) trade; five *depot* which deal in other agricultural produce; five *warung* providing meals and snacks in addition to casual accommodation for itinerant traders; and a small grocery stall. Three of the five *depot* specialize in chillies and the other two in citrus, but all occasionally buy seasonal produce including fruit, soybeans and peanuts. The majority of traders are women, although a few of the larger traders are men. One chilli *depot* is operated by a husband and wife; the second (the biggest and most prosperous) on which my research was centred, is run by three women. The third, which is also relatively large, is owned by two brothers and opens only in peak periods.

Bu Nyai's enterprise grew from very weak foundations. She acquired her early trading experience buying coconuts, and after marrying opened a *warung* selling a range of general goods. About 1955, when two of her five children had been born, she entered the more lucrative chilli trade by establishing a bulking *depot* for chillies in her *warung*. She gradually built up business until she was buying two tonnes of chillies a day during peak periods. In

1977 the premises she rented were placed on the market and as Bu Nyai did not have sufficient finance to purchase them she joined forces with her niece, Bu Sugi, to construct a building in the newly opened Pasar Bengkuwang. At this time Bu Sugi had two young children (she now has six) and about a year's experience as an independent trader in agricultural produce. Her husband, a comparatively rich man who runs a *sate* and curry stall near the railway station, provided finance and the two women established a joint business. Within six months they were joined by Bu Badriyah, the eldest daughter of Bu Nyai, who is now the mother of five children. She had acquired her finance and trading experience during the period that her husband (a retired naval officer, now a farmer) was stationed in Jakarta. She used family connections to airfreight agricultural produce such as onions to Singapore and later to Irian Jaya when her husband was transferred there. Each woman contributed Rp 200 000 to finance their initial trading, and the scale of their present business suggests that this has grown to more than two million rupiah each.

Although the three women are equal partners, each has a different role in the functioning of the *depot*. Bu Nyai, as the most senior, receives and handles all correspondence. Bu Sugi, very outgoing and attractive, is most active in buying produce, while Bu Badriyah spends long hours at the *depot* supervising sales and deliveries. The three also make the geographical distribution of their residences an economic asset. Bu Sugi lives in a hamlet in south Prembun, Bu Nyai in a village two kilometres north of the town, and Bu Badriyah's village is four kilometres to the east. This dispersal gives them a useful range of local contacts, several bases for small-scale accumulation of produce, and facilitates buying on short-term credit.

The *depot* provides work for numerous porters (*kuli*) and ancillary workers, who, like traders, switch spheres of activity with the agricultural cycle. The *depot* regularly employs four porters and has long-standing relationships with three; two have lived in Bu Nyai's house since they were young men and the other is a close neighbour of Bu Sugi. The porters pack and carry produce, as well as negotiate with conductors of buses, minibuses and trucks on behalf of traders. More or less fixed fees are paid for services: Rp 100 for each sack of goods packed and carried (a sack of chillies weighs between thirty and fifty kilograms), and about Rp 125 for arranging transport. Porters are often also given perks such as a handful of chillies or a snack. The two porters who live in Bu Nyai's household transport goods by handcart from her village to the *depot* and run errands of various kinds, in return for free board and lodging. A number of elderly women and young girls dry and sort chillies, and fetch tea and snacks. Those working a full day are paid Rp 350 and provided with one meal, with sometimes a few chillies for household consumption.

A final important aspect of the *depot*'s business is its credit arrangements with two of the five *warung* in the Pasar Bengku-wang. Snacks and meals are sent out and they maintain daily accounts. Javanese businesses seem to run on tea and snacks: the women eat very frequently, and traders, drivers and conductors, not to mention anthropologists, are constantly being invited to eat 'just a little'. A series of small gifts flow back and forth from *depot* to *warung*—a special snack, fruit, chillies etc.—as well as a great deal of information, much of it misleading.

All activity in the *depot* is regulated by the seasonal flow of produce. Peaks in supply keep the *depot* open eighteen hours a day, while troughs demand a mere two hours' work on periodic market days. Income fluctuates accordingly.

The three women describe themselves as an informal business association, which they liken to the Indonesian-Chinese enterprise called a *kongsi*. Both in their own eyes (although Javanese modesty does not allow them to assert it) and in those of other traders, the large scale of their business makes them *juragan* (merchants) rather than *bakul* (traders). The fact that three Javanese women have sustained a flourishing business for more than five years is regarded as unusual by other traders and stories of business alliances collapsing are commonplace. In fact, nineteenth century Dutch reports contrasted the lack of established business alliances among Javanese with the trading networks among Chinese and attributed this to aspects of Javanese society,[2] a point developed by Dewey (1962b). But, although this is the biggest agricultural *depot* run by women in Prembun, similar businesses are becoming more common each year.

At times operating independently, at times in concert, each partner keeps her own accounts, but all profits and losses are split three ways in accord with the Rp 200 000 they each initially in-vested. The business is unregistered, operates without the permits necessary for business firms (*perusahaan*) and shops (*toko*), and maintains a highly flexible organizational and accounting pro-gramme. Kinship links and the fact that each independently acquired trading experience and finance have played an important role in the maintenance of their partnership. While the *depot*'s corporate foundation is weakly developed and its connections with other traders and similar enterprises are not formalized with contracts or legal devices, this lack of corporateness is in a sense a strength. It permits a highly flexible business strategy which enables them to cope with fluctuating seasonal demands.

PATTERNS OF SUPPLY

The small-scale traders (*bakul*) who supply the *depot* buy produce throughout the wider Prembun area, a range of about eighteen kilometres. The clients who buy chillies from the *depot* carry them to large centres up to 100 kilometres away. Goods are also consigned to Cilacap, Semarang, Surabaya and Jakarta, and traders from these and other centres in Java buy chillies at the *depot*. At times the owners of the *depot* themselves buy chillies in Muntilan (about forty kilometres distant) and Secang (sixty-five kilometres away), consigning them to Tegal in north Central Java, and Jakarta.

The types of transport used for carrying the goods vary with both the quantity of produce and the ease of access. The ponycart (*dokar*) is perhaps the most common transport for small-scale *bakul* delivering to the *depot*, but they may also employ a carrier riding a bicycle with attached panniers (*tukang loper*). Larger traders often hire minibuses although, as most villages off the main road have no regular services, they have to charter one especially. Regular bus and minibus services run along the main east–west highway and traders can hail these to transport goods, paying the normal passenger fare plus a negotiated price for the produce. Large-scale traders use the trucks running along the main highway, many of which have one-way loads and rely on casual trade for a backload.

Lombok gede (*Capsicum annum L.*), the large plump chilli for which the Prembun district is well known throughout Java, produces two crops a year, one in the dry season and another in the wet. The latter crop is harvested from mid-February to May and the former, which is the larger, from August to December. The producing area lies between the highway and the south coast with the seasonal flow of produce beginning in the west and moving east. Crops in any particular village are harvested within a six-week period and it is the overlap between small ecological niches which extends the harvesting season to three or four months.

Chillies take about 120 days to mature, and a further period of ten to fifteen days is required for them to ripen and turn red, although the green crop is mature and can be harvested. Red chillies almost invariably fetch a higher price than green, but there are a number of reasons for the sale of the green chillies. Early in the season, the first flowering are slow to redden and should be collected to allow the rest to ripen. Chillies are also highly vulnerable to rain and will rot or fall off prematurely, while the desire to prepare the ground for another crop encourages the plucking of green chillies at the end of the season. It is difficult to determine yields as the crop is progressively harvested during the six-week period with five to ten individual pickings, but farmers claim that a 100 *ubin* (0.14 hectare) plot produces up to three quintal in a season. The dry season crop is grown on rain-fed *sawah* as well as dry land (*tegalan*), while the wet season crop is grown only on *tegalan*.

At the beginning of the wet season harvest in mid-February the *depot* purchases up to three quintal of green chillies a day, and by mid-March the quantity of red and green chillies are more or less balanced at about five or six quintal each. At the height of the season in late April, five tonnes of red chillies are purchased each day with a further three tonnes of green. The *depot* continues to buy chillies during May but the supply rapidly dwindles and the proportion of green to red rises steeply.

The dry season harvesting cycle follows a similar pattern, but the heavier production more than doubles many of the figures. The early pickings in August are mainly of green chillies, but by mid-September the *depot* buys about five tonnes of red and one and a half tonnes of green each day. During the seasonal peak in later September and early October, most days bring in at least five tonnes of red chillies, occasionally more than twelve tonnes. By early November the proportions change to three tonnes of green to five quintal of red, and this remains fairly constant to the end of the season.

Buying strategies within these general parameters of the business year are extremely flexible. In 1979, for example, when a large part of the Prembun wet season chilli crop was destroyed by floods, Bu Nyai remained at the *depot* to collect what produce was available, Bu Badriyah traded independently in coconuts, and Bu Sugi bought soybeans and peanuts for a more extended period than usual. For five years the three collected and bulked chillies from the Secang/Muntilan region, but in 1982 abandoned this activity when increasing profits from their dry season chilli buying made them less inclined to face the extensive travelling.

DISTRIBUTION AND PRICES

The broad parameters of the distribution of chillies to and from the *depot* is set out in Figure 6.1, which is generalized from both wet and dry season operations. Chillies grown in the Prembun region are resold as fresh chillies in Magelang, Wonosobo, Klaten, Yogyakarta and Solo as well as Jakarta and Bandung. Chillies collected from Secang/Muntilan are sent to Jakarta and Tegal. During the dry season harvest, the local market for fresh red and green chillies is flooded and retail prices fall considerably. Large quantities of red chillies are then sun-dried and at the height of the dry season in October there are often more than thirty tonnes of chillies spread out to dry behind the *depot*. During the wet season, when chillies cannot be sun-dried, surpluses are often artificially dried in Chinese processing plants in Kutoarjo, a large town thirteen kilometres away. Many of the dried chillies are purchased by Chinese wholesalers and are consigned to Semarang and Surabaya, with Singapore as a final destination. Others are sent to Jakarta where factories process the dried chillies into powder, generally also for export.

Some indication of the prices at various points in the distribution network is given in Table 6.1. The figures are only indicative of the level of profit at each point and are taken from a single day's trading during the wet and dry season respectively. But the ratios between various points are congruent with my more extensive data.

Although the consequences of this market structure for price setting are discussed in more detail below, some general remarks are appropriate at this point. While modal profits made by the traders (*bakul* and *juragan*) who buy directly from the producer are not high, especially when transport costs are taken into account, windfall profits at times when prices are changing drive average profits well above the figures in the table. The highest profits are made by the *depot* and this reflects two factors: their better access to price information and their ability to resell in a wide range of markets. Sellers at points in the distribution network

142

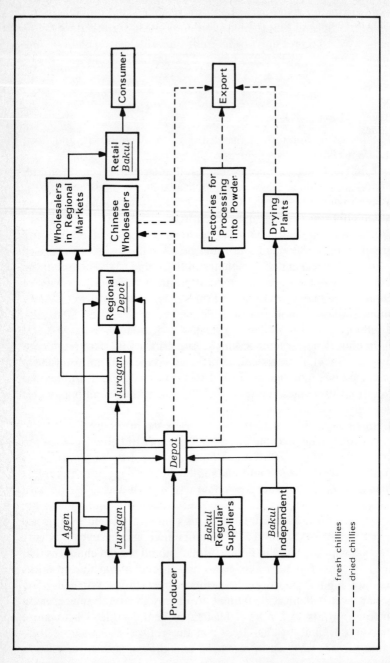

Fig. 6.1. Channelling of Chilli Production through Depot

TABLE 6.1

SELLING PRICES OF RED CHILLIES AT SELECTED POINTS IN DISTRIBUTION
NETWORK

	Wet Season Rp	Dry Season Rp
Producer	200	525
Bakul	275	600
Juragan	275	600
Depot	400	800
Regional Depot	425	850

after the *depot* make relatively small profits on each kilogram and are mainly concerned with maintaining a high turnover. Profits for buyers at points in the network prior to the *depot* are more dependent on their ability to buy cheaply.

Prices for red and green chillies fluctuate markedly throughout the harvest seasons. Some indication of price fluctuations can be gained from the open-ended graphs in Figures 6.2 and 6.3 which show the 1980 base prices paid by the *depot* to their regular suppliers from 24 March to 24 April (the wet season crop) and 7 October to 20 December (dry season crop). The most significant feature is that while prices increase as the season approaches its peak, the price increases are irregular and prices may double in a week. This makes it very difficult to predict prices even one or two days in advance and, as is discussed below, this information edge is a critical determinant of the level of the *depot*'s profits.

During the wet season the average price differential between red and green chillies was 90% with a range of 7% to 169%. But over the dry season (for which I have fuller figures for a longer period) the average price differential was 246% with a range of 6% to 838%. The average price differences, Rp 126 per kilogram for the first period and Rp 346 for the second, are very significant to the small farmer who produces less than 100 kilograms a year. A very important consequence of the strong demand for red chillies is that there is a direct relationship between the level of supply and price: as the season nears its peak the price rises rather than falls. The reason is that the larger supply entices buyers from elsewhere and makes it possible for local traders to send truckloads to more distant markets.

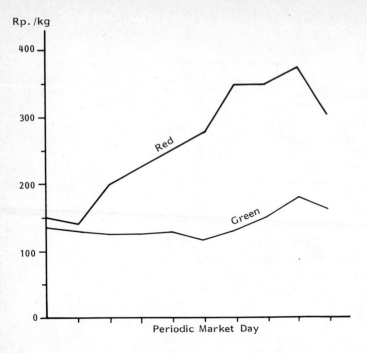

Fig. 6.2.   Base Price of Red and Green Chillies, Wet Season Crop

SUPPLIER BAKUL

The *depot* purchases most of its produce from *bakul* who have bought chillies in their home villages. In the wet season the *depot* has six regular suppliers (five women and one man), but buys from as many as thirty other *bakul*. Two of the regular suppliers are relatives of the three women, links which helped establish the trading ties in the first place. Mbak Ngamini, for example, is a younger daughter of Bu Nyai and lives in one of the major chilli-growing centres. She has sufficient finance to purchase up to three quintal of chillies before reselling and generally buys on the roadside close to the harvest areas, weighing the goods on the spot. Occasionally she purchases chillies directly in the field[3] and during the bi-weekly market in her village sets up her scale near the market place to buy from incoming farmers.

Traders such as Mbak Ngamini normally buy in small lots of less

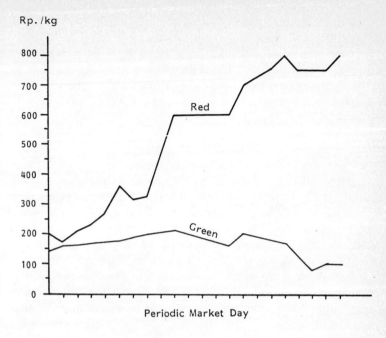

Fig. 6.3. Base Price of Red and Green Chillies, Dry Season Crop

than twenty kilograms. The farmer and *bakul* haggle over prices, with the *bakul* attempting to buy as cheaply as possible. Her knowledge of the previous day's prices gives her an important advantage over the farmer because even though prices may be known to be rising, the extent of the rise is irregular. Mbak Ngamini, like most other *bakul* of this scale, pays cash for purchases because farmer and *bakul* seldom have sufficient knowledge of each other's financial situation to permit credit. At the *depot* all the *bakul* are normally paid in cash, although they may have to wait a few hours. Occasionally, when far more chillies have been purchased than can be resold that day, a *bakul* who is a regular supplier will be given a partial payment and the remainder paid the following day. Daily prices are set by the *depot* and there is very little or no bargaining with these *bakul*.

While the *bakul* who are the *depot*'s regular wet season suppliers make a good living during the season, it must be remembered that for long periods they are either unemployed or deal in less profitable commodities such as coconuts. *Bakul* such as Mbak

Ngamini make an average profit of Rp 2000 on each 200 kilograms delivered to the *depot* but sometimes make as much as Rp 4000. While losses are rare, a flood might prevent them delivering a load of green to the *depot*; such losses may wipe out their trading funds. Early in the season *bakul* may take three days to accumulate a load, but at the peak they deliver five or six days a week.

AGEN AND JURAGAN

The nature of the *depot*'s collection activities alters dramatically during the dry season. Four of their six wet season suppliers now bypass the *depot* and transport chillies directly to larger centres. The reason is that it is now possible for one, occasionally two, *bakul* to accumulate at least a minibus load each day, and they can obtain funds from *depot* in other regions to finance the purchase. The *bakul* have no need for the bulking function of the *depot* and achieve slightly greater profits by selling directly to wholesalers in *pasar* within 100 kilometres. As many as thirty additional *bakul* enter the chilli trade at this time and some become regular suppliers to the *depot*. One woman, for example, trades chillies only during the dry season harvest, but each of her loads of about two quintal is sold to the *depot*.

The important change, however, is that relatively large-scale agents (*agen*) and independent merchants (*juragan*) begin supplying the *depot* with chillies. Some *juragan* are farmers with finance reserved for this purpose, but the majority are full-time traders who in other seasons deal in products as diverse as duck eggs, long beans, coconut sugar and oranges. The defining characteristic of an *agen* is that his trading funds are provided by someone else. Most *agen* are men and are restricted in that they must resell the produce to the providers of their finance, although they appear to receive the same prices as any other trader. They are not paid wages or commission and depend for their livelihood on their ability to buy cheaply from the producers.

During the dry season the *depot* has ten *agen*. Four of the ten are supplied with trading funds by the *depot*, but the other six obtain finance indirectly through *juragan* connected with the *depot*. Most *agen* work in fairly circumscribed areas close to their homes, buying up chillies in the field or having them delivered to their homes by farmers. The *agen* pays cash and arranges deliveries to the *depot*. There is, as one might expect, great diversity in the type and intensity of the relationships between the *agen* and *depot*. For example, a young man, an *agen* of five years' standing, lives in a major chilli-producing village five kilometres south of Prembun, but also buys chillies on behalf of the *depot* thirteen kilometres away in Kutoarjo. He usually pays farmers in cash from a fund of Rp 50 000 supplied by the *depot*, but occasionally acts as a mere go-between, delivering the chillies and returning a bill of exchange to the producer. Other *agen*, however, are given only small advances of around Rp 10 000 at the start of the season and must repay them at the end.

Twenty *juragan* sell regularly to the *depot* during the dry season. One of the major differences between *bakul* and *juragan* is the matter of scale. A *bakul* can buy no more than three quintal each day, whereas the *juragan* handles around a tonne and needs about Rp 500 000 in cash. The other important difference is that the majority of *juragan* are male, mostly affluent as indicated by their motor cycles. Unlike the *bakul*, who will occasionally buy a crop in the field or otherwise make purchases without weighing the goods, *juragan* buy only by the *kilon* system: offering a price per kilogram, weighing the chillies and paying cash. Farmers often bring chillies to the houses of *juragan*, who also buy at the roadside or employ *agen* to do so. Depending on the type and scale of his business, *juragan* trade in chillies any time from six weeks to four months. Farmer/*juragan*, for instance, may choose to trade in chillies for a mere six weeks, whereas full-time *juragan* will buy as long as it is profitable.

Collection and distribution strategies differ among *juragan*. Some deliver chillies to the *depot* every day and employ bicycle carriers to ferry the goods. Others deliver only twice a week. One *juragan*, for example, delivers four times a week. He has an arrangement with a minibus owner to pick up his bulked chillies and distribute them in equal proportions to three different *depot*. Sometimes the minibus takes three separate trips to do so if supplies are heavy. I suspect that most *juragan* supply more than one *depot* on a regular basis, and that the larger the scale of their operation the more likely they are to have links with several *depot*.

All *juragan* later visit the *depot* to collect payment, but they usually receive a portion only and the remainder is paid off when the *depot*'s buyers have paid their accounts. Payment is never entrusted to the bicycle carrier or minibus driver, for price information is best kept secret as possible. Occasionally a large-scale buyer from outside the district may bypass the *depot* and send trucks directly to the villages, although it is difficult for buyers without prior contacts to buy a truckload of chillies quickly enough to make this worthwhile. More commonly the *depot* acts as an intermediary, arranging with *agen* and *juragan* to fill such trucks directly in the producer villages. During late September and early October, when the area south of Prembun is flooded with chillies, Bu Sugi herself accompanies the trucks to the fields, bypassing both *juragan* and *agen* in an effort to maximize profits. Her *agen* may have arranged some of the preliminary bulking, but Bu Sugi negotiates the payments.

In both seasons a few farmers choose to sell directly to the *depot*, but this produce is a miniscule proportion of its business. In the hope of gaining a higher price for their produce or because they wish to visit the Monday or Thursday market, farmers or their wives may approach the *depot*. Quantities tend to be small, not more than thirty kilograms, so that they can be carried with the aid of the basket (*kranjang*) and sling (*slendang*) used by women, and the baskets on a pole (*pikulan*) used by men. Farmers have to haggle strenuously to obtain the prices paid to *bakul* and few succeed. For most the reward is a mere Rp 20 per kilogram more than they would have obtained in the village, but this at least covers the expense of a trip to the market.

The relationship between the *depot* and the *juragan* and *bakul* who are its regular suppliers is reciprocal, but competitive: it has an almost exclusively economic base, even when the persons involved are kin or neighbours. These *bakul* and *juragan* do not sell all their goods to one *depot*, although they do have a hierarchy of *depot* and over the season will sell most of their produce at one place. At the beginning and the end of the season they sell all their produce to a single *depot* and this provides the main economic advantage to the *depot*: a guaranteed flow of produce. From the supplier's point of view the main advantage of a regular relationship is price information. They usually know a day in advance the minimum price they will receive and this is an important edge in bargaining with farmers. Regular suppliers do not have to haggle to obtain the ruling price and thus can dispose of their produce quickly and return to buy more. Other *bakul* who are not regular suppliers can and do obtain similar prices, but they have to spend considerable time haggling.

The relationship between *agen* and *depot* approaches, but still falls well short of, a patron–client relationship. In providing an *agen* with finance, the *depot* makes it possible for him to increase substantially the scale of his buying. The finance is, in effect, an interest-free loan for which the *agen*'s only economic obligation is to resell to the *depot* at the same prices he would obtain elsewhere —a considerable economic asset in a society where well-paid work is in very short supply. It is not surprising that potential *agen* are very carefully scrutinized and that most have prior kin or residence ties with members of the *depot*. There is some evidence that members of the *depot* attempt to reinforce these ties with their *agen* by maintaining social contacts during the off-season, but there is no evidence of the use of such relationships for other purposes. Whereas rights to participate in agricultural harvests are often tied to obligations to provide labour for activities such as housebuilding, I know of no similar examples with *agen–depot* relationships.

DEPOT SALES

The selling strategies of the *depot* also vary with the seasons. During the wet season four regular buyers, three women and one man, all of whom live in the wider Prembun area, transport chillies from the *depot* to other regions. Two of these, a man and a woman, regularly sell chillies in Magelang and Wonosobo. The two (who are, as far as I know, unrelated) run separate businesses but usually combine forces to transport the goods. Because they are dealing with larger quantities of goods than the supplier *bakul*, they, like the large-scale suppliers of the dry season, are usually termed *juragan*. Other *juragan* distribute chillies to Klaten, Yog-yakarta and Solo, occasionally purchasing chillies from another *depot* to make up a full load. In all cases the produce is usually transported by charter minibus. Such buyers are described by the women in the *depot* as their *langganan tetep* (see Chapter 5. Cf. Forbes 1978:221; Siegel 1969:209). They buy on a system of one-day credit, collecting chillies one day and paying, generally in full, the following day. In other words, a payment is made each day, but for the previous rather than the current purchase. They deal only in fresh chillies, both red and green, and sell mainly to wholesalers in other regional markets. All have one or more *lang-ganan tetep* in the regional *pasar* to whom they sell most of their load and they are generally paid immediately in cash. Regular buyers from the Prembun *depot* pay a fixed daily selling price. Regular customers do not bargain to obtain this price—indeed this would be impossible for those who have goods consigned to them—but casual buyers have to haggle vigorously and only the knowledgeable will obtain it. The redistributors in turn negotiate prices with their *langganan tetep*. But bargaining here is also usually restricted: firstly, because the regional wholesaler is anxious to maintain supply lines and, secondly, because both have a very good understanding of retail prices in the market.

During the wet season each *juragan* buys between five quintal and a tonne of chillies daily and they account for the bulk of the produce passing through the *depot*. Apart from moving the chillies, the distributors also supply much of the price information on which the *depot*'s further buying depends. To some extent they are an uncertain source, for it is in their interest to report lower prices so as to ensure their own profits. But the *depot*'s use of several distributors, experience in market conditions, and general skills in assessing information and bargaining diminish the room for manoeuvre.

Mbak Ngamini, the close relative mentioned earlier, has special privileges. During the chilli season in her home region she brings in a full load (two quintal or more) most days of the week, but on Monday and Thursday market days, and on Saturdays, she travels to Yogyakarta by bus or minibus with two quintal of chillies to sell to a *langganan tetep* there. If she has not bulked sufficient chillies from her village she purchases enough to make up a load from the *depot*. Mbak Ngamini is unusual in being permitted to play this double role, for the *depot* attempts to maintain a strict division between its buyers and sellers, in part to maintain high turnovers and in part to control price information.

Dry season redistribution shares many features with the wet season. While the *depot* uses its local networks to streamline the bulking process, the regular buyers maintain their role in the redistribution of chillies and do not increase the scale of their activity.[4] Instead the *depot* uses its extra-local trade links with large wholesale merchants to dispose of its increased purchases. A *langganan tetep* in Tegal takes the largest proportion of their produce, sometimes transporting as much as eight tonnes a day to Tegal and Jakarta. Another important buyer comes from Semarang where he runs a business dealing in chillies, potatoes and onions. He, unlike the Tegal *langganan tetep* who uses his own trucks, relies on the *depot* to consign goods to him on receipt of a letter or telegram placing the order. A large number of other smaller scale merchants and wholesalers also order by telegram, but personal contact is maintained because payments are made by hand, usually within a day of delivery.

CREDIT

Although the combined funds (*modal*) of the three women are little more than six million rupiah, it is clear that at many points during the dry season the *depot* owns chillies worth more than twenty million rupiah. The women's success, indeed their continued existence as large-scale traders, depends upon their ability to maintain a balance between credit and debt so as to maintain a constant cash flow. The most important way of achieving this is to carefully mix types of suppliers and distributors. On the supply side, small *bakul* who must be paid almost immediately are joined with *juragan* to whom payment may be delayed for a day or two. Similarly, the *depot*'s ability to consign chillies to profitable but distant markets with consequent delays in payment presupposes other large distributors who will pay cash immediately. The scale of the *depot*'s operations depends upon credit, but the credit is intended to be very short term, three days at most, and a temporary halt in cash flow may ripple through the system bringing activities to a standstill.

Given the standard of communications in Java, short pauses in cash flow do occur, and these are met with loans from the numerous official and unofficial credit sources in the *pasar*. The interest rates are high, and because of bureaucratic delays loans from official sources are normally arranged through a broker with consequent additional expenses, but as the loan period is very short the interest rate is relatively unimportant. It is worth pointing out that loans are not used as a source of purchasing funds (*modal*)—in part because of a reluctance to become involved with government agencies, and in part because the system of producer and supplier interest-free credit reduces the need for such funds.

Nevertheless chillies are a highly perishable and therefore risky commodity and not even the most careful management can guarantee against natural disasters. In 1980 a considerable proportion of the *depot*'s immediate cash flow was generated by sales to their Tegal *langganan tetep* who was making payments of up to five million rupiah each day within twenty-four hours of buying the produce. But on one trip at the height of the season, a truck was halted by a washed-out bridge, the load was innundated by heavy rain, and most of the chillies rotted. The Tegal purchaser subsequently defaulted on a payment of more than two million rupiah. For a time the *depot*'s situation seemed precarious, but they made up for some of the short-fall with bank loans, another trader advanced funds for them to buy as his *agen* and the Tegal buyer gradually paid the deficit over the next four months.

The major function of credit is to speed up the flow of trade, allowing those at the centre of trading networks to increase the scale of their businesses and thus their incomes. It provides additional gearing for those with finance rather than allowing those without finance to become traders. The risk of default is minimized by carefully regulating persons to whom credit is given and its duration. The credit system inhibits both suppliers and distributors from constantly seeking better prices at one of the competing *depot* and thus maximizes the flow of produce. Credit relationships gradually built up over the season are critical in reactivating trading links in the succeeding season. The credit arrangements reinforce aspects of production which encourage the *depot* to establish a few, relatively stable-links with substantial buyers and sellers. But there is a strong countervailing tendency: the risks of default encourage a relatively widespread distribution of credit in relatively small parcels.

PRICE SETTING

When I began research into the chilli *depot*, I was frustrated by the women's insistence that they set selling prices only slightly above the prices they paid to their suppliers, although they were very reluctant to specify the figures for any given day. Although their claim of standard mark-ups was consistent with my observations that many transactions were concluded without obvious price negotiations, it was incongruent with the vigorous haggling which I saw on other occasions. With hindsight their reluctance is not surprising, for it gradually became apparent that profits in selling agricultural produce are a function of success in maximizing turnover while concealing price information.

As was noted earlier, *bakul* and *juragan* who are regular suppliers to the *depot* essentially receive a fixed price without bargaining. Other *bakul* may obtain the same price, but will have to haggle strenuously. Similarly, *juragan* who are regular buyers for distribution to other areas meet with fixed prices, whereas itinerant buyers must negotiate a price. Although regular *juragan* seldom haggle over prices at the point of sale, indeed they often order by post or through an intermediary, they sometimes claim to have made a loss and seek a reduction at the time of payment. While this is seldom granted, they may be given extended credit for a portion of the debt.

As the locus of transactions moves away from the *depot*, the intensity of haggling increases. Bargaining between *bakul* and farmer is both intense and protracted because, while the *bakul* has a reasonably clear notion of the price she will obtain on resale, her income depends on buying as far below this level as possible. *Juragan* selling to wholesalers in regional markets also bargain strongly, although bids are exchanged very rapidly.

The *depot*, therefore, serves the critical function of articulating the supply and distribution networks, which it accomplishes by setting maximum buying prices and minimum selling prices. The women initially told me that selling prices were set about Rp 10–25 above the buying price after expenses are taken into account, and observation suggests that, in a stable market at times when prices are low, profit margins approximate the higher figure per kilogram. But price setting is not the mechanical process which this statement suggests. At times when supply and demand conditions are stable, prices do not fluctuate much from day to day and the profit margins are also constant. But when prices are rising in the regional markets, the *depot* makes much larger profits by delaying price increases to their suppliers. There is always a two or three day delay before the higher prices received by the *depot* are translated into higher prices for *bakul*. Similarly, at times in the year when prices are known to be falling, the prices to the *bakul* drop more steeply than the prices received by the *depot*.

The *depot* is able to set prices because of its strategic position at the crossroads of the flow of information.[5] While many other traders have accurate information on prices in their particular sector of the market, only the *depot* operators have sufficient information from both supply and distribution networks to reconstruct the price system as a whole. The two or three days it takes for information to percolate throughout the system is the information edge which provides high profits. It is the supplier *bakul* who provide most of this higher profit margin, although they in turn benefit from the day it takes for price information to reach the farmers. The reason for the *depot*'s extraction of profit from the *bakul* is that not only do *bakul* who resell mainly to the *depot* have limited sources of information, but the *depot*'s ability to lift the selling price to distributing *juragan* is inhibited by its desire to maintain the stable relationships which maximize turnover. The major constraint on the prices set for both the *bakul* and *juragan* is that the *depot* must not appear to be treating its own suppliers worse than the other *depot* in town. But while competing *depot* do not confer on prices, it is in their individual interest to keep in step with their competitors.

The intensity of bargaining is less a function of the scale of the transaction or the opportunity cost of time than of the point in the information network where the transaction takes place. Where there is recognized to be little shared information, as between *bakul* and producer, bargaining is intense and protracted; where information is held almost in common, as with the *depot* and *juragan*, fixed prices are normal. An additional indication that it is the recognition of shared information rather than the scale of the purchase or the opportunity costs of the trader's time which determines bargaining, is that strangers always have to haggle. Farmers selling direct to the *depot*, *bakul* who are not regular suppliers, and *juragan* who are not regular customers must all bargain intensely to obtain a reasonable price. The reason why a member of the *depot* will always bargain vigorously with the farmer trying to sell twenty kilograms, or with a *bakul* buying 100 kilograms for retail in a regional market, is less because the profit in such a transaction is significant, than because information on prices at the extremity of the market system is invaluable.

MAKING A PROFIT ON CABBAGES

The extent to which access to information also determines profits on the distribution side of the marketing system is difficult to demonstrate through an analysis of chilli retailing in Kebumen. Because chillies are grown locally, price information is widely shared and potential buyers have numerous sources of supply. For this reason, I use the retailing of cabbages, a commodity whose marketing system was described in Chapter 3, for illustrative purposes.

The cabbage trade in Kebumen is controlled by two whole-salers, Pak Dul and his younger brother's wife, Bu Warti, who supply thirty-two of the thirty-four cabbage retailers in the Kebumen market. Pak Dul, who has been married seven times and divorced twice, currently lives with his youngest wife, but four other wives retail cabbages which they obtain from him. Bu Lamirah, his third wife, works on the Prembun–Kutowinangun–Kebumen market circuit. In Kebumen she mainly retails, whereas in Kutowinangun and Prembun most of her stock is sold to other *bakul*. In Prembun, Bu Lamirah sells cabbages to twelve of the twenty-three retailers including the five largest. Five of her regular customers are her siblings and another is the wife of a sibling.[6]

Although Bu Lamirah is very quick at mental arithmetic, she is illiterate, and her niece records the sales. As with many other assistants in the market, the niece is not paid wages, but she dips into the daily proceeds for snacks, receives small presents, and often eats at Bu Lamirah's house.

Bu Lamirah visits Kebumen each day, transporting her allocation of cabbages—which may be as little as a quintal or as much as one and a half tonnes—by minibus to Prembun or Kutowinangun. Sometimes she pays her husband in cash, but normally she buys on one-day credit, paying for the previous load as she collects the next: the *ngalap-nyaur* system described in Chapter 5. Occasionally, when she wants at least a tonne of cabbages, one of the *juragan* who supplies her husband delivers direct to her in Prembun.

The cabbage retailers in the Prembun market (high season twenty-three, low season seventeen) get most of their income from this source, but also sell beans, chocos or carrots. As long as Bu Lamirah has ample supplies, she sells to twelve *bakul* in addition to *warung*, but otherwise gives preference to her six relatives. When she has only a few cabbages, she retails them herself.

Bu Lamirah seldom bargains with the *bakul* she supplies regularly, often giving a Rp 5 discount to her relatives, but haggles vigorously with other *bakul*. When she is retailing, Bu Lamirah always bargains and will not drop her price below that paid by *bakul*. Unlike retailers specializing in more frequently purchased vegetables such as onions or chillies, cabbage sellers bargain strongly with most of their customers. In the *pasar*, cabbages are weighed and sold intact at a price per kilogram but, as they are an expensive commodity, most will be cut up and resold in *warung* to direct consumers. Leaves which have dropped off or have been cut off to make the cabbages seem fresher, are sold in bundles.

Table 6.2 tabulates the salient features of Bu Lamirah's accounts for two weeks. The figures were recorded on my behalf by her assistant. Week One (January 1980) was towards the end of the season when supplies were still plentiful and the price had fallen to a low level. Sales average a little more than one tonne a week, with 70% wholesaled to *bakul* or *warung* and the remaining 731 kilograms retailed by Bu Lamirah and her assistant. The total profit over the two weeks was Rp 19 130 with an average of Rp 1366 per day or Rp 8 per kilogram.

Looked at *in toto*, these figures appear to support the assertions of Bu Lamirah and other cabbage wholesalers that they make only Rp 5 per kilogram profit and that they set the prices to *bakul* at a level which will enable them to share the profits. Although I do not have detailed figures, it is likely that the profits of the retail sales also averaged about Rp 8 per kilogram so that the greater income achieved by Bu Lamirah might be seen as a function of the scale of her business. Cabbage retailing thus seems a classic example of the 'shared poverty' ethic described by Geertz (1956a:141) and implied by Dewey (1962a).

But a more detailed examination of the accounts suggests some problems with this interpretation. In the two weeks under review, not only does daily income range from the profit of Rp 5545 to a loss of Rp 1500 but also the profit per kilogram ranges from Rp 2 to Rp 15. The level of Bu Lamirah's income is not a function of her turnover for, although on both Tuesday and Friday in Week One she sold 250 kilograms of cabbages, her profit was Rp 825 higher on the Tuesday. While transport costs vary with the distance from Kebumen, these are less than half her overheads and do not account for the variations in profit.

A more convincing interpretation is that Bu Lamirah is taking advantage of her access to both wholesale and retail price information. On Monday in Week One she bought 217 kilograms at Rp 130, wholesaling 182 kilograms to *bakul* at Rp 140, and retailing thirty-five kilograms herself at an average price of Rp 150. After overheads were deducted this gave a profit of Rp 920. The next day she bought 250 kilograms at the same price she had paid on Monday, but lifted the price by Rp 10 a kilogram, and increased her profits more than threefold. By Wednesday the wholesale price had risen to Rp 140 and Bu Lamirah would probably have made only a small profit if she attended the market. But on Thursday she sold two days' supply, at prices which implied that

TABLE 6.2

BU LAMIRAH, DAILY SALES

Day	Quantity Bought/Price		Sales to Bakul/Price		Daily Profit	Profit per kg.
	Kg	Rp	Kg	Rp	Rp	Rp
WEEK ONE —						
JANUARY						
Monday	217	130	182	140	920	4
Tuesday	250	130	240	150	3 725	15
Wednesday	—	—	—	—	-1 500[a]	—
Thursday	551	150	315	160	5 545	11
Friday	250	152	240	170	2 900	12
Saturday	—	—	—	—	—	—
Sunday	100	160	87	170	660	7
Total	1 368	144 (av.)	1 064	158 (av.)	12 250	10 (av.)
WEEK TWO —						
MARCH						
Monday[b]	300	67	188	75	2 580	7
Tuesday	150	60	125	70	250	2
Wednesday	150	60	90	70	1 400	9
Thursday	200	70	100	80	675	3
Friday[c]	200	75	145	90	—	—
Saturday	—	—	—	—	1 225	6
Sunday	75	60	—	—	750	10
Total	1 075	65 (av.)	648	77 (av.)	6 880	6 (av.)

[a] Bu Lamirah did not attend the market, but suffered a loss as she had to pay Rp 1500 to porters for unloading and reloading cabbages.
[b] Quantities for the day are an estimate only as the scales were out of action. 200 cabbages were bought and of these 125 sold to bakul.
[c] 35 kg. remained for sale on the following day.

the wholesale price had reached Rp 150 a day earlier than it did, and again made a large profit.

In Week Two, when cabbages were plentiful but prices were low and stable, Bu Lamirah adopted different methods to maintain her income. Whereas in Week One she had wholesaled 77%, in Week Two she limited this to 60%.

If she had set prices to *bakul* at levels which evenly split the margin between wholesale and expected retail prices, Bu Lamirah would have obtained a very small return on the finance invested in her business. Instead she maximizes the value of her superior sources of information. Her daily trips to Kebumen inform her of wholesale prices a day in advance, while retailing part of her stock is an accurate way of testing the local market. She makes her greatest profits in the season when the disjunction between her knowledge and the *bakul*'s is greatest: when prices are fluctuating and particularly when, despite the fall in prices, supplies are increasing. With each price change, the scale of profits increases greatly for a day or two, before slipping back to the average, and it is the large profits on these days that make cabbage selling a viable enterprise. My observations suggest that similar conditions apply to other, non-staple vegetable traders. While profits on most transactions are extremely low and a poor reward for the long hours spent in the *pasar*, the trader can make considerable profits during the short periods when buying and selling prices are out of kilter.

MARKET HIERARCHIES

The hierarchical model outlined earlier does have some heuristic value in understanding the operation of Bu Nyai's *depot*. The critical feature of the flow of produce is that chillies are a seasonal crop, susceptible to rapid spoiling, and grown by numerous small producers. The first two aspects require a marketing system which can quickly shift variable quantities to retailers, while the third provides numerous opportunities for the entry of very small traders. It is notable, however, that during the main season when greater quantities are available, the *depot* bypasses the lower steps in the hierarchy through the *agen* and *juragan* system. On the distribution side, the characteristics of chillies facilitate a hierarchy of numerous small-scale traders who prevent particular regional markets being flooded and shift the chillies before they rot. But once again this network of traders is not used for the main season's production, much of which is sold directly to relatively few buyers. There are also far more 'horizontal' sales than the hierarchical model might suggest: not only from the *depot* to *depot* in other regions, but between traders on lower steps in the marketing structure. In sum, the hierarchical model is most applicable to the slow trading at the beginning and end of the season, but it has little relevance to the main crop.

More significantly, however, this account throws considerable doubt on the view that the structure and trading practices of the *pasar* are inimical to economic growth. As described by Geertz (1963b), the *pasar* deals with goods which are not bulky, are easily transportable, and permit small marginal alterations in the scale of trade.[7] Where the nature of the goods requires discontinuities in trading scale (as with agricultural produce), the *pasar* traders control only the lower stages and large-scale trade is completely controlled by the Chinese. Because prices are set by haggling, traders are 'perpetually looking for a chance to make a smaller or larger killing, not attempting to build up a stable clientele or a steadily growing business' (ibid:35). Although traders are bound together by a complex and ramified network of credit balances which 'stabilize more or less persisting commercial relationships' (ibid:36), both profits and risks are fractionalized, even on very small deals which traders could finance on their own: '[Traders] lack the capacity to form efficient economic institutions, they are entrepreneurs without enterprises' (ibid:29).

Most of the elements in Geertz's account are contradicted by the material presented above. Bu Nyai and her partners now deal in very large quantities of perishable agricultural products and have gradually built up their business over many years. Prices in the larger transactions are not set by haggling and the *depot* constantly attempts to set up a stable network of both suppliers and distributors. Nor are profits and risks fractionalized. Profits are not continuous throughout the system and 'windfall' profits resulting from lack of information are regarded as legitimate and desirable. While some members of the trading network are relatives and friends, and such links are used to expand the business, there is no evidence of favoured treatment with regard to price. Buying prices are set as low, and selling prices as high, as the market will bear.[8]

It is difficult to ascertain the extent to which the differences are the result of the thirty years between the two periods of fieldwork, or specific characteristics of the field sites in Central and East Java respectively. No doubt developments in transport, the economic recovery after the war for Independence, and especially the restriction on Chinese participation in some areas of trade have had important consequences. But nevertheless, it is clear that Javanese entrepreneurs have been able to develop substantial enterprises which remain firmly grounded in the trading practices of the *pasar*. The view that the structure of the *pasar* economy prevents economic growth, or that the poverty of rural Javanese results from the internal structure of their economy rather than the relationship of their economy to other sectors of the Indonesian state, receives no support from this study.

The aspects of Bu Nyai's chilli *depot* which are characteristic of the *pasar* and which are usually attributed to particular aspects of Javanese culture or social structure can be readily understood in terms of the organization of the trading network of which the *depot* is the centre. The large number of independent traders, the hierarchy of trading functions, the relatively equal profit splitting at some points in the distribution network and the widespread use of credit are not products of a Javanese peasant ethos—a form of 'shared poverty' (see Geertz 1956a; cf. Alexander and Alexander 1982). They are outcomes of entrepreneurial activity constrained by conditions of very low finance, dispersed markets, perishable products and discontinuous information.

1. Two broad types of hierarchy have been described. One, in which the commodities flow directly to the next level of the system until they reach the urban centres, is characteristic of Guatemala (Smith 1975) and north-east Brazil (Forman and Riegelhaupt 1970). The other, which involves more horizontal flows, is found in China (Skinner 1964/65) and Java. The structure of the first type has been attributed to colonialism (Plattner 1975) but the inclusion of Java in the second type suggests the explanation is more complex (cf. Mintz 1956; 1960). For additional accounts of Javanese markets using this model see Anderson (1980) and Chandler (1981).

2. Cf. Fruin (1938:114) '. . . the ineptness of the natives where money matters are concerned has given rise, more particularly in Java, to the above described class of Chinese traders and moneylenders'. One example of the 'ineptness' of the Javanese mentioned in passing by Fruin is that during the 1930s Depression, the Dutch exported fl.158 000 000 of bullion obtained by melting down unredeemed pledges at government pawnshops!

3. *Penebas*, persons who buy crops prior to harvest, seldom purchase chillies, although they are the major buyers of citrus, yam beans and green vegetables. The major reason is that chilli crops are seldom harvested as a unit and, in contrast to green vegetables, for example, where the decision of how many plants are bound into a bundle (*ikatan*) markedly affects returns, marketing skills other than bargaining have little relevance.

4. The constraint on their buying is transport. Such buyers can handle only one load each day and the size of the load is limited by the capacity of the minibus they use.

5. Forman and Riegelhaupt (1970) point out that in north-east Brazil the *armazen*, which seem very similar to *depot*, set prices, but attribute this to the fact that most *armazen* are run by urban residents.

6. My choice of examples may give a misleading impression of the importance of kinship links in organizing market trade. Cabbage selling and the copperware trade (see Chapter 7) are the only sections in the Prembun market dominated by groups of kinsmen.

7. While the general characterization is true, many of the commodities dealt with by *pasar* traders are both bulky and difficult to transport: bricks, tiles, *kranjang* (bamboo baskets) etc.

8. This should not be read as a claim that Javanese traders lack compassion. Individual traders cut prices when selling to very poor customers, give gifts to relatives, neighbours and the poor, and attempt to help others establish businesses. Whether such activities are more common than in other societies, I am unable to say. The point, however, is that they are the actions of individuals, not norms of *pasar* behaviour.

7

An Ethnography of Bargaining

BARGAINING is at once the most obvious, and the most elusive, activity in the peasant market place. The rapid-fire patter of the *pasar* trader and the lively haggling between buyer and seller both bewilder and attract those accustomed to the more circumspect manners of the industrialized economy. This intriguing topic deserves more attention than it has received, for Cassady's (1968; 1974) model of negotiated price fixing, on which subsequent accounts have drawn heavily (Beals 1975; Cook 1982; Geertz 1979), is most applicable to the special case of markets where a high proportion of vendors sell goods which they have produced themselves. Cassady's model is of less value in the more sophisticated markets, such as those of Java, where most vendors buy all their stock.

Although studies of Javanese markets have given some attention to bargaining, they also contain problematic assertions concerning both particular aspects and the general phenomenon. Geertz (1963b:35), for example, saw the uncertainties inherent in bargaining as inducing traders 'always to get as much as possible out of the deal immediately at hand', and therefore, as inhibiting the possibility of building a larger business. Peluso (1982:10–15) noted that higher prices are asked from apparently wealthy customers, a point confirmed by my observations, yet she did not pursue the question of whether such women actually paid more.[1] Handbooks for tourists (Dalton 1978:48) suggest that they offer half, three-quarters, or some other set proportion of the seller's initial bid which, as will become apparent, at least explains why selling to tourists can be so profitable.

Dewey's influential account of Javanese markets drew on neoclassical economic theory to explain the intensity of bargaining in terms of the qualities of the commodities and variations in supply: the more standardized the commodity and the more regular the supply, the narrower the range of bids and the less intensive the bargaining (1962a:74–6). Consequently, agricultural produce, which varied greatly in both quality and supply, attracted a much wider range of bids than factory processed cigarettes. Similarly, when market conditions were stable, bargaining for a commodity was limited, but in a fluctuating market, both the range of prices and the intensity of bargaining increased. Dewey (1962a:128) also noted that bargaining was more common in transactions between small traders than between larger traders, and related this to the greater opportunity costs of the larger traders' time. My data confirm Dewey's empirical points, especially if the discussion is confined to single commodities. As goods are sold in progressively larger quantities through the bulking process, bids are fewer and are exchanged more rapidly. But it should remain an open question whether the character of bargaining is sufficiently explained by the characteristics of the commodities, fluctuations in supply, and the opportunity costs of traders' time. For while it takes only a few seconds to finalize retail prices for unstandardized vegetables, which are variable in supply, it may require an entire day to buy copperware which, although expensive, is relatively standardized and without supply variations. A trader herself put it succinctly: 'You can't buy copper goods like you buy chillies; all over in a minute'.

OBSERVING BARGAINING

In many cases, when it is limited to a brief rapid interchange of prices, bargaining is relatively easy to observe and to record in writing. Other transactions, however, involve bargaining of such duration and complexity that tape recordings are required for fruitful analysis. *Bakul* were initially reluctant to allow a detailed investigation of their professional skills and it was only after many months sitting alongside them in the market, when our conversations indicated that I understood the broad features of their bargaining strategy, that they were happy with my use of a tape recorder. By this time customers were also familiar with my presence and most paid little attention to the unobtrusive cassette recorder.

Obtaining useful recordings, however, was far more difficult than I anticipated. The *pasar* is usually busy and noisy: lorries and buses roar past on the highway, cassettes and loudspeakers blare forth music and sales patter. My tape-recordings are often lop-sided with the seller's voice clearer than the buyer's, in part because the recorder was closer to the seller and also because buyers, hesitant to commit themselves, mumble their bids. But the major problem in obtaining useful recordings is that when deciding to tape a particular interaction one never knows whether a sale will eventuate.[2] Customers wander off only to return five, ten or thirty minutes later and it is frustrating to match recordings. Moreover, sellers of expensive commodities make few sales each day. As well as the recording, analysis requires detailed notes on the items being sold. Both buyers and sellers, but more particularly sellers, frequently switch bids from one item to another, leading to very sudden changes in the prices mentioned in the recordings.

The analysis in this chapter is mainly based on my observations of hundreds of bargaining sessions. The two dialogues and graphs reproduced below have been selected to illustrate points of my analysis; they are not the basis for it. But they are certainly not atypical of the general process of bargaining in Javanese markets. Both the buyers in the transactions used for illustrative purposes are particularly skilful; most buyers are rather less aggressive but just as stubborn.

BUYING COPPER POTS: DIALOGUE ONE

Copperware traders in the Prembun market are descendants of two brothers who actively assist one another in haggling with customers. The seller(S) in this dialogue, Bu Bariyah, shares a stall with her husband; he and her mother, who is located in a stall to her left, drop in the occasional remark.

There are three main considerations in buying copperware: weight, durability and craftsmanship. In theory, copperware is sold at a price per *ons* (100 grams) and the weight is marked inside the vessel. Durability is enhanced if the vessel is forged in one piece. A repaired pot has brass forging along the seams, but as pots are sometimes covered by paste to protect the surface, joins are difficult to identify. A well-crafted pot is symmetrical and the copper is heavy and of even thickness throughout.

The buyer (B) is a very worn-looking man about sixty, wearing black work shorts tied up with a rubber band and sandals made from rubber tyres. He is carrying an unloaded *pikulan* (probably indicating that he had brought produce to the market to sell) which has been left in the care of Bu Bariyah's husband half an hour previously. He is accompanied by two women, one in her mid-fifties and the other about forty. The second woman, his daughter, who is in fact buying the pot, leaves the bargaining to her father, but frequently murmurs in support. The transaction took about fifty minutes, but five minutes were spent bargaining with another trader, and ten minutes with a third.

line

S. *Njaba gira, ya ora apa-apa. Barang pandean ora disambung.*

Inside or out, it doesn't matter. It's forged in one piece. (Copper goods are often built up out of old pieces and thus consist of two pieces joined together. Such pots are less durable.)

B. . . .

(An indistinct mumble from the buyer.)

5 S. *Ya, ora disambung, ora dilombo. Ya, ora disambung, ora disambung, puton.*

Yes, there's no join, I'm not lying. Yes, there's no join, no join, it's made in one piece.

B. . . .

(Again an indistinct mumble indicating disbelief from the buyer.)

S. *Astafirallah haladin! Mengko nek tembelan ora usah dibayar!*

God forgive me! If you can discover a repair there's no need to pay!

10 B. . . .

(Strong objections, but it is not clear what they are. He moves away, then turns back.)

S. *Eh, eh, 'Yu . . . Ya, puton. Kiye telung kilo, kiye ya telung kilo, ora ditumbuk.*

Eh, he, 'Yu (she thumps the pot to emphasize her point). Yes, made in one piece. This is three kilos, this one, yes, it's three kilos, no dents.

S. *Eh, eh, eh, Pak. Kene, Pak,*
15 *lungguh . . . ora kaya tuku lombok. Niki puton, ora disambung. Niki disambung, bangunan. Ora bangunan, 'nggeh temenan! La, nyong karo bapake*
20 *nglombo karo anake wadon mengkene.*

Eh, eh eh, *Pak*. Come here, *Pak*, sit down. (She again thumps the pots.) It's not like buying chillies. This is made in one piece, there is no join. This one has a join, has been remade (pointing to another pot). It's not renovated, yes truly! How could I lie to you and your daughter!

B. . . . *kasar* . . .

. . . rough . . . (He grumbles away indistinctly.)

S. . . . *ya, puton, nek sambungan balekaken ngene. Ora nglombo*
25 *karo sampeyan.*

(She also grumbles, then raises her voice.) . . . yes, made in one piece, if there's a join bring it back here. I'm not lying to you!

S's mother

   Inggeh, ora nglombo karo
   sampeyan, yakin!

Yes, she's not lying to you. I swear it! (A wheedling tone changes to one of indignation.)

S. *Barang-barang isih tembaga anyar,*
   ya, isih kasar. Nek wis dienggo,
30   *ya, alus. Barang iki durung tau*
   dienggo, dudu bodolan, akeh
   lebune.

Newly made copper goods are still rough. Once they are used they become smooth. This one has never been used, is not second-hand, has much dust.

S. *Kiye gede, nek kiye semendon*
   cilik. Iki regane telung puluh pitu
35   *teng. Kiye, ya kiye sing alus. Kono*
   gari milih!

This one is big, this one rather small. This one (the large one) costs Rp 36 500.[1] This one, yes this one is fine quality. It's up to you to choose! (She again thumps the pots to emphasize her point.)

S. *Nek nglombo ora usah dibayar.*
   Dandang tembelan ora usah
   dibayar. Dandang sing anyar. Eh,
40   *'Yu. Dandang niki kasar, iki sing*
   alus, niki bangunan.

If I'm lying there's no need to pay. No need to buy a patched pot. This is a new pot. Heh, *'Yu* (as they go to move off), this is a poor quality pot, this is a fine one, and this is a repaired one.

B. *Pitung ewu.*

Rp 7000[a] (pointing to the large pot).

S. *Sampeyan kok malah bingung,*
   'nggeh.

You're becoming increasingly confused, aren't you (irritation mounting in her voice).

45 S. *Puton, puton temenan! Niki sing*
   kaya niki ora bagus. Kiye
   disambung. Oh allah!

Made in one piece, made in one piece, truly! One like this is not a good one. This one is a repaired one. Oh god!

S. *Jajal ditiliki. Anak panjenengan*
   sing dibayar. 'Nggeh, wis.

Look closely! It's your daughter who is buying. Yes, that's enough! (Sound of horn in the background and the seller rests a minute.)

S's mother

50   *Eman, eman, eman!*

Oh, what a pity!

S. *Kiye sing enteng. Eh, iki sing*
   enteng piyambak. Dandang, ora
   apa-apa. Oh, allah! Barang-barang
   niki ora ditempel, ora disambung.
55   *Nek ora bagus aja tuku karo*
   nyong, aja tuku maning.

This one is a light one. Eh, and this one is the lightest. A pot, it doesn't matter. Oh, god! These pots aren't patched, aren't repaired. If they are no good, don't buy from me, don't buy from me again. (Referring to the fact that he had previously bought one for himself.)

S. *Heh, heh, heh, Pak. Kiye ora*
   bangunan kaya kiye. Olehe gawe
   bae saking angele.

Heh, heh, heh, *Pak* (as he moves off yet again). This one isn't repaired like this one. It's very difficult to make one this way (meaning in one piece).

60 S. *'Nggeh, regane murah. Milih! Pada*
   bae niki bagus.

Yes, the price is cheap. Choose! (He points to one and she thumps it three times.) The same, it's a good one.

S's mother

   Coba 'jenengan, ngendikane pira?

Come on, you, name a price!

S. . . . *ora ditambung, ora diboros,* *tambahi duwit. Regane pira, sih?* Kiye regane pitung lima, ngenyang *oleh pitung ewu ngono. Kiye,* *Bapake, ora mblondrokna.*	(mumbling away) . . . not dented . . . not wasteful . . . raise your offer. How much, you. This one is Rp 7500[2] and you can offer Rp 7000[3] for that one over there. (Neither of these two small pots—*kendel*—is mentioned again.) This one, *Bapak*, I'm not misleading you.

65

B. *Sepuluh ewu!*	Rp 10 000[b] (he points to the large pot yet again; his previous offer was Rp 7000. The seller ignores him.)

S. *Niki bangsane niku. Niki sing* gede. Milih. Uwis. Digaweni pada *bae. Kaya kiye bae ora bisa* *sepuluh ewu. Ngene, Pak, regane* *tak pasna bae.*	This one is the same as this. This one is a big one. Make your choice. Yes, they're made the same way. You can't get one like this (indicating the large pot) for Rp 10 000. Come here, *Pak*, I'll give you the right price.

70

S. *Wong tuku dandang ora kaya milih* trasi, kaya milih getuk, sedela dadi. *Wong, la kiye bae tunggale kiye.* *Kilon bae, 'nggeh sekilo limalas,* *sekilo limalas, limang ringgit.* *'Nggeh, Kang, sewelas ewu ora* oleh.	You don't buy copper pots in the same way as you buy fish paste or cassava sweetmeats, in just a moment. Why yes, this one is the same kind as this. Just by kilo, yes, one kilo Rp 15 000, one kilo Rp 15 000, Rp 12 500. Yes, *Kang*, you can't buy it for Rp 11 000.

75

80

B. *Ayah! Sewelas ewu!*	What! (exclamation of incredulity changes to tone of determination). Rp 11 000.[c]

S. *Sewelas ewu rega mriyen karo siki* *ya ora oleh!*	Rp 11 000 is the old price, you can't buy it for that nowadays.

B's daughter Sewelas!	Rp 11 000.[d]
S. *Ora wani. Wani pas, cap jempol* *sewelas ewu!*	I wouldn't dare. Ha (contempt), number number one quality Rp 11 000?

85

S. *Panjenengan, kiye nyong ora* nglombo, ora tuku dandang karo *nyong, kiye bagus, kiye bagus.* *Nyong karo kakange nglombo, aja* *tuku maning. Isin temen nyong* *nganti nglombo, yakin!*	You, I wouldn't deceive you, don't buy a pot from me, this is a good one, this is a good one. If I'm lying to you, don't buy another one. I'd be extremely ashamed if I was lying to you, truly!

90

B. . . .	. . . (more indistinct mumbles.)
S. *Oh, allah!*	Oh, god!
	(The buyers move off for the first time and the three spend some five minutes with Bu Lurah, the older sister of Bu Bariyah. Both of the women appear more comfortable with her, but they return.)

S. *Kene karo lenggah! 'Nggeh ora* *kena, ya? Niki karo lenggah.* *Bapake ngenyang nem ewu tekan* *pitung ewu ora oleh.*	Come on and sit down! Didn't buy one, eh? Come on, sit down. You can't bargain Rp 6000 to Rp 7000, you can't do it. (The seller is referring to the prices they had offered to Bu Lurah.)

95

	S. *Kene karo lenggah, Bapak.*	Come on and sit down, *Bapak.*
100	*Limalas ewu. Ya nganah-nganah dandang isih regane sepuluh ewu kaya kiye ya, ora oleh.*	Rp 15 000[4] (for a small, good quality pot). Wherever you go you won't get one like this for Rp 10 000.
	B. *'Nggeh, sampun! Pira? Pitung ewu.*	Yes, that's enough! How much? Rp 7000[e] (for the Rp 15 000 pot directly above).
105	S. *Mbok ya o sing titen nek milih. Ngene, ya, aja nganah tak omongi ngeneh.*	Please be careful how you select your goods. Come here, don't go there, I will advise you.
110	S. *Ngene, Kang, tak pasna bae. Wis tak pasna bae selawe ewu.*	Come here, *Kang*, I will give you the right price. Now this is the right price (for the large pot), Rp 25 000.[5]
		(There is no reply from the buyer who looks sourly at the seller.)
	S. *Punjul pira? He, Kang, kene, kene, kene karo lenggah. Aja nganti kliru oleh sing sambungan. Nek kiye ora disambung.*	Going to raise your offer? Heh, *Kang*, come, come, come here and sit down. Be careful you don't make a mistake and buy a repaired one. If it's like this it isn't repaired.
115	B. *Ora kena*	Can't.
120	S. *Mbok, ya nganah-nganah dandang durung sepuluh ewu ya ora oleh. Sepuluh ewu bayar pundi, ora kaya batik, Kang. Bingung! Oh, allah! Ana tembelane! Eh, Kang, aja tuku mengkene, eh Kang, pasna bae selawe. Kene, kene, kene karo lenggah.*	Please, wherever you go you won't get one for less than Rp 10 000. Where would you pay Rp 10 000 for one? It's not like *batik* cloth, *Kang*. Confused! (Referring to the state of the buyer.) Oh, god, there's a patch! (Exclamation as she examines it more closely.) Eh, *Kang*, don't buy there. Eh, *Kang*, the right price is only Rp 25 000.[6] Come and sit down.
125	S's mother *Kula ngenyang kalih dasa kirang.*	I offer less than Rp 20 000. (It is not clear whether she is interfering in the bargaining process or giving her own price.)
	S. *Kadar neng ngenyang ora oleh, ora nggawa.*	All that's left is to decide the price; if you don't offer a price you won't get it and take it home.
130	S. *Aja nganti ngenyang bakule njaluke selawe ewu. Ngenyang aja angel, angel. Bakul bae isih seneng. Milih karo lenggah. Janji wong ngenyang dandang rong puluh kurang, tetep ora oleh.*	You don't need to make a counter-offer; I ask Rp 25 000.[7] Bargain, don't make it difficult. I'm still happy. Make your choice sitting down. If you bargain less than Rp 20 000 for a pot, of course you won't get it.
135	S. *Pitung ringgit, ya ora. Limalas ringgit, limang ringgit, sewelas ringgit, ya ora.*	Rp 17 500, no way. Rp 37 500, Rp 12 500, Rp 27 500, no way. (She won't sell it for any of these prices; the order and number are somewhat nonsensical.)

S. *Nganah lunga sing adoh ora
undang maning. Engko gampang
dibaleni maneh.*

If you go away I won't call you back. It's
easy to come back again.

140　S. *Ngono kuwi ya kena, kiye ya kena.
Tak ora sisan gawe kesuh aku.*

Over there you can, here you can. I'm
very ashamed when you make me angry.
(She is becoming increasingly vexed
because the bargaining is going on for a
long time.)

S. *Ngene, Pak, kuwi ya kena kiye
ya kena. Wong sing jenenge
lurahku, tuku dandang bae*

145　*nganti ping lima.*

Come back, this one you can, that one
you can. There's a man, my village
headman, who has bought pots from me
as many as five times.

S. *Kae ngenyang rong puluh kurang
bae urung oleh. Mundut pira?
Agi tak jajage sepiro jerone
kaline.*

If you offer less than Rp 20 000 for that
one, no way. Come on and make an
estimate. How much do you want to
offer?

150　B. *Kiye nyong ukur sepuluh ewu
tok!*

For this one I offer only Rp 10 000![f] (for
the small good quality pot he had
previously offered Rp 7000 for.)

S. *Dandang kaya kiye sepuluh ewu.
Nyong tak kulak sepuluh. Sepuluh
ewu yakin wis. Lorolorone ajek*

155　*punjule pira?*

A pot like this for Rp 10 000. I can't buy
it wholesale for Rp 10 000, Rp 10 000,
truly! Come on both of you, how much
more are you prepared to offer.

B. *Aja nglombo karo nyong, sewelas.*

Don't lie to me, Rp 11 000![g]

S. *Ngene, tak omongi mengko kliru
sambungan. Kae bae wis njaluk
sewelas ewu.*

Come here, I'll advise you so you don't
make a mistake and buy a repaired one.
For that one over there you've already
offered Rp 11 000 (for the large pot).

B's daughter
160　*Sepuluhe tak imbuhi limang atus.*

Rp 10 500.[h] (For the large pot, she
offers Rp 500 less than her father's
previous offer for it.)

B. *Njaluk sewelas, limang atus
maneh, uwis.*

Rp 11 000,[i] five hundred more, that's
it!

S. *Ngene, ngene, ngene, Pak, takon
dewek ngenyang pira? Tuku*

165　*dandang sewelas ewu, mboten kaya
kiye, Pak. Niki karo lenggah.
Limalas, patwelas, telulas ora
wani.*

Come, come, come here, *Pak*, ask
yourself, how much do you offer. If you
pay Rp 11 000 for a pot you won't get one
like this, *Pak*. Come on and sit down.
Rp 15 000, Rp 14 000, Rp 13 000 I wouldn't
risk it!

B. *Ah, sampeyan!*

Ah, you (raising his voice impatiently, but
interrupted before he had a chance to
continue).

170　S. *Oh jelas, ora wani. Dilunas!*

It's plain, I won't risk it. Pay up!

B's daughter
Sewelas.

Rp 11 000.[j]

S. *Sangalas, ngene, ngene, ngene,* Rp 19 000,[8] come here, *Pak.* Come
 Pak. Kene takon nyong. Kae here, ask me. That one over there,
 pirang ewu? how much?

B's daughter
175 *Wis lah!* That's enough! (price implied—
   Rp 11 000[k].)

S. *Nganah engko tindak maneh.* Oh, you'll go away then come back here
  again. (The buyer wants a good pot, but
  refuses to raise his offers.)

B. *Ora bayar, Bu.* I won't pay that, *Bu.*

S. *Ngenyang dandang sepuluh ewu* No matter how far you go you won't get a
 endi sing bakule adoh lah! trader who'll offer a pot for Rp 10 000.

180 S. *Gari mbayar limalas, ora larang,* Just pay Rp 15 000,[9] that's not expensive.
  wis, uwis! Enough, enough!

B. *Wis sewelas ora oleh tak tinggal.* Rp 11 000[l] is enough, I leave it at that.
  (The seller's bid is for the small good
  quality pot, but the buyer's is for the
  large one.)

S. *Sewelas ora wani. Pira, Mas?* I can't risk Rp 11 000. How much, *Mas?*

  (The buyers wander off to Bu Darmo, a
  cousin of this seller, the man picking up
  his carrying pole—*pikulan*—from Bu
  Bariyah's husband as he goes. They spend
  some ten minutes with Bu Darmo then
  return again.)

S. *Ngono golek liyane, engke tindak* Over there seeking another, then
185 *ngene maning. Gari mbayar bae.* returning here again. All that remains is
 Tak pas pitung ringgit. Dilunas. to pay for it. Precisely Rp 17 500.[10] Pay
 Nek kiye nembelas ewu setengah. up! This one over here is Rp 16 500.[11]
  (The more expensive one is the pot the
  buyer is after, and the cheaper one, a
  lighter one not previously mentioned.)

B's daughter
 Sampeyan . . . You . . .

B. *Pira? Pira? Sewelas!* How much? How much? Rp 11 000.[m]

190 S. *Oh, allah! Kari mbayar bae,* Oh, god! Just pay Rp 16 000[12] (referring
 nembelas ya kena. Kaya kiye to the Rp 16 500 pot above), you can.
 limang ringgit. Ngene tak omongi Like this one; Rp 12 500[13] (referring to
 disik. Ngene, ngene, ngene, Pak. the small good quality one). Come here,
 Eh, nyong ora omong limang I'll advise you first. Come here, *Pak.* Oh,
195 *ringgit. Nyong omong limalas.* I don't say Rp 12 500. I say Rp 15 000.[14]
 Patwelas, ora wani. (She corrects her previous bid.)
  Rp 14 000, I wouldn't risk that.

B. *Kula . . . wis semanten.* I . . . that much is enough! (Price
  implied—Rp 11 000[n].)

B's daughter
 Kiye enteng. This is a light one (in a complaining
  tone).

S. *Ora ana sing bayar nembelas ewu.*
200 *Nganggo barang sejam, rong jam isih awet barange. Niki nembelas pas. Dilunas!*

There is no one who pays Rp 16 000. For one that price you use it for only an hour or two. This one is durable. Precisely Rp 16 000.[15] Pay up!

B's daughter
Pada bae.

Same price (as before, i.e. Rp 11 000[o]).

S. *Ngene, ngene, ngene, Pak!*

Here, here, here, *Pak!*

205 B. *Rolas teng.*

Rp 11 500.[p] (pointing to the large pot; the seller ignores him.)

S. *Limang ringgit. Wis suwe, malah bingung.*

Rp 12 500[16] (for the lighter one). The longer you take the more confused you get.

B's daughter
Kula mawon mboten purun diparingaken limang ringgit.

I myself do not want to give Rp 12 500. (for the lighter one).

210 S. *Ya, upamane, limang ringgit, limang ringgit ora gelem.*

Yes, typical! Rp 12 500, Rp 12 500, you don't want it for that (in a tone of disgust).

B's daughter
Pun, pun, kula pun pol Ibune.

Enough, enough, that's the limit for me (price implied—Rp 11 000[q]).

S. *Limang ringgit ya wis.*

Rp 12 500,[17] yes, that's enough!

B. *Pun, pun, bolak-balik.*

Enough, enough (price implied Rp 11 000[r]), from both sides.

215 S. *Ngene, ngene, ngene, Pak, ngene, ngene, ngene, Kang.*

Here, here, here, *Pak*. Here, here, here, *Kang.*

B. *Teng ngriko-ngriki tiyang tuku onten bobote.*

Here, there, there is a limit to what people will pay.

S. *Bobote mboten namung semanten.*

There's not only one limit!

220 B. *Pun, angsal mboten, Bu? Nek siyos 'nggeh kula mbayar nek mboten 'nggeh empun. 'Nggeh napa pripun. Pada bae.*

Enough, can I or can't I, *Bu*? If it's still on I'll pay, if not, no. I've had enough. Yes or no? The same offer (i.e. Rp 11 000[s] for the lighter pot).

S. *Limang ringgit wong kena tok!*
225 *Kiye mung nempilaken kono, Pak. Kiye nukokna tok yu sampeyan. Ngandel ya wis, ora ya wis. Tuna. Asale bakule ora nyekel duwit?*

Rp 12 500,[18] that's it! There is no profit in it for me, *Pak*. Pay for this, you. You believe me, yes or no, that's enough. A loss! If traders don't make money . . .?

B's daughter
Sewelas ewu. Siji, loro, telu,
230 *papat, lima.*

Rp 11 000.[t] One, two, three, four, five. (Counting out money in Rp 1000 notes. She hands over Rp 11 000 for the lighter pot. The seller is reluctant to take it.)

S. *Kiye pirang-pirang duwit. Eman, eman tok!*

This is a lot of money. What a pity, what a pity!

B. *Nggo niki jujul limang atus. Nyong*
235 *duwe jujul bae ora, ora duwe*
duwit. Jujule wonten napa mboten,
nek mboten kula tukaraken.
Langganan wis lawas, kon ora dadi
karo nyong?

The change for this is Rp 500, (i.e.
Rp 11 500[u] as he hands over a further
Rp 1000 note and indicates the slightly
better original pot as he does so.) Do you
have the correct change. I'll change it
elsewhere. I've been a customer for a
very long time; why do you quibble with
me?

(The seller had now agreed to sell the
lighter pot for Rp 11 000, but then agrees
to the buyer's request that he get the
better pot for Rp 11 500.)

S. *Sampeyan wis murah karo nyong.*

You've got a cheap price from me.

240 B. *Janji niku dienggo sepisan borot*
kula mbalekaken. Nek borot kula
buang. Kula tutor maleh. Saniki
kula kantun tumbas kendel. Kula
isih butuh kendel gede. Kula gadah
245 *kendel gede.*

I promise you this, if I use it once and it
develops a leak I'll return it to you. If it
has a leak in it I'll throw it away and
fetch another. Now all that remains is to
buy a different kind of pot. I have a large
pot. (This passage is delivered in a joking
manner.)

B's daughter
Kendel gede nggo jangan tewel
ora maen!

Large pots are no good for cooking
unripe jackfruit!

(There is general laughter from all the
nearby sellers as well as the three buyers.
All shake hands and take their leave.)

S's mother
Eman, eman, eman banget.

How regrettable!

S. *Kesel, kesel banget!*

How tired I am!

(The above *dandang* weighing 28 metric
ounces was sold for Rp 11 500. Bu
Bariyah's husband had sold another of the
same weight and similar quality earlier in
the morning, for Rp 16 000, which is the
top end of the normal price range.)

This dialogue illustrates some general features of bargaining.
The seller does most of the talking, keeping up a constant flow of
patter which the buyer answers or, more commonly, ignores.
Bu Bariyah stresses the generally high quality of her goods, but
occasionally points to low quality pots among her stock so that she
can represent herself as an adviser rather than an antagonist (*45–7*;
51–63; *65–7*; *105–7*). Talking almost constantly, she wheedles
(*11–21*), feigns indignation (*8–9*; *23–5*; *152–5*) and tries to intimidate (*43*; *185*) her customer. She also attempts to confuse him by
switching her offers to other goods on sale (*64–6*; *186–7*). The

seller makes most of the bids. Despite the fact that the buyer had purchased a similar pot from her at Rp 11 000 not long before, her initial bid is well beyond this mark (*34–5*), and even when the bargaining is well advanced she is still asking more than double (*122*; *129*). During the second session, Bu Bariyah's offers hover around Rp 15 000 and once she drops this by a quarter the sale is quickly concluded. The seller, confident in his price knowledge because he had made a recent purchase, reiterates his initial serious bid, with occasional bids for other pieces of copperware. Bu Bariyah claims his information is outdated (*82*) and that he is not making sufficient allowance for variations in quality (*52–4*; *178–9*), but the buyer is sufficiently confident to persist. In fact, at the end of the transaction, Bu Bariyah is momentarily confused and sells a high quality pot for only Rp 500 more than an inferior one.

BUYERS AND SELLERS

Javanese differentiate two aspects of bargaining or negotiating prices. The initial stage where the buyer or seller, usually the seller, makes an offer[3] or series of offers is called *ngenyang* (*Ngoko*) or *ngawis* (*Krama*). Once an exchange has been initiated, the 'haggling' as the buyer and seller exchange offer and counter-bid is referred to as *nyang-nyangan* (*Ngoko*) or *ngawis-ngawisan* (*Krama*).[4] This is not merely a transition from single to double verb forms, but a clear distinction between testing the waters and entering reasonably serious negotiations.

Javanese conceptions of the bargaining process do not share one important connotation of the English work 'bargain': obtaining goods below the usual price. Prices within the *pasar* are always conceptualized as a range: *reregan pasar*. Nor is there a distinction between wholesale and retail prices, for while most purchases intended for resale will be in the bottom half of the price range, skilful consumers can buy at the same price and traders sometimes buy dearly. Except at the times when prices are widely recognized to be falling (immediately after the major holiday of Lebaran, for example) a good price for a Javanese buyer is a price at the lower end of the currently prevailing price range. The clever buyer is *terlaten* (painstaking): she—Javanese regard this as a predominantly female characteristic[5]—repeats her bids and only raises them little by little. Traders describe prices at the bottom of the range as *tempil*, implying that they have bought and sold at the same price, and their aim is to sell at as high a price as possible (*bati apik*, lit. good profit). The seller's bargaining strategy is intended to lead the unwary or uninformed buyer into a bid above the current price range.

The ideal *bakul* is friendly (*ramah*) and lively (*rame*). These characteristics are demonstrated by constant chatter and are especially important for traders selling expensive commodities such as cloth. *Bakul* selling frequently purchased items need less time to finalize sales and can afford to be more abrupt in manner. Little emphasis is placed on the vendor's honesty for, given the competitive nature of bargaining, it is expected that both buyer and seller will make unreliable assertions in the process of bluff and counter-bluff. It is frequently asserted that pious Muslims seek just prices and are more circumspect in their claims, but it is commonly recognized that lying is widespread in the *pasar* and is an integral part of haggling. The only honesty demanded in the *pasar* is that the *bakul* provide the agreed quantity of goods and that the customer pay the agreed price.[6]

A clever buyer therefore attempts to obtain information about current prices before beginning bargaining, but this is recognized to be a difficult task. In an economy where prices are seldom marked on goods or displayed on market stalls, where advertising is almost unknown, where production or overhead costs are seldom calculated, and where commodities are both unstandardized and subject to marked fluctuations in supply, the interest which people take in prices amounts almost to an obsession. Javanese carrying new goods are invariably asked, often by total strangers, how much they paid and how they conducted the bargaining. The answers are seldom accurate: buyers quote lower prices because they fear being thought foolish for paying too much. The inability to obtain prices which others have reported, may be one reason why Javanese folklore is replete with tales in which peasants are cheated by traders.

While bargaining itself might be regarded as price research, aborted sales normally only tell the buyer that her price knowledge is incorrect for it takes considerable skill to infer the usual price range from incomplete transactions. More accurate information can be obtained from observing sales, but the muttered bids, the rapid decrease in price in the last few seconds of bargaining, and the practice of concealing the payment in the palm of the hand, limit opportunities for observation.

Bakul take considerable pains to conceal price information, especially if they feel a buyer is bargaining to test the market. Among the most successful are the copperware traders who make the largest profits in the *pasar*, occasionally 100% on a single item. Copperware sellers claim that they do not bargain over prices: copperware is sold at a set price for each *ons* (100 grams) of copper it contains, plus a small allowance for workmanship. This system of pricing was also used for the silver and gold jewellery which many of them sold before the steep price increases in the mid-seventies. As each pot is marked with its weight, and will be weighed at the buyer's request, there appears to be little room for manoeuvre. But the *bakul* are very successful in concealing the current price of an *ons* of copper. As the price is known to fluctuate and householders seldom purchase more than one pot in a decade, buyers are aware that their information may be outdated. Nor can they test it by comparative bidding with a number of traders; all copperware *bakul* are descendants of two brothers and co-operate in bargaining. Moreover, copperware manufacture in the Prembun region is localized in a single village and the producers are close relatives of the traders. Nor surprisingly, bargaining for copperware involves more suspicion, even hostility, than trade in other commodities.

INFORMATION SEARCH

Three structural features of the *pasar* have important consequences for information search and hence for bargaining: the heterogeneity of commodities, the concentration of sellers, and the institution of *langganan* (regular customers).

As in other peasant markets (e.g. Beals 1975; Geertz 1979; Khuri 1968; Szanton 1972) commodities in the *pasar* are not standardized and prices are heavily influenced by seasonal factors in ways which are not always obvious to the uninitiated. For example, whereas the price of rice and other crops sold mainly on the local market falls at harvest times, chilli prices rise at peak harvest because the increased scale attracts distant buyers and reduces unit transport costs. Prices of foodstuffs and clothing commonly rise at Lebaran and other major festivals when such goods are in especially high demand, while prices of some individual items are correlated with specific seasons: the price of *tandung* (woven hats worn when harvesting) increases by a third approaching the harvesting season. After-harvest buyers have money in their pockets and *bakul* believe they are less careful in bargaining, especially over commodities which are not purchased regularly. Customers are also more likely to be men as farmers bring small quantities of produce to the market to sell. *Bakul* therefore ask higher prices and bargain more strenuously, knowing that because the volume of sales increases during such periods, if their more aggressive bargaining techniques antagonize one buyer, they will benefit from another. In slack times, however, they are resigned to accepting lower prices to maintain turnover.[7]

The heterogeneous nature of most commodities in the *pasar* poses considerable problems for buyers.[8] A villager may have some knowledge of the current price of *su'un* noodles, for example, and be able to distinguish the three major grades on the basis of colour. But it takes the expert knowledge of the trader to make further distinctions within these grades. Similar problems arise with most commodities and are particularly apparent in the case of cloth. The widespread use of the scale has reduced some of the uncertainty in the sale of foodstuffs. Prices are normally given in terms of a kilogram or *ons* and while some small-scale sellers stick to 'traditional' methods of measurement such as the half coconut shell and the tin, or simply arrange their goods in small piles on a bamboo tray, they are prepared to weigh goods if customers request it. But differences in quality remain, and the value of a kilogram of onions will be far different if the customer allows the *bakul* to fill the scale than if she does so herself.

Javanese markets concentrate sellers of each commodity in discrete sections of the *pasar*. In Prembun, for example, 270 cloth and clothing traders occupy adjoining stalls in five large open sheds; 364 vegetable traders are squeezed into a space half this size, while the nine copperware traders have a shed of their own. Traders prefer a central locality with access to a four-way flow of traffic, but rights are established by use and newcomers are limited to the least desirable sites. Nevertheless, say the *bakul*, each seller will gain a fair share of customers for if one buyer neglects them the next will not. *Bakul* can compensate for an undesirable site by an attractive display of goods, but noisy solicitation of customers is unusual and it is only when a prospective customer is sidling doubtfully past that a trader draws attention to a particular item.[9]

Localization of traders is critically important (Geertz 1978:30–1). It brings prospective buyers and sellers into quick contact and avoids a laborious search for the buyer of a particular commodity. Buyers can immediately see the range of goods on offer and compare style, quality and craftsmanship. In some cases, especially commonly purchased vegetables of low value, customers can also obtain relatively accurate price information by soliciting offers from a number of vendors; but for expensive commodities, where the price range is greatest and bargaining is most important, this is not possible. Whereas in West Asia (Geertz 1979; Khuri 1968:702) buyers survey prices in several shops before beginning intensive bargaining with their usual supplier, Javanese see such procedures as unproductive. *Bakul* will not quote offers which indicate current price ranges until they are sure that the customer wishes to purchase a specific item of their stock.

As Geertz (1978:31) points out, a definitive feature of the bazaar economy is that extensive search is ancillary to intensive search. Rees (1971:109; cf. Stigler 1968:171–80) used the contrast between used car markets in industrialized economies to illustrate the differences between the two concepts. In the new-car market, where products are assumed to be identical, buyers search extensively by obtaining quotations from numerous dealers and comparing such factors as price, after-sales service, and credit. But with used cars, where no two are identical, sensible buyers search intensively, asking numerous diagnostic questions about the characteristics of a particular car. Another way of making the same point is to emphasize that whereas in an industrialized economy the main locus of competition is between sellers—the buyer searches for the vendor with the best price—in a bazaar economy price competition is between a specific buyer and a specific seller.[10]

Once a *bakul* begins bargaining with a customer, other traders do not intervene, and a customer may only bargain with one trader at a time, although customers will often move from one trader to another and back again. One indication of the strength of this convention is that a vendor who does not have the specific commodity her customer requires, often borrows it from another stall, splitting the proceeds with the owner. When business is brisk, vendors often bargain with several customers simultaneously, but they attempt to keep each transaction separate. If one customer buys a specific good at a specific price, bystanders who attempt to buy immediately at the same price may well be told that no other items exactly the same are available.

The best way for a customer to obtain reasonably accurate price information is to make as many purchases as possible from the same trader: 'clientelization' (Geertz 1978:30).[11] Accounts of the Javanese *pasar* have reported that Javanese traders do not attempt to build a steady clientele (Dewey 1962a; 1962b; Geertz 1963b), but this is not true of contemporary Central Java.

Bakul describe three categories of customers. *Sing tuku* is a casual buyer whom the vendor may never see again. Social interaction is devoid of anything other than the desire to exchange products or services, and transactions are strictly directed towards the goal of gaining a good price. A *langganan*, or *langganan biyasa*, is a customer who buys on a regular, but not necessarily exclusive, basis. Transactions with such customers are always cordial and the seller's initial offer is often pitched at a level which limits bargaining to a single counter bid. Concessions on quantity may be granted on cheaper items. *Langganan biyasa* merge in many respects with *langganan tetep*, although with the latter credit is extended to the customer for periods ranging from a day to a month. As *langganan* relationships of both kinds require regular transactions, it is not surprising that the most common loci are retail stalls (*warung*) both in the villages and the towns.[12] The *bakul* involved in *langganan* relationships with consumers trade almost exclusively in regularly purchased foodstuffs, especially vegetables and meat, prepared foods, sweetmeats and drinks. It is difficult to estimate the proportion of consumer transactions which involve *langganan*, but it probably approaches half for stallholders in the daily market and is higher in village *warung*.

It is transactions with *sing tuku* which most closely approximate Dewey's (1962a) and Geertz's (1963b) characterization of *pasar* behaviour. Intensive bargaining accompanies every transaction. The *bakul* attempts to maximize the price and although she will try to convince buyers that they have bargained cleverly so as to encourage them or their friends to return, she will not offer concessions in price, quantity or quality. Buyers of the more expensive items which villagers require but which they purchase infrequently—mats, textiles, most household items, clothes and manufactured goods—are almost always *sing tuku*. It is for these items that the price range is greatest and bargaining is most highly developed.[13]

BARGAINING TECHNIQUES

In transactions for items of daily use, especially food, bargaining is seldom protracted: buyer and seller rapidly exchange three or four bids and the sale is concluded. With expensive commodities such as textiles, clothing or copperware, however, more elaborate techniques are required. Buyers must be attracted to the stall, their desire for a particular item must be encouraged, the depth of their knowledge of prices established, and the sale concluded in a way which will encourage them to return or to recommend the trader to their friends or neighbours. Although much bargaining is noisy and aggressive, sometimes acrimonious, *bakul* usually attempt to finalize sales with elaborate thanks and handshakes.

Javanese are generally regarded, and regard themselves, as reserved and restrained in their behaviour, but norms of behaviour in the *pasar* differ from other social contexts. A successful trader's manner is often *kasar* (vulgar), a characteristic which is negatively contrasted with *alus* (refined) in other contexts (Geertz 1960:232), but the *pasar* itself has the positive attribute of being noisy and crowded (*rame*). It is partly for this reason that the market is always thronged with people, many of whom have no intention of making a purchase. There is an air of excitement surrounding the *pasar* and traders do their best to entice their customers to surrender to it.

Traders differ, of course, in marketing-skills and personality, and this affects the way in which they bargain, but there are some well-established bargaining techniques which are used by all *bakul*. Two of these might be described as verbal techniques: maintaining sales patter and switching currency units. The other three are non-verbal: interchanging items, 'walking off', and *tambahan/tombokan* ('adding extra').

SALES PATTER

Sales patter designed to attract, stimulate and maintain the interest of potential customers is a very important asset for traders in expensive commodities. Although the initial intention is to convey the trader's friendly personality and to persuade the buyer to enter serious negotiations, once bargaining has commenced the aim is to confuse the buyer, although not to the extent that she walks away. Traders in commodities such as cloth, clothing and copperware are aware that the successful are fluent talkers, and observation confirms this.

Negotiations in the *pasar* are nearly all conducted in Javanese rather than the national language, Indonesian. Most market place participants have some knowledge of Indonesian, although this may be rudimentary among the older women, but only the occasional government employee or student uses Indonesian when bargaining. Village women often said that the reason they preferred the *pasar* to the *toko* was that in shops one should speak Indonesian, although their (mistaken) belief that one cannot bargain in shops was also important.

While seven levels or styles of Javanese have been delineated, they can be regarded as variations on two main speech styles (Geertz 1960:253; Horne 1961:xxi–xxv; Koentjaraningrat 1960:197; Wolff and Soepomo 1982:4). *Ngoko* is the basic, informal style used when speaking to someone of lower status and with close friends. This is the usual form of speech among Prembun villagers. *Krama* is the formal style used when speaking to strangers and distant acquaintances. *Krama Madya* is a less formal version of *Krama*. The dialect of Javanese used in Prembun is less formal and refined than the standard of the court centres. There are subtle differences in some vowels and numerous regional variations in vocabulary. While recognizing *Krama* forms, most villagers are not themselves adept at manipulating language levels, and frequently comment that their Javanese is deficient.

My initial hypothesis that manipulation of speech levels to gain a status advantage would be an important bargaining technique proved unfounded (cf. Wolff and Soepomo 1982:26). While there are differences in the language levels used in the recorded transactions, there is no evidence of attempts to manipulate language levels to gain a bargaining advantage. In most cases the language level used at the beginning continued to the end. Although *bakul* used more respectful language if their customer was obviously older than themselves, the speech level appeared to reflect education rather than social status. *Krama Madya*, and particularly *Krama*, was used only when both speakers were well educated. Internal variations appeared to be due to mistakes arising from unfamiliarity with high level language forms, although there was some tendency for sellers to use less polite forms towards the end of a protracted exchange. Most transactions are conducted in *Ngoko* with occasional *Krama Madya* and the subtle status distinctions inherent in much of Javanese life are muted.

Kinship terms are the most common mode of address and usage is governed by age. *Bakul* address most male adults as *pak* (lit. father) and females as *bu* (lit. mother), young women as *mbak* or *'yu* (lit. older sister) and young men as *mas* or *kang* (lit. older brother). Elderly men and women are occasionally addressed as *'mbah* (lit. grandfather/grandmother). These terms are the polite and acceptable forms of address for all strangers and do not appear to be used for rhetorical purposes.[14]

The copper sale in Dialogue One is replete with examples of patter designed to stimulate the haggling to a successful conclusion. The initial friendly atmosphere was not maintained for long. Under the stress of bargaining, Bu Bariyah's friendliness and willingness to give advice (*1–2*) rapidly switches to impatience (*4*), feigned anger (*8, 23–5, 152–5*), disparagement (*69–83*), and even ridicule (*206–7*). At times her sales talk degenerates into a nonsensical babble: she spits out a series of prices (Rp 17 500, Rp 37 500, Rp 12 500, and Rp 27 500) in rapid and illogical form, stating that she will not sell at any of them (*134–6*). In fact, two of these prices are above her current offer of Rp 25 000 and two below. The content of sales patter is extremely varied and includes accusations or denials of lying and deception (*19–21, 24–5, 37*). All of the above references are the seller asserting her honesty, but the buyer also accuses her of lying (*156*). As might be expected, exclamations are frequently scattered through the passage, as are words emphasizing the truth of a statement: *yakin* (*92*) and *temenan* (*45*) are examples. The seller frequently calls upon the name of God, usually in the form of '*Oh, Allah!*', but the expression '*Astafirallah haladin*' meaning 'God forgive me!' is also used once (*8*). Even for the expert, talking continuously can lead to mistakes and the trader inadvertently reduced her offer from Rp 15 000 to Rp 12 500 in one breath (*190–6*). She immediately corrected herself, however, and the slip appeared to pass unnoticed.

Bu Bariyah is a quick-tempered woman who often becomes impatient with her customers and attempts to intimidate them into buying. Bu Menik, the cloth trader in Dialogue Two (see Appendix), is much closer to the ideal of a *bakul*: polite, non-aggressive, patient and very successful. She usually attempts to portray herself as an adviser, more concerned with meeting the customer's requirements than making a sale. Whereas Bu Bariyah tends to expose her impatience with either real or feigned anger, Bu Menik often relieves tension by giggling, a common Javanese reaction to stress. But faced with a skilful customer Bu Menik becomes insistent (*44–63*), and sarcastic (*67*). In this transaction she showed an uncharacteristic lack of courtesy in failing to farewell her customer, and later excused herself to me with a comment on how exhausting it was to bargain with a *terlaten* customer in an almost empty market.

CURRENCY UNITS

A second important verbal bargaining technique is to manipulate the currency units. The purpose is to bewilder the buyer and force her to switch between various methods of calculating prices, or to force more rapid increases in bids.

The only currency unit officially used in Indonesia is the *rupiah*, and the smallest coin is five *rupiah*. Nevertheless, the terms *ringgit* (lit. Rp 2.5) and *talen* (lit. 25 cents) derived from market Malay during the colonial period remain in common usage. Prices are frequently expressed in multiples of these terms which have come to have the same meaning. For example, *pitung talen* (lit. 7 x 0.25 = 1.75) can mean in the contemporary context Rp 175, Rp 1750 or Rp 17 500. Similarly, *limang ringgit* (lit. 5 x 25 = 125) means Rp 125, Rp 1250 or Rp 12 500. Two examples from the Dialogue illustrate the usage of the term *ringgit*. In the first, the seller reels off a series of numbers: seven *ringgit* (17 500), fifteen *ringgit* (37 500), five *ringgit* (12 500) and eleven *ringgit* (27 500) (*134–6*). The intention here is to force the buyer into mental arithmetic in the hope that he will make a mistake. Later the seller switches in successive offers from 'fifteen' (Rp 15 000) for one pot, to 'seven *ringgit*' (Rp 17 500) on another, to 'sixteen and a half thousand' on yet a third pot (*180–7*).

Further complications arise with the use of the word *tengah*, meaning 'half'. The three forms commonly used are *teng*, *tengah*, and *setengah*. While *teng* and *tengah* imply that half a unit is taken off the sums named, the use of *setengah* means half a unit is added to the figure.

The first form, *teng* appears very clearly (*34–5*) in Dialogue One, when the seller quotes the price '*telung puluh pitu teng*', thirty-seven less a half (Rp 36 500), and later (*205*) when the buyer offers '*rolas teng*' (*rolas* = twelve) meaning Rp 11 500. Up to this point the buyer has consistently bid '*sewelas*' or '*sewelas ewu*', Rp 11 000, and by switching to the *teng* form is able to increase his bid by Rp 500, rather than Rp 1000.

Tengah is interpreted in the same way: *kalih tengah* (*kalih* = two) means one and a half. A brief passage illustrates a slightly complicated version of the usage:

S. *La, meniko kalih tengah.*   Well then this one if Rp 1500.
B. *Meniko karo tengah paron.*   This is Rp 1500 halved (lit. two minus a half, halved.)

On yet other occasions, prices are expressed in terms of a unit minus (*kurang*) or plus (*tambah/punjul*) another unit, as in Dialogue Two (*17–20*) in Appendix.

B. *La, niki pinten niki?*   Well then, this one, how much is this one?
S. *Regine sekawan setengah.*   The price is Rp 4500.
B. *Loro punjul?*   More than two (thousand)?
S. *La, ya, loro punjul loro.*   Well, yes, two plus two.

Another potentially profitable technique is to quote prices in figures without a qualifier of a hundred or a thousand. For instance, 'five' may mean five hundred, or five thousand, or even fifty. The advantage of quoting a price of Rp 5000 as 'five' becomes apparent when the buyer replies with a good round figure of 'two'. The temptation is to raise the bids in the sequence of 'three, four', meaning Rp 3000, Rp 4000 rather than increments of less than Rp 1000. But a clever buyer often switches units again, replying to an offer of 'five' (5 x 1000) with a bid of 'twenty' (20 x 100), which enables her to raise her bids in units of 100 rather than a thousand.

INTERCHANGING ITEMS

The practice of switching currency and numerical units discussed in the previous section is a verbal strategy to manipulate prices. But not all techniques of price manipulation are verbal, and buyer and seller negotiate many variables other than price. While a *bakul* may eventually lower her offers in response to a customer's refusal to increase her bids, she may also offer another item at the same price, increase the quantity of goods, add a cheap bonus item or, more rarely, suggest some form of credit. Negotiating non-price variables is not discussed here, for it seldom occurs in bargaining between traders and consumers for the expensive commodities which are the focus of this chapter. The strategies termed 'interchanging items' and 'walking off' are common in protracted bargaining interchanges, while *tambahan* is the usual bargaining technique when purchasing small quantities of foodstuffs.

The strategy of interchanging items can be illustrated from the transcribed copper sale (see also Figure 8.2). In the course of the transaction, the seller draws attention to five different copper pots (of three qualities) and manages to entice bids for three of them. The trader has various aims in introducing new items: to emphasize the high quality of the main pot (*1*); to try to revive bargaining which has stalled (*4*); and to attempt to switch a reiterated bid to lower quality pots (*16*). Somewhat ironically, a last minute substitution by the buyer (*u*) results in a sale at the bottom of the normal price range. Even with a relatively standardized commodity such as copper pots, interchanging items may give considerable advantages to the trader. Not only can she hold offers constant while altering the quality, or *vice versa*, but the wide range of items and prices may well confuse the buyer and lead her to make an indiscreet bid. Skilful buyers, however, can make use of the same technique.

The strategy of interchanging items is most highly developed in the cloth trade, where important variables in addition to price and quality include such subjective matters as colour, style, design and finish. Moreover, because of the wide range of cloth, potential buyers are less likely to have firm preconceptions of quality, style and appropriate price, and may be swayed by the trader into placing most weight on colour, design or finish. The front of the stall is soon heaped with pieces of cloth and it requires considerable concentration to recall which bids applied to particular items.

Dialogue Two which is graphed in Figure 8.3 is an unusually clear example of the gains, and pitfalls, of the switching strategy. The seller's initial offer is Rp 4500 for a Solo cloth and the buyer indicates her interest by repeated bids of around Rp 1500. In an attempt to reduce the price gap, the seller introduces a cheaper Sablon cloth for which she asks Rp 2250. The buyer bids twice for the Sablon cloth (*d,e*), which she has no intention of buying, but then responds to offers for the Sablon cloth with bids for the Solo cloth (*f . . . p*). Consequently the buyer's and seller's prices quickly come together (*k*), although the bids are for different pieces of cloth. At this point the buyer is bidding Rp 2000 for the Solo (the same price as the seller wants for the Sablon) and is bidding only Rp 250 less for the Sablon. When the buyer's argument that there are only minor differences between the two pieces of cloth is rejected, and the seller refuses to reduce her initial price of Rp 4500 for the Solo, the customer walks off.

Immediately the customer returns, the seller drops to Rp 2500 on the Solo, while maintaining the price of Rp 2000 for the Sablon (6). The buyer (*m*) responds by lowering slightly her earlier bid for the Solo cloth (from Rp 2000 to Rp 1750) but then increases it in small increments. When she reaches Rp 2000 for the second time the seller accepts.

Although it was the seller who introduced the cheaper cloth, eventually the tactic rebounded against her. By cleverly adjusting her bids so that the initial wide difference in the prices of the two cloths was rapidly narrowed, the buyer isolated the seller's offer of Rp 4500 for the Solo cloth. To continue negotiations the *bakul* was forced to half her price in one step, thus losing her tactical advantage of making small reductions.

WALKING OFF

Walking off is a simple, but widely used, bargaining technique. Although sometimes seen in sales of small quantities of foodstuffs where the trader and the customer have had little previous acquaintance, the more protracted the bargaining the more likely that the buyer will walk away at least once. Walking off differs from the strategies discussed above in that it is used solely by buyers, although traders may also put a temporary halt to negotiations by feigning an interest in conversations with bystanders or a neighbouring stallholder (see Dialogue Two *63*; *69*; *71* in Appendix).

Walking off does not have a single goal. Among sophisticated buyers, the intention is often to persuade the seller that one is no longer interested in the commodity and thereby induce her to lower her price by a substantial amount. This is seldom effective unless the customer's bids are already well within the current price range. More commonly, the *bakul* simply calls the customer back, often by drawing attention to a new item. Occasionally a trader makes a small reduction as the buyer moves off, but it is rare for such customers to receive a substantial price reduction on their return, for the return itself indicates continued interest.

Among sophisticated buyers walking off serves other purposes. A common motive is simply to gain a breathing space: some time to consider negotiations so far and to gain strength for another protracted session. Such buyers often leave the *pasar* and may not return for some hours. For other buyers (see Figure 8.2) the intention is to reinforce the signal that the buyer is confident that her knowledge of prices is correct. Such buyers usually walk off for only a few minutes, often spending the intervening period making similar bids for similar quality items at an adjoining trader's stall. When they return, the trader has a clear indication that she must reduce her offers to the imputed price range or forego the sale.

TAMBAHAN

The most common purchase in the market is a small quantity of foodstuffs where the crucial variable in bargaining is not price, but the quantity and quality of the *tambahan*. The *tambahan* may be an extra handful of chillies, a piece of soybean cake (*tempe*), or a bunch of coriander if the customer has purchased some cabbage.

In such transactions where price knowledge is widely shared, the seller's initial offer is much the same for all customers, other than her *langganan*, and there is usually only one counterbid. One morning, an onion seller replied to all price queries with Rp 150. While some customers did not bargain, the majority bid Rp 140, which she accepted. But all customers bargained over the quality of the onions and over the *tambahan*. Customers who had selected their own onions to make up the usual selling unit of 250 grams, attempted to place a further handful on the scale. The *bakul* invariably threw them back but, after some haggling, added three or four good onions or a handful of inferior onions from a pile she had near her scale. Customers who allowed the *bakul* to fill the scale initially were more likely to obtain a *tambahan* with little haggling, but in all cases considerably more attention was given to the *tambahan* than the price.[15]

Tambahan is most important when the value of the commodity is low, or the selling unit is very small. The smallest coin is five *rupiah*, followed by ten *rupiah*. When the selling unit is in this price range, it is difficult to haggle over prices and buyers seek a discount for multiple purchases. The term *tambahan* is used also for the additional quantity which comprises this discount. When spinach, for example, is priced at Rp 10 for a variable sized bunch, buyers who bargain strenuously may obtain three bunches for Rp 25. *Tempe* is Rp 5 a piece, but purchasers of ten pieces can obtain extra pieces as a *tambahan*. Probably the largest *tambahan* are provided by the meat sellers. Meat is very expensive, more than Rp 2000 a kilogram, and customers always bargain strongly over the price. Once the price is agreed, there is an equally prolonged negotiation for the *tambahan*, and a skilful bargainer who has made the usual purchase of fifty grams of meat may obtain an additional twenty grams of fat.

A final bargaining strategy for foodstuffs might be regarded as simply short-changing. Having accepted the purchase, the buyer hands over a series of small coins and walks off before the trader can count them. In the cases witnessed, the amount was always only one coin short, and usually involved a mature *bakul* buying from a younger woman. Although *bakul* complain that this practice is dishonest, it is sufficiently common to be regarded as a regular bargaining technique and it is countered by traders refusing to hand over the purchase until the price is paid.

1. Katzin (1960:325–6) makes a similar point for Jamaican markets. Perceptions of social status affect prices asked, but experienced shoppers know this and, if prepared to persist, pay within the normal price range.

2. I was unable to arrive at reliable figures on how many bargaining sessions result in sales, in part because it was difficult to decide whether a particular customer was a serious buyer, and in part because there are considerable variations between commodities. My impression is that if the buyer makes a serious bid for cheap items a sale will eventuate, but that with expensive commodities only about a quarter of bargaining sessions conclude with a sale.

3. Prices introduced by the seller have been termed 'offers'; those by the buyer 'bids'.

4. These Javanese words have Indonesian equivalents: *menawar* means to make an offer and *tawar-menawar* to haggle.

5. Male traders and other men who visit the *pasar* regularly are likely to be as skilful bargainers as women, but the statement is valid because three-quarters of the traders and even more of the customers are women. Men of high status feel that it is undignified to bargain and will pay the asking price, but it is rare for such men to make purchases in the *pasar*. For the same reason, men with reasonably large areas of land often leave it to their wives to negotiate sales of agricultural produce and pay harvesters.

6. Although there are sufficiently regular exceptions to make even this statement doubtful (see p. 187).

7. A particularly quiet market is *sepi*, in contrast to an active market where goods are in demand (*laris*).

8. For a description of the large number of units of measure used in Haitian market places and a demonstration that customers nevertheless have an 'informed view of the relationships of quality to price', see Mintz (1961b).

9. The major exceptions are vendors of factory-produced 'traditional' medicines (*jamu*) whose stalls often include powerful sound systems.

10. Cassady's (1974:72) observation that the nature of competition in peasant markets 'involves rivalry among sellers for the patronage of buyers' is not only empirically misleading, but directs attention away from the critical analytical point which Cassady (1968:71) himself makes elsewhere. Similarly the use of fixed

marked prices—which creates competition between sellers, rather than between a buyer and a seller as with bargaining—in the St. Louis public market studied by Plattner (1982; 1983) makes it difficult to apply his conclusions to peasant markets.

11. For discussions of clientelization in different contexts see Geertz (1979) and Khuri (1968) for the Middle East; the *suki* relationship in the Philippines discussed by Anderson (1969), Dannhaeuser (1977), Davis (1973), and Szanton (1972); and Mintz (1961a) on *pratik* in Haitian markets.

12. It is probable that most studies of the rural Javanese economy underestimate the importance of *langganan* relationships between trader and consumer because they concentrate on the *pasar*, the market place proper, at the expense of the other loci of economic transactions. *Langganan* are most important in transactions for agricultural produce with *depot* (see Chapter 6), in retail sales at stalls (*warung*) situated in both towns and villages, and in supplying *bakul* with stock (see Chapter 5).

13. The lack of clientelization in the retailing of commodities such as cloth might also increase bargaining. Anderson (1969:654) notes for the Philippines that 'bargaining (*tawal*), for instance, is always permitted among *suki*. However, an element of *hiya* (embarrassment) enters to reduce progressively the amount and kind of bargaining and makes it more respectful as the frequency of reasonably satisfactory transactions and the quality of trust develop'. See also Forman and Riegelhaupt for Brazil (1970:197). But Javanese do not appear to regard bargaining between *langganan* as disrespectful, and do not emphasize non-economic relationships between *langganan*. They describe *langganan tetep* as an economic relationship which conveys advantages to both parties and which does not require additional moral backing.

14. According to Khuri (1968:701), Middle Eastern vendors often address prospective customers by kinship terms as a mark of respect or affection, and by doing so hope to create a feeling of informality and mutual trust. But people of obviously higher status than the seller are addressed by a title indicating a formal relationship in which it is expected no haggling will take place. The Javanese use of kin terms is clearly not instrumental. On very rare occasions when a man of considerable status finds himself in a context where bargaining is usual, he may be addressed by his title, and feel that it is undignified to bargain. The Headman from our village often noted that trishaw drivers would address him formally and then request double the usual fare.

15. The lack of price-bargaining for small quantities of foodstuffs seems a general feature of peasant market places (see Katzin 1960:318; McGee 1973:152; Szanton 1972 and Uchendu 1967:45). But in each case a convention similar to *tambahan* is important.

8

Conclusion:
Bargaining as Information Testing

THE *pasar* in some ways approximates the perfectly competitive market postulated by neoclassical economics: there is relatively free entry, large numbers of small-scale buyers and sellers, and few cartels. A significant departure from the model, however, is the absence of perfect information, for in the *pasar* price and other information is differentially allocated and difficult to acquire. Information is restricted by both the qualities of the commodities and the nature of trading practices. The lack of standardized commodities, seasonal fluctuations in supply, and the numerous sources of supply operating within differing production constraints create unstable prices. The absence of advertising, even in such a simple form as displaying a price on a stall, combines with ubiquitous bargaining to inhibit access to current price ranges. As Geertz (1978:30) reminds us, 'The search for information—laborious, uncertain, complex, and irregular—is the central experience of life in the bazaar'.

Bakul have the best access to information, and not simply on the goods which they themselves stock. During slack periods in the *pasar*, prices are a constant topic of conversation as *bakul* question their friends, their neighbours, and their own and other trader's customers, weighing the often misleading answers against their experience of market trends. But the *bakul*'s position in a trading network is the most important constraint on the quantity and quality of price information available to her. *Langganan*, and other relatively sustained economic relationships, provide not only commodities and credit, but also reliable price information. The desire to widen channels of knowledge—to balance information obtained from several sources—is one reason why *bakul* dealing in

189

variable supply commodities seldom obtain all their stock from one supplier. For the same reason, traders wholesaling agricultural produce prefer to sell to several buyers. But while each participant in the trading network is attempting to gain information, she is simultaneously attempting to conceal her own knowledge. Information is not equally distributed throughout the trading network, which is the major reason why the allocation of profit is discontinuous. The largest profits are made at the points where the two participants in a transaction recognize that their access to information is unequal: between farmer and *bakul*; at the point of articulation of supply and distribution networks, which is usually a *depot*; and between *bakul* and consumer.

Viewed from this perspective, protracted bargaining for a specific item between a serious buyer and a market vendor is less the last stage in the buyer's search for information, than a process in which the quality of a buyer's information is evaluated. Exchanging offers and bids, switching attention from one item to another, making claims and counter-claims, are devices by which both participants test the information which the buyer has obtained. If the buyer's information is inaccurate, then either no sale will eventuate or the buyer will pay at the top of the price range. If the trader is convinced that the buyer is confident of the accuracy of her information, then the sale will occur towards the bottom of the price range.

NEGOTIATED PRICEMAKING

This approach suggests some changes to the widely applied theoretical account of bargaining which was developed by Cassady (1968; 1974). Based on neoclassical economic theory, leavened with extensive observations of Mexican markets, Cassady's general model[1] is reproduced in Figure 8.1.

Under market conditions where demand is stronger than supply, the general model still holds but the price will be skewed towards the vendor's initial offer; conversely when supply outstrips demand, the skewing will be towards the buyer's counter-offer.

Cassady's model incorporates several conventions which are generally accepted as typical of bargaining in bazaar economies: the seller bids first, bids alternate, backward moves are forbidden, and accepted bids must be honoured (Geertz 1979:227). These

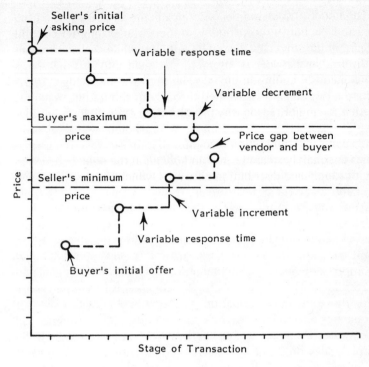

Fig. 8.1.   Basic Behavioural Pattern of Sellers and Buyers in their
Price-negotiation Activities (after R. Cassady 1968:54)

conventions also broadly characterize bargaining in Java although,
with the exception of the last, they are frequently broken. Buyers
and sellers often make backward bids usually by switching offers to
another item; the seller normally makes many more bids than the
buyer; and while the seller usually does make the initial offer, she
may attempt to inveigle the buyer into bidding first.

Cassady's model, which only approximates transactions he observed (1974:57–60), is heavily influenced by two theoretical assump-
tions.[2] First, that the seller's initial asking price establishes the
parameters of the bargaining. The spread between the initial offer
and the buyer's counter-bid, both of which are relatively equidistant from the final negotiated price, is determined by the type of
goods involved. Secondly, that both buyers and sellers have previously calculated price limits and a sale is only possible when
there is overlap between the two.

The initial price asked by the seller is the critical factor in this model of the bargaining process, for it is in the region between the seller's initial offer and the seller's minimum price that any sale will take place (Cassady 1968:55). Vendors aim to pitch initial offers sufficiently high to prevent subsequent haggling lowering it below a buyer's maximum price, but not so high as to inhibit negotiations. This seems plausible, but to be convincing it also requires some account of how the vendor calculates the vital initial offer. Cassady (ibid:57–60) suggests that retailers selling items which they have purchased recently will add something—say 20%—to cover their overheads and thus fix their minimum price. They may then add a further 50% to calculate their initial offer. He notes that the relationships between the initial offer and the minimum price will be affected by such variables as the level of demand, the type of goods and the presumed status of the customer, but does not discuss how the vendor uses such information to calculate an appropriate percentage. Some Javanese vendors do calculate prices in this way—sellers of single cigarettes, for example, sell at 50% above their cost price, but it is precisely in such cases that bargaining seldom occurs.

In Cassady's model the buyer's strategy is conceptualized as the mirror image of the seller's: buyers pitch their counter-bid as far below their maximum buying price as they believe the seller's offer was above the minimum selling price. If the buyer calculates correctly, then subsequent haggling, all things being equal, will produce a sale at the midpoint between the minimum selling price and the maximum buying price. While bargaining skill plays some part, the major determinants of the sale price within the par-ameters created by the initial offer and counter-bid are the oppor-tunity costs of time and the level of supply. In a busy market with limited supplies, buyers have to lift their bids rapidly and sharply to conclude a sale. In a slow market with excess supply, the seller will make most offers and decrease the price by the larger amount.

Cassady's model has proved an effective way of ordering a wealth of data on peasant markets, but as an explanation of bargaining it depends upon the validity of the central assumption: that buyers and sellers enter negotiations with pre-calculated maximum and minimum prices.[3] In the Javanese case it is very doubtful that most *bakul* could calculate an accurate minimum price. This is not because they are unskilled in mental arithmetic, but because the overheads of their business are difficult to establish with any accuracy. Storage costs, market fees and transport expenses are relatively fixed; snacks, porterage fees and gifts to beggars are not. Moreover, some of these fees must be paid irrespective of the level of sales, while others are sales dependent. Nor is stock bought in large quantities at set prices. A cloth trader, for example, may have 400 pieces of cloth bought at a hundred different prices over a period of six months. While *bakul* show remarkable skill in recollecting the prices they paid for cloth, it would be very difficult for them to remember prices and add margins for overheads, as they switch between items while bargaining with a customer.

The most important point, however, is that traders operating in a market where goods are both bought and sold by bargaining would be foolish to calculate minimum selling prices by adding overheads to the purchase price.[4] A trader's profits depend almost as much on her bargaining skills when she buys as when she sells, and traders, like consumers, buy at varying points within the ruling price range. Because competition in such markets is not between sellers, but between a particular buyer and a particular seller, a trader who had bought cheaply would simply relinquish potential profit if she aimed to regain her purchase price plus a standard markup for overheads.

In as much as Javanese traders use a concept of a minimum selling price, it is not the purchase price plus overheads, but the replacement price: the price she expects to pay for the same or similar item. And her bargaining strategy is not directed to obtaining a particular price, a 'target price' as Cassady assumes for Mexican traders (cf. Cook 1982:257–67), but the highest price possible. *Tempil*, the Javanese term for a sale at a price approaching replacement cost, has very negative connotations for traders. In deciding whether they will accept a low price, the primary consideration of the traders is that their *modal* should not be diminished. The usual translation of *modal* (or *pawitan*) as 'capital' (Horne 1974:381) is misleading because *bakul* regard their *modal* as a quantity of goods, ten *kodi* (bundles) of cloth, for example, not a sum of money. A striking example of the implications of this difference are the actions of retailers of kerosene whose *modal* may consist of five drums (400 litres). When price rises are foreshadowed, kerosene retailers withdraw their stock from sale on the grounds that if they sell at the old price they will not be able to maintain their *modal*. From the government's point of view such actions are profiteering: from the retailers' point of view they are essential to avoid reductions in their *modal*.

Given the problems inherent in the seller's calculations, it is impossible to accept that potential customers, with the far more limited information available to them, could calculate a maximum buying price. Having observed a series of complete transactions, it is not difficult to sketch hypothetical minimum and maximum prices outside which the sale would probably not have eventuated. But whereas in some contexts the question of whether such prices have psychological validity for the actors is not a relevant test of the economic analysis (Hefner 1983:670–4), in the case of bargaining this point must be demonstrated if the analysis is to be sustained (cf. Ortiz 1979:76). Accounts of bargaining, such as Cassady's, which aver that such prices lie at the heart of bargaining strategies are unconvincing if they do not include at least plausible evidence that the participants make such calculations.

AN ALTERNATIVE MODEL

The alternative model draws on *bakul*'s explanations of the differing strategies they use when buying and selling, and on the graphs of complete negotiations for expensive commodities where bargaining skills are most apparent. Despite differences in the range of prices, the number of offers and bids, and the time taken to conclude negotiations, the two graphs reproduced in Figures 8.2 and 8.3 have a common form which was repeated in the scores of transactions recorded.

The form of these graphs bear out the *bakul*'s claims that there are clear differences in the bargaining strategies of buyers and sellers. Buyers are consistently *terlaten*: increasing bids by only small amounts and often merely reiterating them. Consequently their initial bid is usually within 70% of the final price and their bids fall along a relatively straight line of the graph. Sellers also repeat offers but, especially in the early stages of negotiations, commonly drop prices considerably with each offer. As a result, their initial offer is frequently three times the final price. The intersections of these two strategies produces right-angled triangles rather than the equalitateral triangle of the conventional model.[5]

The graphs also suggest that there are three stages in completed

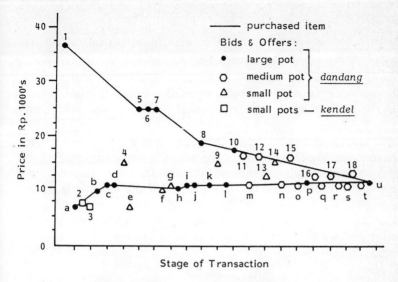

Fig. 8.2. Bidding Sequence for Copper Pot

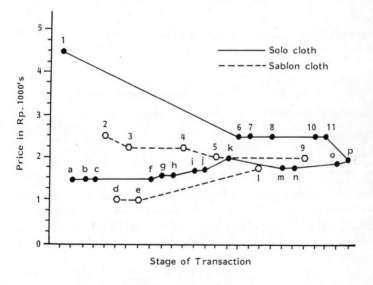

Fig. 8.3. Bidding Sequence for Solo Cloth

transactions:[6] the Initial stage where the seller drops the price
considerably with each offer; the Plateau stage where both participants reiterate prices; and the Settlement stage characterized by

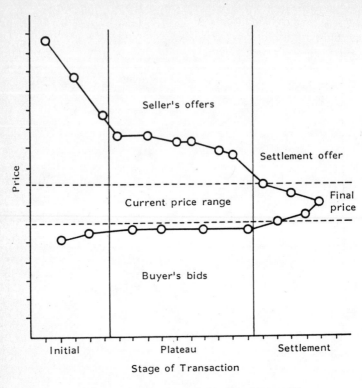

Fig. 8.4. A Three-Stage Model of Bargaining

matched bids of relatively equal increments culminating in the agreed price. These features, with the addition of broken lines to indicate the current price range, are generalized in the model presented in Figure 8.4.

During the Initial stage (*ngenyang*) the vendor tests the buyer's prior knowledge. If a trader feels her customer may be ignorant of current prices—she is a stranger, is too well-dressed, is buying a rarely purchased item, or the market is fluctuating—then her initial offer will be at least three times above the current price range. If the buyer appears knowledgeable, then the initial offer will be lower, or will be quickly followed by a more realistic offer. This stage is very difficult for customers who are aware that their information may be faulty. A bid which is too low, in addition to indicating their lack of information, is met with ridicule and if persisted with inhibits further negotiations; but a high bid leads to an expensive purchase. Not surprisingly, such buyers often avoid direct bids, responding to the seller's offers without mentioning a price or mumbling so it cannot be heard clearly. A customer confident of her knowledge, however, can limit bargaining and ensure a reasonable price, by initially bidding just below the ruling range, raising it a little, and then reiterating it in response to the seller's offer.

While the boundaries between the stages are necessarily fuzzy, the Plateau stage (*nyang-nyangan*) is reached when successive offers by the vendor do not involve substantial price reductions and where the buyer is reiterating a single bid. The *bakul*'s tactics at this point depend on what has been revealed previously. If the buyer's offers are well below current prices, the *bakul* ceases negotiating and resumes only if the buyer makes a new and higher offer. Where the buyer's bid is already well within current prices, the *bakul* attempts to move directly to settlement. A common situation, however, is that depicted in the model where the buyer has conveyed her relatively accurate price information through a series of bids slightly below the current price range. The *bakul* then abandons hope of windfall profits and tries to maximize the price within the current range by persuading the buyer to pay a premium for quality. It is at this stage that the skills of a very good *bakul* become apparent. She introduces large numbers of additional items into the discussion, manipulating factors such as colour, size, quality and currency units, while maintaining a continuous flow of sales patter. Her strategy has two goals: either to transfer the bids under discussion to lower-value items, or to persuade the buyer to raise her bid by demonstrating the high quality of the goods for which she is bidding. Vendors at this stage of the bargaining only decrease their offers by small amounts and try to insist that any drop is matched by at least a token increase on the part of the buyer. Buyer's tactics are almost solely defensive: if they raise their bid, it is by just sufficient to continue the negotiations.

The Settlement stage is initiated by the seller when she offers a price significantly below her previous offer. The signal for this 'Settlement' offer is normally the buyer's refusal to increase her bids in response to slight decreases by the *bakul*, plus a clear understanding of the exact item which is being negotiated. If a sale eventuates (and most negotiations which have proceded this far are concluded), the price will usually be equidistant between the seller's settlement offer and the buyer's previous bid, for at this stage *bakul* are unwilling to drop their price by more than the increase in the buyer's bid. Hesitant customers will be asked to increase their price ('*Tambahi maleh*' or '*Punjule pira?*') or to state an alternative ('*Pinten?*' or '*Pira?*'). In most cases the settlement bid effectively matches buyer's and seller's expectations and a rapid exchange of two or three prices is enough to seal the bargain.

While considerable differences in the buying and selling prices at the Plateau stage are cancelled out during the Settlement stage, most of this is accomplished by the single settlement offer which effectively determines the final price. The *bakul*'s accuracy in calculating the appropriate amount for the settlement offer is not surprising: not only has she had considerable experience, but she has had up to an hour to decide how much this particular customer is likely to pay. There are two major exceptions to the pattern of quick equidistant settlements. A stubborn customer may occasionally force a tired *bakul* eager to complete a sale to make a second settlement offer and thus unilaterally drop her price, although in some cases the *bakul* is only feigning tiredness and the sale will still be in the upper range of prices. Less commonly, a *bakul* faced with a customer who persists in bidding below the ruling price range may offer a price within this range and refuse to alter it.

INFORMATION TESTING

The first two steps of this model—the Initial and the Plateau stages—can be readily conceptualized as a process of information search or, more precisely, information testing. In the initial bidding the buyer's knowledge of prices of a commodity is tested: if they are too low the transaction is aborted. The Plateau stage involves bluff and counter-bluff as the *bakul* attempts to convince her customer that while her general information may be correct, she must make allowances for variations in the specific items being discussed. During these stages the customer may believe that she is acquiring additional information—a *bakul*'s anger or indifference may be interpreted as a signal that her offers are too low, and the *bakul*'s eagerness that her offers are perhaps a little too high—but in most cases she is mistaken. It is the *bakul* who is acquiring information about her customer's knowledge of prices.

The settlement offer marks both the beginning of the Settlement stage and the end of information testing. At the point at which she makes the settlement offer, the *bakul* has a clear idea of what she thinks the customer will pay: a price equidistant between her offer and the buyer's last bid. In most cases the bargain is rapidly concluded at this point.

In the Javanese context, at least, the phenomena which Cassady's model explains is not the bargaining process as a whole, but only the Settlement stage. It is the Settlement stage for which 'negotiated price fixing' is an appropriate term, for it is here that the differences between buyer's and seller's prices are negotiated. Both parties have set the parameters for the final negotiations and both pay some heed to the convention that the final price should be reached by equal movements. If the buyer feels that this price is too high—because she cannot afford to pay it, because she thinks that the *bakul* may be induced to make a second, lower, settlement bid, or because she feels she could do better by beginning again with another trader—then the transaction will terminate or return to the Plateau stage. If the buyer feels that the price is appropriate, then it will be reached by steps approximating Cassady's model, although the buyer may try to obtain a slight discount.

The most significant difference between the two models is that the alternative model does not require the assumption of maximum buying prices and minimum selling prices. Both buyer and seller approach the transaction in terms of their particular knowledge of the current price range. The seller's aim is to obtain a price in the upper region or above this range, although she may sell below it in a falling market. The buyer's aim is to obtain the bottom price within the current range, and it is the *bakul*'s task to convince her customer that whatever price she pays is at that level.

A major advantage of the model developed here is that it explains variations in the intensity and duration of bargaining for specific commodities under specific conditions. Factors such as the heterogeneous nature of commodities, marked fluctuations in supply and demand, repetitive purchases from a single vendor, and the social status of customers, which have been used to explain the form and process of bargaining, are important mainly because of their influence on a second variable: the extent of shared information.

At one end of the continuum, where sellers recognize that their customers have accurate price information, either fixed prices prevail or bargaining is limited to a settlement offer and counterbid. Sales in village stalls, regular purchases of foodstuffs and common household items, payments for minor services, and many transactions in which both participants are *bakul*, fall into this category. Consequently, despite its importance in setting prices within the marketing system as a whole, bargaining is muted or absent in the majority of individual transactions between Javanese.

Bargaining is most intense and protracted when the difference in access to price information between buyer and seller is recognized to be at its greatest. This both prolongs bargaining and produces a greater range of prices, which in turn increases the buyer's difficulty in obtaining accurate information. The *bakul* can be said to have perfect information: a very clear understanding of both long- and short-term prices for the commodities in which they deal. Three broad factors govern the extent to which this information is available to the customer: the nature of the commodities, the structure of the market, and the social status of the customer.

The two most important qualities of commodities which affect price information are value and the degree of homogeneity. At one extreme is hand-produced *batik* cloth, a very expensive item no two pieces of which are exactly the same; at the other are cigarettes, cheap identical items. To some extent the two factors may cancel each other out: although vegetables purchased for home consumption differ considerably in quality, they are purchased in very small amounts, so that price disparities are not very significant. Such considerations are important in pricing services as well as commodities: a school child who takes a trishaw to and from school each day need not bargain, nor do most travellers bargain on buses. But a *bakul* chartering a minibus, or a Javanese hiring a trishaw at a bus station, can expect prolonged haggling.

The marketing system in some commodities creates very rapid price fluctuations which markedly affect the ability of customers to obtain price information. Among the important variables are the seasonality of supply and demand, and the extent to which the marketing structure incorporates fixed-price transactions. Some agricultural commodities, including the chillies and cabbages discussed in previous chapters and most fruit, have sharp seasonal production peaks. Some non-agricultural items also have seasonal peaks in demand: consumer items for which demand increases around Lebaran, for example, or building materials for which demand drops during the wet season. Conversely, commodities which are produced in large industries or whose distribution is controlled by government regulation often enter the *pasar* system at a fixed price which is widely known. Cigarettes, machine-made textiles, kerosene and rice are important in this regard.

The final important variable is the social status of the customer: people who do not regularly purchase a commodity have few opportunities to obtain accurate information on prices. It is for this reason that well-dressed women, who are presumed to be infrequent visitors to the market, are greeted with high initial offers. At one extreme is the tourist buying an item of craftware;[7] at the other is a *bakul* selling agricultural produce to a *depot*.

Taken together these factors explain the range of bargaining in the *pasar*. Negotiations between copperware or cloth traders and their customers are protracted because these are situations where the disparities in price information are at their greatest. Bargaining between *bakul* for large quantities of agricultural produce is swiftly concluded, not because the opportunity costs of the *bakul*'s time are so high that they will make price concessions to speed negotiations, but because the level of shared information is recognized to be so great that little remains to be negotiated.

1. The model is reproduced in Cassady (1974) and Beals (1975:191) and is also used by Geertz (1979:226) with a new title: 'Bargaining: The Basic Model'.

2. A possible reason for the lack of fit between Cassady's model and behaviour he observed in Mexican market places is that many of the vendors were only part-time traders: farmers and artisans selling their own produce (1968:58–9). Such vendors do not have good access to price information, and the disparity between the buyer's and seller's information, characteristic of the Javanese *pasar*, is much reduced. See note 5 below.

3. But see Cassady (1968:75) for some general comments on buyer behaviour, and the recognition that the concept of a buyer's minimum price is unrealistic. At one point (ibid:74) he appears to recognize that the notion of minimum selling prices must be an *ex post facto* assumption. He also notes that vendors are apt to be the most aggressive bargainers, but does not pursue the question.

4. This point also has important consequences for information access. Because she is constantly buying new stock, the vendor has a very sound idea of current prices, whereas her customers, who purchase the commodity infrequently, have few reliable sources of information. For ease of exposition the seller's information is consistently treated as superior to the buyer's, but this is not always true. When producers are selling to *bakul* or *depot*, the position of buyer and seller are reversed, and the seller adopts the conservative strategy. For similar strategies employed by fishermen selling to fish traders see Firth (1946:191–3) and Alexander (1982:170–5).

5. Cook's (1982:272) study of the graphs of 108 sales of *metate* in the Octolan market gives opposite results: 49% were asymmetrical in favour of the buyer and 28% were symmetrical. But taking into account that many sellers were producer-vendors and many buyers were urban wholesalers, and that in such cases the information edge lies with the buyer, the results are not incompatible with my model.

6. Others have pointed to three stages in bargaining, although their interpretations differ: Geertz (1979:227); Uchendu (1967:40).

7. *Bakul* who regularly sell to foreign tourists recognize that their customers' access to price information is too poor to permit bargaining and often mark fixed prices (*harga pas*) on their goods. Javanese buyers treat such prices as the vendor's initial offer.

Appendix: Dialogue Two

Bu Menik (see Chapter 5 for a description) is the seller, and the buyer is a middle-aged woman reasonably well-dressed in regional costume. The transaction takes about half an hour to complete and the seller later described the customer as a diligent bargainer, one who raised her offers in Rp 100 lots.

The buyer bustled up to Bu Menik's stall and pointed in the general direction of a Solo *jarik* which Bu Menik pulls out for her to look at.

line

B. *Sing resik, Bu, sing resik.*

A flawless one, *Bu*, a clear one. (The buyer examines the cloth, while the seller hails another prospective customer.)

S. *Tindak mriki, Bu, ngersakaken menapa? Apa selimut napa, Bu? Mangga, Bu, liyane napa*
5   *maleh.*

Bu, come over here. What do you want? A blanket, *Bu*? Come one, *Bu*, something else. (The second buyer, a young middle-class woman comes over, looks at a sash, then moves one.)

B. . . . *neng niki napa?*

. . . but this one?

S. *'Nggeh, keliri pepek, inggeh.*

Yes, a full range of colours, yes.

B. *Karo siki?*

In this one?

S. *Inggeh, neng satunggal. Nek*
10   *ngandap mboten enten. Sak nggangge le napa? Niku sing sae. Kandel, kandel sedaya 'nggeh napa.*

Yes, but only one. If there isn't one below. A pocket or not? That one is a good one. All of them are thick, yes.

S. *Mboten enten, Embah. La, pun*
15   *sae. La, kuwi keliri dipipeki, ujare bakule.*

There isn't, *Embah*. Yes, a good one. Why that one, a complete range of colours, so says the trader.

B. *La niki, pinten niki?*

And this one, how much for this one? (The buyer holds up a Solo *jarik*.)

S. *Regine sekawan setengah.*

The price is Rp 4500.[1]

B. *Loro punjul?*

More than Rp 2000?

20 S. *La, ya, loro punjul loro.*

Well yes, two plus two (thousand).

203

B. *Punjuli pira?*

How much more?

S. *La, 'jenengan ngenyang lumrahe niku.*

Come on you, bargain in the normal way.

B. *Limalas.*

Rp 1500.[a]

25　S. *Ya, ora dadi, ya sing seregane ya morine pada uwis.*

Yes, no way, yes, you pay for the quality you get.

B. *Loro punjul pira?*

How much more than Rp 2000?

S. *Ya, lorone punjul. Nek loro kurang, ya ora dadi encer.*

Yes, more than Rp 2000. If less than Rp 2000 it won't come off, truly!

30　B. *Kula ngawis limalas, wis limalas.*

I offer Rp 1500, yes, Rp 1500.[b]

S. *Ya, oleh ngenyang. Mengkene limalas ora oleh, nek neng kono loro setengah kaya kiye. Nek loro kurang terang ora dadi.*

Yes, you may bargain. But even here you can't offer Rp 1500, even over there you have to pay Rp 2500 for one like this. If less than Rp 2000 it's clear it won't come off.

35　B. *Limalas, niki punlah!*

Rp 1500, that's enough![c]

S. *Ya, ora ana jarik niku limalas. Ora ana temen, nyong ora gara.*

There is no *jarik* like that for Rp 1500. There's none like that, truly, I'm not lying.

B. *Mboten saged limalas?*

I can't get it for Rp 1500?

S. *Mboten, ora oleh niku lorone*
40　*punjul. Loro setengah.*

No, not for that, Rp 2000 plus. (The seller indicates a factory-print Sablon) Rp 2500.[2]

B. *Ora awet, sewu.*

That's not hardwearing, Rp 1000.[d]

S. *Rong ewu seprapat, wis seregane!*

Rp 2250, that's the price![3]

B. *Neng larang niki. Sewu!*

But that's expensive. Rp 1000![e]

S. *Mboten ora oleh sewu mboten*
45　*angsal. Pinten jajal? Niki mawon malah apik, 'nggeh. Wiron nggo.*

I can't give it to you for Rp 1000. How much, have a try? It's just that this one is better (indicating the Solo *jarik*), the edge can be worn folded (for formal wear the edge is always folded, and a *jarik* needs to be of a generous length for this.)

S. *Niki ora tawa akeh. Nek bocahe malah seneng kiye kena nggo wiron, resik. La nek wis dienggo*
50　*masa kon niliki jerone.*

This one, there's no need to offer a lot. A young girl would be happier if she could wear it with the edge pleated, a clean one. Why if it has already been worn, look at the inside.

B. *Limalas, niki mawon sedengan apik.*

Rp 1500, just this one, it's good enough.[f]

S. *Mboten angsal 'nggeh, Bu. Mboten.*

I can't do that, *Bu*. No.

55　B. *Carane pinten, Bu?*

This style, how much, *Bu*?

S. *Ya, oleh ngenyang. La lember niku nembe gedine pada.*

Yes, you can make an offer. That length is the same size.

B. *Nembelas!*

Rp 1600.[g] (The seller ignores this offer and the buyer walks off for the first time. She is away a matter of minutes before she returns.)

B. *Mboten angsal nembelas? Pinten?*

Can't buy it for Rp 1600.[h] How much?

60 S. *Temen, Embah, ora tawa bola-bali. Pokoke lorone punjul, ora isa kurang. Kiye, kiye rong ewu seprapat.*

Truly, *Embah*, don't bargain by wandering back and forth. Essentially it's Rp 2000 plus, you can't get it for less. This one, this one is Rp 2250.[4] (The seller indicates the Sablon cloth.)

(The seller turns to a friend going past and chats to her for several minutes about her daughter's education.)

B. *'Nggeh napa pitulas?*

What about Rp 1700?[i]

65 S. *Temanan, ora oleh.*

Truly, you can't.

B. *Kurang selawe wis lorone.*

Rp 1750![j]

S. *Matur nuwun. Lorone kurang ora dadi. Ajeng kalih tumbas niki. Rasukane?*

Thank you (sarcastically). Rp 1750, no way. You can buy this for a price approaching Rp 2000.[5] (The seller turns to her friend again and continues the conversation, which is now about some cloth she has purchased.)

70 B. *Niki, sing niki!*

This one, this one!

S. *Seragam, seragam, Dharma Wanita. Seragam napa? Putih napa?*

A uniform, a Dharma Wanita uniform. You want a uniform? A white one? (Dharma Wanita is a women's organization which has a *jarik* and *kebaya* of fixed colour and design. The trader addresses the question to her friend and they have a brief discussion. She turns to the buyer again.)

S. *Kulake bae ora oleh semono.*

Even wholesale you can't get it for that. (Referring to previous offer of Rp 1750 for Sablon.)

75 B. *Cobi pintenlah?*

Come on, how much? (referring to Solo *jarik*.)

S. *La, sampeyan punjuli pira? Mbayar!*

Oh you, how much do you add to your offer? Pay up!

B. *Lorone, ampun punjul.*

Rp 2000, no more.[k]

S. *'Nggeh, mboten saged. Nya saniki*
80 *kersa nggo tak caosna nek niku ora dadi. Mborongi, Embah, rong ewu setengah ora ana nek kelarangan. Timbang mayeng-mayeng ora serega ora oleh iki sing resik. Iki*
85 *bae wis maen.*

No, you can't. Now you want one to wear, I'll search it out for you, if that one, no way. Buy up wholesale, *Embah*. Rp 2500[6], if it's too expensive no need to buy it. Think about it, you won't get a nice one for a price like this if you go from place to place. (The buyer starts to wander off.) This one is a good one. (The buyer ignores her and she turns to her friend again.)

S. *Wis karo klambine sisan. Ukarane pirang meter? Kae klambine wis pas bae. Kur kari pirang meter?*

Together with a *kebaya*. How many metres for the *kebaya*. That *kebaya* (meaning the one the friend is wearing) fits well. How many metres do you have? (The buyer returns and interrupts the conversation with the trader's friend.)

B. *Disukakaken pinten niki?*

How much are you selling this for?

90 S. *Rong ewu punjul limang atus. Sampeyan dilampau mayeng-mayeng. Pokoke ora serega masa olehe.*

Rp 2500.[7] You walk from place to place. It's not possible to find a price like this.

B. *Pinten?*

How much?

95 S. *La, sampeyan pinten nek arep munjuli.*

Oh you, if you'll increase it, how much?

B. *Nyong ngenyang pitung talen.*

I offer Rp 1750.[1]

S. *Pitung talen mbayar ora oleh.*

Rp 1750, you can't pay that.

B. *Angsal napa mboten?*

Can I or can't I?

100 S. *Mboten.*

No.

B. *Niki pinten jajal.*

How much is this, make an effort.

S. *Pokoke lorone punjul. Loro kurang ora oleh, matur nuwun.*

Essentially it's more than Rp 2000 (i.e. Rp 2500)[8]. Less than Rp 2000 no way, thanks very much.

B. *Saestu? Mboten temenan. Kula kesah.*

105

Truly? You're not in earnest. I'm off.

S. *'Nggeh, mlayu bae.*

Yes, walk off. (The buyer stalks off for the third time, but returns almost immediately.)

B. *Pitung talen. Angsal napa mboten niki?*

Rp 1750.[m] Can I or can't I?

S. *Nboten.*

No.

110 B. *Kiye wolulas bisa apa ora?*

This one for Rp 1800[n] or not?

S. *Ya, ora oleh.*

Yes, you can't.

S. *Rong ewu kene kari mbayar pasna.*

Rp 2000[9], here all you have to do is pay on the dot. (For the cheaper Sablon *jarik*.)

B. *Sing apik.*

For the good one.

115 S. *Wong, rong ewu setengah ya ora tunggale.*

Rp 2500,[10] they're not of one kind.

B. *Niki kali niki tuli tunggale.*

This one and this one are the same kind.

S. *Niki sejen, wong bakul siji-siji.*

This one is different, I judge them one by one.

B. *Bangsane niki?*

The same as this.

120 S. *Ya, ora bangsane bae, wong regane bae sejen.*

Yes, they're not the same, the prices are different.

B. *Tunggale napa sejen?*

The same or different?

S. *Sejen.*

Different.

B. *Takoni ora ngaku. Takoni semono*
125 *kok ora ngaku. Pinten?*

I question someone and it's not acknowledged. Question so much, why is it not acknowledged? How much?

S. *Rong ewu setengah, kari tambah.*

Rp 2500,[11] it's up to you to increase the price.

B. *Olehe pinten niku?*

How much for that?

S. *La, sampeyan, piralah, namung*
takon bakule bae, ngenyang
130 *wolulas, Wolulas ya, ora oleh.*

Well then, you, how much? You only ask the trader, you offer Rp1800. Rp1800, no you cant'.

B. *Nyong ngenyang sangalas.*

I offer Rp 1900.[o]

S. *Mboten.*

No.

(The buyer walks away for the fourth time, but returns in less than a minute.)

B. *Rong ewu, punlah!*

Rp 2000,[p] that's enough!

(The seller makes no reply, but accepts the proffered Rp 2000 and wraps the parcel. The buyer then drifts off, and most unusually no farewell greetings are exchanged. The seller complains that she is tired (*kesel*) and that the buyer had bargained diligently (*terlaten*).

References

Abendanon, J.H.   1904
'Vergardering te Poeworedjo voor de Afdeelingen Poeworedjo en Kebumen op 24 Maart, 1904, des Morgens te 9 ½ uur', *Rapport van den Directeur van Onderwijs, Eerendienst en Nijverheid*. Batavia.

Adam, L.   1916
'Hoe bakoels aan bedrijfskapitaal komen', *Koloniale Tijdschrift* 5:1604–7.

                                                   1929
'Enkele Gegevens Omtrent den Economischen Toestand van de Kaloerahan Sidoardjo (District Kabonangan, Regentschap Bantoel, Afdeeling Jogjakarta)', *Economische Beschrijvingen* 2:I & II. Batavia: G. Kolff & Co.

Alexander, J.   1985
Pasar, Pasaran. Unpublished PhD Dissertation, University of Sydney.

Alexander J. & P. Alexander   1979
'Labour Demands and the "Involution" of Javanese Agriculture', *Social Analysis* 3:22–44.

                                                   1982
'Shared Poverty as Ideology: Agrarian Relationships in Colonial Java', *Man* 17:597–619.

Alexander, P.   1981
'Shared Fantasies and Elite Politics: The Sri Lankan "Insurrection" of 1971', *Mankind* 13:113–32.

                                                   1982
Sri Lankan Fishermen: Rural Capitalism and Peasant Society. Canberra: Australian National University Monographs on South Asia, No. 7.

Anderson, A.G.   1978
The Structure and Organization of Rural Marketing in the Cimanuk River Basin, West Java. Bogor: Agro Economic Survey, Rural Dynamics Series No. 3.

                                                   1980
'The Rural Market in West Java', *Economic Development and Cultural Change* 28:753–77.

Anderson, J.N.   1969
'Buy-and-Sell and Economic Personalism: Foundations for Philippine
Entrepreneurship', *Asian Survey* 9:641–68.
Angelino, P. de Kat   1930
Batikrapport. Part II. Weltevreden: Landsdrukkerij.
(ARA Bagalen)   1832
Nr. 3 Bagalen, Residentie Bagalen. Algemeen Rijks Archief Ministrie
van Kolonien 1814–1849.
Ardener, S.   1964
'The Comparative Study of Rotating Credit Associations', *Journal of
the Royal Anthropological Institute* 93:201–29.
Beals, R.L.   1975
The Peasant Marketing System of Oaxaca, Mexico. Berkeley and Los
Angeles: University of California Press.
Boeke, J.H.   1926
'Inlandsche Budgetten', *Koloniale Studien* 1:229–334.
                                        1954
*Economics and Economic Policy of Dual Societies as Exemplified by
Indonesia*. New York: Institute of Pacific Relations.
Burger, D.H.   n.d.
'Vergelijking van den Economischen Toestand der Districten Tajoe en
Djakenan (Regentschap Pati, Afdeeling Rembang)', *Economische Be-
schrijvingen* 4.
                                        1930
'Het niet-officieele crediet in het Regentschap Pati in 1927', *Koloniale
Studien* 14:395–412.
                                        1939
De Ontsluiting van Java's Binnenland voor het Wereldverkeer. Wage-
ningen: H. Veenman & Zonen.
                                        1948/49
'Structuurveranderingen in de Javaanse samenleving', *Indonesie* 2:381–
98, 521–37, 3:1–18, 101–23, 225–50, 381–89, 512–34.
Cassady, R.   1968
'Negotiated Price Making in Mexican Traditional Markets: A Concep-
tual Analysis', *América Indígena* 28:51–79.
                                        1974
Exchange by Private Treaty. Austin: The University of Texas.
Castles, L.   1967
*Religion, Politics and Economic Behaviour in Java: The Kudus Ciga-
rette Industry*. Cultural Report Series No. 15, Southeast Asian Studies,
Yale University.
Chandler, G.N.   1979
Village Markets in D.I. Yogyakarta, Indonesia. B.A. (Hons) thesis
submitted to Dept of Geography, Monash University, Melbourne.
                                        1981
Market Traders and the Sale of Clothing in Rural Java. Monash: Centre
of Southeast Asian Studies, Working Paper No. 25.
                                        1982
Periodicity, Mobility and the Distribution of Consumer Durables: A

Study of Village Market Trade in D.I. Yogyakarta, Indonesia. M.A. thesis submitted to Dept of Geography, Monash University.

1984
Market Trade in Rural Java. Monash: Centre of Southeast Asian Studies, Monash Papers on Southeast Asia No. 11.

Chayanov, A.V.   1931
'The Socio-Economic Nature of Peasant Farm Economy', in Sorokin, P.A., C.C. Zimmerman & C.J. Gilpin (eds.) *A Systematic Source Book in Rural Sociology*, Vol. II pp. 144–7. Minneapolis: The University of Minnesota Press.

Collier, W.L.   1978
'Food Problems, Unemployment, and the Green Revolution in Rural Java', *Prisma* 9:38–52.

Cook, S.   1982
Zapotec Stonecutters: The Dynamics of Rural Simple Commodity Production in Modern Mexican Capitalism. Lanham: University Press of America.

Dalton, B.   1978
Indonesian Handbook. Vermont: Moon Publications.

Dannhaeuser, N.   1977
'Distribution and the Structure of Retail Trade in a Philippine Town Setting', *Economic Development and Cultural Change* 25:471–503.

Daumont, V.   1977
'Un Monopole Féminin Menacé: Le Commerce des Jamu', *Archipel* 13:263–6.

Davis, W.G.   1973
Social Relations in a Philippine Market: Self-Interest and Subjectivity. Berkeley: University of California Press.

Deventer, C.T. van   1904
Overzicht van den Economischen Toestand der Inlandsche Bevolking van Java en Madoera. 's-Gravenhage: Martinus Nijhoff.

Dewey, A.   1962a
Peasant Marketing in Java. Glencoe: Free Press.

1962b
'Trade and Social Control in Java', *Journal of the Royal Anthropological Institute* 92:177–90.

1964
'Capital, Credit and Saving in Javanese Marketing', in Firth, R. & B.S. Yamey (eds) *Capital, Saving and Credit in Peasant Societies*, pp. 230–55. Chicago: Aldine Press.

Does, A.M.K. de   1893
'Toestand der Nijverheid in de Afdeeling Bandjanegara', *Tijdschrift voor Indische Taal-, Land en Volkenkunden* 36:1–112.

Doorn, C.L. van   1926
Schets van de Economische Ontwikkeling der Afdeeling Peorworedjo, Residentie Kedoe. Weltevreden: Kolff.

Droste   1921
'Verslag omtrent den Inlandschen Handel in de Residentie Madoera', *Blaadje voor het Volkscredietwezen* 11:198–220.

Epstein, T.S.   1982
Urban Food Marketing and Third World Development. London:
Croom Helm.
Firth, R.   1946
Malay Fishermen: Their Peasant Economy. London: Kegan Paul,
Trench, Trubner & Co.
Forbes, D.   1978
'Urban-Rural Interdependence: The Trishaw Riders of Ujung Pan-
dang', in Rimmer, P.J. et al (eds) *Food, Shelter and Transport in
Southeast Asia and the Pacific*, pp. 219–36. Canberra, ANU Press.
                                      1979
The Pedlars of Ujung Pandang. Monash: Centre of Southeast Asian
Studies, Working Paper No. 17.
Forman, S. & J.F. Riegelhaupt   1970
'Market Place and Market System: Towards a Theory of Peasant
Economic Integration', *Comparative Studies in Society and History*
12:188–212.
Fruin, T.A.   1938
'Popular and Rural Credit in the Netherlands Indies', *Bulletin of the
Colonial Institute of Amsterdam* 1:106–115, 161–75.
Geertz, C.   1956a
'Religious Belief and Economic Behaviour in a Central Javanese Town:
Some Preliminary Considerations', *Economic Development and Cul-
tural Change* 4:134–58.
                                      1956b
The Social Context of Economic Change: An Indonesian Case Study.
Cambridge, Mass.: Massachusetts Institute of Technology.
                                      1960
The Religion of Java. Illinois: Free Press of Glencoe.
                                      1962
'The Rotating Credit Association: A "Middle Rung" in Development',
Economic Development and Cultural Change 10:241–63.
                                      1963a
Agricultural Involution: The Process of Ecological Change in Indonesia.
Berkeley: University of California Press.
                                      1963b
*Peddlers and Princes: Social Change and Economic Modernization in
Two Indonesian Towns.* Chicago: University of Chicago Press.
                                      1965
The Social History of an Indonesian Town. Cambridge, Mass.: MIT
Press.
                                      1978
'The Bazaar Economy: Information and Search in Peasant Marketing',
American Economic Review 68:28–32.
                                      1979
'Suq: The Bazaar Economy in Sefrou', in Geertz, C., H. Geertz & L.
Rosen, *Meaning and Order in Moroccan Society: Three Essays in
Cultural Analysis*, pp. 123–313. Cambridge: Cambridge University
Press.

Geertz, H.   1961
The Javanese Family: A Study of Kinship and Socialization. Glencoe:
Free Press.

Gelpke, J.H.F.S.   1901
Naar Aanleiding van Staatsblad van 1878. No. 110.

Gille, H. & R.H. Pardoko   1965
'A Family Life in East Java: Preliminary Findings', in Berelson, B. *et
al.* (eds) *Family Planning and Population Programmes*, pp. 503–23.
Chicago: University of Chicago Press.

Gutem, V.B. van   1919
'Tjina Mindering: Eenige Aanteekeningen over het Chineesche Geld-
schieterwezen op Java', *Koloniale Studien* 106–50.

Handbook of Netherlands East-Indies 1930
Batavia: G. Kolff & Co.

Hart, G.P.   1977
Patterns of Household Labour Allocation in a Javanese Village. Mimeo.
                                              1978
Labour Allocation Strategies in Rural Javanese Households. Unpub-
lished PhD Dissertation. Dept of Agricultural Economics, Cornell
University, Ithaca, New York.

Hatley, B.   1984
Prominent? Dominant? The Situation of Women in Javanese Society.
Paper presented at the Fifth National Conference Asian Studies Associ-
ation of Australia, University of Adelaide, May 13–18, 1984.

Hefner, R.W.   1983
'The Problem of Preference: Economic and Ritual Change in Highlands Java', *Man* 18:669–89.

Hering, B.B. (ed.)   1976
Indonesian Women: Some Past and Current Perspectives. Bruxelles:
Centre d'Etude du Sud-Est Asiatique et de l'Extrême Orient.

Hill, P.   1984
'The Poor Quality of Official Socio-Economic Statistics relating to the
Rural Tropical World: with special reference to South India', *Modern
Asian Studies* 18:491–514.

Horne, E.C.   1961
Beginning Javanese. New Haven and London: Yale University Press.
                                              1974
Javanese-English Dictionary. New Haven and London: Yale University
Press.

Hull, T.H.   1975
*Each Child Brings its own Fortune: An Inquiry into the Value of
Children in a Javanese Village.* Unpublished PhD Dissertation. Dept of
Demography, Australian National University, Canberra.
                                              1977
'The Influence of Social Class on the Need and Effective Demand for
Children in a Javanese Village', in Ruzika, L.T. (ed.) *The Economic
and Social Supports for High Fertility*, pp. 287–386. Canberra: ANU
Press.

Hull, V.J.   1975
Fertility, Socio-Economic Status and the Position of Women in a Javan-

ese Village. Unpublished PhD Dissertation. Dept of Demography, Australian National University, Canberra.

1976

Women in Java's Rural Middle Class: Progress or Regress. Yogyakarta: Population Studies Centre, University of Gadjah Mada, Working Paper No. 3.

1979

A Women's Place . . . Social Class Variations in Women's Work Patterns in a Javanese Village. Yogyakarta: Population Studies Centre, University of Gadjah Mada, Working Paper No. 21.

Isaac, B.L.   1981

'Price, Competition and Profits among Hawkers in Pendumbu, Sierra Leone: An Inventory Approach', *Economic Development and Cultural Change* 29:353–73.

Jay, R.   1969

Javanese Villagers: Social Relations in Rural Modjokuto. Cambridge, Mass.: MIT Press.

Jellinek, L.   1976

The Life of a Jakarta Street Trader. Monash: Centre of Southeast Asian Studies, Working Paper No. 9.

1977

The Life of a Jakarta Street Trader: Two Years Later. Monash: Centre of Southeast Asian Studies, Working Paper No. 13.

1978a

'Circular Migration and the Pondok-Dwelling System: A Case Study of Ice-Cream Traders in Jakarta', in Rimmer, P.J. *et al.* (eds) *Food, Shelter and Transport in Southeast Asia and the Pacific*, pp. 135–54. Canberra: ANU Press.

1978b

'The Rise and Development of a Vegetable Trading Enterprise', *Indonesia Circle* 15:29–38.

Kahn, J.S.   1980

Minangkabau Social Formations: Indonesian Peasants and the World-Economy. Cambridge: Cambridge University Press.

1982

'From Peasant to Petty Commodity Producers in Southeast Asia', *Bulletin of Concerned Asian Scholars* 14:3–15.

Kantor Sensus dan Statistik   1978

Statistik Tahunan 1978. Kabupaten Kebumen: Pemerintah Daerah dan Kantor Statistik.

1980

Statistik Tahunan 1980. Kabupaten Kebumen: Pemerintah Daerah dan Kantor Statistik.

1981

Statistik Tahunan 1981. Kabupaten Kebumen: Pemerintah Daerah dan Kantor Statistik.

Katzin, M.F.   1960

'The Business of Higglering in Jamaica', *Social and Economic Studies* 9:297–331.

Keers, J.   1928

'Het Pandcrediet op Java', *Koloniale Studien* 12:367–418.

Kertanegara 1958
'The Batik Industry in Central Java', *Ekonomi dan Keuangan Indonesia* 11:345–401.

Khuri, F.I. 1968
'The Etiquette of Bargaining in the Middle East', *American Anthropologist* 70:698–706.

Koentjaraningrat 1960
'The Javanese of South Central Java', in Murdock, G.P. (ed.) *Social Structure in Southeast Asia*, pp. 88–115. Chicago: Quadrangle Books.

1967
'Tjelapar: A Village in South Central Java', in Koentjaraningrat (ed.) *Villages in Indonesia*, pp. 244–80. New York: Cornell University Press.

Koloniaal Verslag 1892
The Hague, Ministry of Colonies.

Liem Twan Djie 1947
De Distribueerende Tusschenhandel der Chineezen op Java. s'Gravenhage: Martinus Nijhoff.

Loriaux, C.L. & C.L. van Doorn 1923
'Economische Beschrijving van de Desa Wiroen in Betrekking tot de Credietverhoudingen onder de Bewoners', *Blaadje voor het Volkscredietwezen* 11:1–33.

McGee, T.G. 1973
Hawkers in Hong Kong: A Study of Planning and Policy in a Third World City. Hong Kong: Centre of Asian Studies, University of Hong Kong.

1978
'An Invitation to the "Ball": Dress Formal or Informal', in Rimmer, P.J. *et al.* (eds) *Food, Shelter and Transport in Southeast Asia and the Pacific*, pp. 3–27. Canberra: ANU Press.

Marzuki, J. 1966
Batik, Pola dan Tjorak. Djakarta: Djambatan.

Mears, L.A. 1961
Rice Marketing in the Republic of Indonesia. Jakarta: P.T. Pembangunan.

1978
'Problems of Supply and Marketing of Food in Indonesia in Repelita III', *Bulletin of Indonesian Economic Studies* 14:52–62.

(Mindere Welvaart)
Onderzoek naar de Mindere Welvaart der Inlandsche Bevolking op Java en Madoera.
Subreports:
VIa   *Overzicht van de Uitkomsten der Gewestelijke Onderzoekingen naar den Inlandschen Handel en Nijverheid en daaruit gemaakte gevolgtrekkingen*, I. Batavia. 1909.
VIb   *Overzicht van de Uitkomsten der Gewestelijke Onderzoekingen naar den Inlandschen Handel en Nijverheid en daaruit gemaakte gevolgtrekkingen*, II. Batavia. 1909.
VIf   *Overzicht van de Uitkomsten der Gewestelijke Onderzoekingen*

*naar den Niet-Inlandschen Handel en Nijverheid en daaruit ge-
maakte gevolgtrekkingen*, VI. Batavia. 1912.

IXb3   *Overzicht van de Uitkomsten der Gewestelijke Onderzoekingen
       naar de Economie van de Desa: Verheffing van de Inlandsche
       Vrouw*, III. Batavia. 1914.
IXc   *Overzicht van de Uitkomsten der Gewestelijke Onderzoekingen
       naar de Economie van de Desa en daaruit gemaakte gevolgtrek-
       kingen*, III. Batavia. 1911.
—   *Samentrekking van de Afdeelingsverslagen over de Uitkomsten
       der Onderzoekingen naar Handel en Nijverheid in de Residentie
       Kedoe*. Batavia. 1907.
—   *Samentrekking van de Afdeelingsverslagen over de Uitkomsten
       der Onderzoekingen naar de Economie van de Desa in de Re-
       sidentie Kedoe*. Weltevreden. 1908.
Mintz, S.W.   1956
'The Role of the Middleman in the Internal Distribution System of a
Caribbean Peasant Economy', *Human Organization* 15:18–23.
                                     1960
'Peasant Markets', *Scientific American* 203:112–22.
                                     1961a
'Pratik: Haitian Personal Economic Relationships', *Proceedings of the
1961 Annual Meeting of the American Ethnological Society, Seattle*, pp.
54–63.
                                     1961b
'Standards of Value and Units of Measure in the Fond-des-Negres
Market Place, Haiti', *Journal of the Royal Anthropological Institute*
91:23–38.
Ochse, J.J. & G.J.A. Terra   1934
'Het Onderzoek naar den Economischen en Landbouwkundigen Toes-
tand en het Voedselverbruik te Kutowinangoen', in Ochse, J.J. *et al.
Geld- en Producten- Huishouding, Volksvoeding en Gezonheid te Koe-
towinangoen*, pp. 1–226. Buitenzorg: Department van Economische
Zaken.
Ortiz, S.   1979
'Expectations and Forecasts in the Face of Uncertainty', *Man* 14:64–80.
Palmier, L.H.   1960
Social Status and Power in Java. London: Althone Press.
Peacock, J.   1973
Indonesia: An Anthropological Perspective. Pacific Palisades, Califor-
nia: Goodyear.
Peluso, N.L.   1981
*Survival Strategies of Rural Women Traders or a Women's Place is in the
Market*. International Labour Organization, World Employment Pro-
gramme Research Working Paper.
                                     1982
Occupational Mobility and the Economic Role of Rural Women. Yogya-
karta: Population Studies Centre, University of Gadjah Mada Report
Series No. 39.
Penny, D.H. & M. Singarimbun   1972

'A Case Study of Rural Poverty', *Bulletin of Indonesian Economic Studies* 8:79–88.

1973

Population and Poverty in Rural Java: Some Economic Arithmetic from Sriharjo. Ithaca, New York: Cornell University Press.

Plattner, S.   1975

'Rural Market Networks', *Scientific American* 232:66–79.

1982

'Economic Decision Making in a Public Marketplace', *American Ethnologist* 9:399–420.

1983

'Economic Custom in a Competitive Market Place', *American Anthropologist* 85:848–58.

Raffles, T.S.   1817

The History of Java. Vol. 1. London: John Murray.

Rees, A.   1971

'Information Networks in Labor Markets', in Lamberton, D.M. (ed.) *Economics of Information and Knowledge*, pp. 109–18. Middlesex: Pelican.

Rens, M.C.   1980

Breastfeeding and Female Employment in Rural Java. Unpublished PhD Dissertation, University of California at Davis.

Rostow, W.W.   1960

The Stages of Economic Growth. Cambridge: Cambridge University Press.

Rouffaer, G.P.   1904

'De Voornaamste Industrieen der Inlandsche Bevolking van Java en Madoera', in Deventer, C.T. van *Overzicht van de Economischen Toestand der Inlandsche Bevolking van Java en Madoera*. 's-Gravenhage: Nijhoff.

Rouffaer, G.P. & W.H. Juynboll   1900

De Batikkunst in de Nederlandsch-Indie en haar Geschidenis. Haarlem.

Sajogyo   1975

Usaha Perbaikan Gizi Keluarga. Bogor: Institut Pertanian Bogor.

1977

Garis Kemiskinan dan Kebutuhan Minimum Pangan. Bogor: Mimeograph.

Sajogyo, P.   1983

Peranan Wanita dalam Perkembangan Masyarakat Desa. Jakarta: C.V. Rajawali/Yayasan Ilmu-Ilmu Sosial.

Siegel, J.   1969

The Rope of God. Los Angeles: University of California Press.

Singarimbun, M. & C. Manning   1976

Fertility and Family Planning in Mojolama. Yogyakarta: Population Institute, University of Gadjah Mada.

Sitsen, P.H.W.   n.d.

Industrial Development in the Netherlands Indies. The Netherlands and Netherlands Indies Council of the Institute of Pacific Relations.

Skinner, G.W. 1964/65
'Marketing and Social Structure in Rural China', *Journal of Asian Studies* 24:3–43, 24:195–288, 24:363–99.

Smith, C.A. 1975
'Examining Stratification Systems through Peasant Marketing Arrangements: An Application of some Models from Economic Geography', *Man* 10:95–122.

Soewondo, N. 1968
Kedudukan Wanita Indonesia dalam Hukum dan Masyarakat. Jakarta: Timun Mas N.V.

1977
'The Indonesian Marriage Law and its Implementing Regulation', *Archipel* 13:283–94.

Stigler, G.J. 1968
The Organization of Industry. New York: Irwin.

Stoler, A. 1975
'Some Socio-Economic Aspects of Rice Harvesting in a Javanese Village', *Masyarakat Indonesia* 2:51–87.

1977
'Class Structure and Female Autonomy in Rural Java', *Signs* 3:74–89.

1978
'Garden Use and Household Economy in Rural Java', *Bulletin of Indonesian Economic Studies* 14:85–101.

Szanton, M.C.B. 1972
A Right to Survive: Subsistence Marketing in a Lowland Philippine Town. Pennsylvania: Penn. State University Press.

Terra, G.J.A. 1932
'De Voeding der Bevolking en de Erfcultuur', *Koloniale Studien* 16:552–93.

Uchendu, V.C. 1967
'Some Principles of Haggling in Peasant Markets', *Economic Development and Cultural Change* 16:37–50.

Veldhuizen-Djajasoebrata, A. 1972
Batik op Java. Rotterdam: Museum voor Land- en Volkenkunde.

Verslag der Nijverheidscommissie 1933

Vreede de Steurs, C. 1960
The Indonesian Woman: Struggles and Achievements. 's-Gravenhage: Mouton.

Vries, E. de & H. Cohen 1937
'On Village Shopkeeping in Java and Madura', *Bulletin of the Colonial Institute of Amsterdam* 1:263–73.

White, B. 1975
'The Economic Importance of Children in a Javanese Village', in Nag, M. (ed.) *Population and Social Organization*, pp. 127–46. The Hague: Mouton.

1976a
'Population, Employment and Involution in Rural Java', *Development and Change* 7:267–90.

1976b

Production and Reproduction in a Javanese Village. Unpublished PhD Dissertation, Columbia University, New York.

1979

'Political Aspects of Poverty, Income Distribution and their Measurement: Some Examples from Rural Java', *Development and Change* 10:91–114.

Wieringa, S.   1979

'Javaanse Batiksters', in Creyghton, M. & P. Geschiere (eds.) *Zij en het Patriachaat: Ontmoetingen met Vrouwen uit Afrika en Azie*, pp. 73–83. Maasbree: Corrie Zelen.

Wiradi, G.   1978

Rural Development and Rural Institutions: A Study of Institutional Changes in West Java. Bogor: Agro-Economic Survey Rural Dynamics Series No. 6.

Wolff, J.U. & P. Soepomo   1982

Communicative Codes in Central Java. Ithaca, New York: Southeast Asia Program, Dept of Asian Studies, Cornell University, Data Paper No. 116.

Index